THE CLASSICS
OF WESTERN
SPIRITUALITY

JOHN RUUSBROEC
THE SPIRITUAL ESPOUSALS AND OTHER WORKS

INTRODUCTION AND TRANSLATION BY
JAMES A. WISEMAN, O.S.B.

PREFACE BY
LOUIS DUPRÉ

PAULIST PRESS
NEW YORK • MAHWAH • TORONTO

Cover Art:
K. DUPRÉ is an artist specializing in stained glass who resides in Miami, Florida.

Library of Congress
Catalog Card Number: 85-62400

ISBN: 0-8091-2729-6 (paper)
      0-8091-0364-8 (cloth)

Published by Paulist Press
997 Macarthur Boulevard
Mahwah, New Jersey 07430

Printed and bound in the
United States of America

CONTENTS

CONTENTS

THE LITTLE BOOK OF CLARIFICATION

Editor of this Volume

JAMES A. WISEMAN, O.S.B., was born in Louisville, Kentucky, in 1942. After undergraduate studies at Georgetown University in Washington, D.C., he spent a year doing graduate study abroad at the University of Freiburg im Breisgau and then returned to Washington to enter the Benedictine community at St. Anselm's Abbey. He was ordained to the priesthood in 1970 and served the community for one term as abbot (1975–1983), after which he was appointed novice master. His doctoral dissertation in spiritual theology at the Catholic University of America was on the theme of love in *The Spiritual Espousals* of John Ruusbroec. At the 1981 Ruusbroec Colloquium at Louvain, he delivered a paper on that theme, subsequently published in the colloquium's proceedings. He has also written articles on Edward Schillebeeckx, T. S. Eliot, and Ralph Waldo Emerson.

Author of the Preface

LOUIS DUPRÉ is the T. L. Riggs Professor of the Philosophy of Religion at Yale University. He is a member of the editorial board of this series and an expert on the mystical literature of the Low Countries. Among his many writings are *Transcendent Selfhood* (1976) and *A Dubious Heritage* (1977).

PREFACE

Fourteenth-century Brabant provides an unlikely setting for the most articulate Trinitarian mystic of the Western Church. In a succession of social and doctrinal crises, the imposing structure of Europe's spiritual culture was rapidly disintegrating. Philosophy and theology were abandoning Aquinas's system of balanced rationality for the uncertainties of nominalist scholasticism. Moral abuses disfigured ecclesiastical life and the need for a religious reformation began to emerge. Rome found itself, once again, in a state of spiritual and civil disarray that rendered it unfit to function as center of the Christian world: In 1309 the popes took up residence in Avignon. In the prevailing climate of unrest, movements of spiritual renewal or eschatological expectation sprang up everywhere—feverish, intense, undisciplined: the Franciscan "Spirituals," Beghards, reborn Waldensians—all of them extremist in claims and aspirations. Brabant provided no shelter from this turbulence. The once sleepy duchy under the remote sovereignty of the German emperor was rapidly, though less radically than the adjacent county of Flanders, becoming an arena of hot disputes between the municipalities and suzerain. Spiritually also, Brabant passed through a period of upheaval, albeit with less violence than southern France or northern Italy.

First as an assistant parish priest in Brussels and later as a canon regular in the wooded solitude of Groenendaal, Ruusbroec wrote his majestic summa of Christian life in the spirit—at once daringly speculative and remarkably balanced. In a time of utter confusion he achieved the kind of synthesis normally reserved to those privileged moments of tranquillity so rare in history. In that respect he evokes a comparison with his older contemporary, the author of the *Divina Commedia*. I shall leave the discussion of Ruusbroec's theological system to the competence of Dom James Wiseman. Here I wish to highlight only one facet of Ruusbroec's oeuvre: its unique Trinitarian character.

Basic differences separate Western from Eastern theologies. The Latins, on the basis of psychological introspection or metaphysical speculation, tend to start from the one God and later, as far as possible, add the Trinitarian distinctions. The Greeks, more spiritually oriented, begin with the revealed mystery of the three Persons. They assume that the order of salvation and revelation directly expresses God's *internal* relations. For centuries the West neglected this rich Trinitarian tradition, despite a sizable output of treatises on the Trinity. Augustine's influential theology all too often led his followers to abstract, numerical speculations performed on the basis of essentially monotheistic concepts. He himself, however, especially in the later period when he wrote *De Trinitate*, went beyond such a psychological monotheism. In surpassing the self and reflecting upon it in the light of revelation, the mind comes to recognize its own internal structure as the imprint of a divine Archetype. Thus the mind's own relations, functioning together and separately in the discovery of the revealed God, present more than an external analogy of an incomprehensibly triune God. They directly reflect the divine reality in which they partake.

Only relatively late in our tradition did we become aware of this deeper vein in Augustine's thought. Indeed, a genuine Trinitarian spirituality did not emerge in the West until the twelfth-century Cistercians (especially William of St. Thierry) and the Victorines in Paris. In Ruusbroec the movement reached its classical completion. The Flemish mystic uniquely synthesized Greek spiritual theology with Augustinian introspection. Eckhart had attempted a similar synthesis—with remarkable results. But the final destination of the Rhineland mystic's spiritual journey had been a darkness beyond distinction. In his theology God, in the end, ceased to *manifest* and revelation lost its definitive authority. For him, the Trinity referred beyond itself to an absolute Oneness in which no further relations obtain. The problem of an insurmountably negative theology seems inherent in the introspective method itself: Once the mind surpasses all human categories, no further determinations are available.

With one stroke, Ruusbroec removed the difficulty. For him, God's being is dynamic, never at rest and, hence, never permanently withdrawn in its own darkness. Granted, the soul begins by moving into God's silence. But this divine silence itself is not a terminal point: It is pregnant with the Word. And so, the contemplative, having reached "the dark silence," moves with the Father's generative act into the perfect Image of the Son and out into the divinely posited otherness of the creatures. Indeed, for Ruusbroec also, the land where God dwells is "wayless" and dark. But "in this darkness an incomprehensible light is born and shines forth; this is the Son of God, in whom a person becomes able to see and to contemplate eternal life."[1] Ruusbroec overcame the ultimate negation by refusing to posit a unity beyond the Trinity, as Eckhart had done. For Ruusbroec the One is the *Father*, that is, a unity that becomes fertile, a silence that must speak, a darkness that yields light: "This sublime Unity of the divine nature is both living and fruitful, for out of this same Unity the eternal Word is ceaselessly begotten of the Father" (*Esp*. II.2/3.C).

The Flemish mystic fully accepted the view of the Greek Fathers that the soul's relation to God partakes in the movements *within* God. Hence, once arrived in the desert of the Godhead, the contemplative mind moves with the same divine dynamism with which the Father moves into his divine image and into the multiplicity of creation. The words in which he describes this intra-Trinitarian movement of the soul are as daring as any ever written: "To comprehend and understand God as he is in himself, above and beyond all likenesses, is *to be God with God*, without intermediary" (*Esp*. III. Intro.). And yet Ruusbroec was never seriously challenged by Church authorities. Indeed he was beatified. He knew how to make the necessary distinctions: "We cannot wholly become God and lose our creaturely state—that is impossible. But if we remained entirely in ourselves, separated from God, we would be miserable and deprived of salvation. We will therefore feel ourselves as being entirely in God and entirely in ourselves" (*The Sparkling Stone* 2.C).

What enables Ruusbroec to present the mystical union between God and man as being so intimate is that it always remains a unity of persons, not an identity of nature. The daring consistency of his Trinitarian theology paradoxically preserved him from lapsing into the kind of mystical pantheism that hovered over his less-discerning contemporaries. No charge, then, would be less justified than that Ruusbroec's mysticism lacks the intimate interpersonal quality of later writers. True, he never developed a *psychology* of the interpersonal spiritual exchange as we find in some Franciscans and, later, in the Spanish Carmelites. Yet at the very basis of his theory lies a theology of the interpersonal.

Once the soul is admitted into the inner life of the blessed Trinity, the mystical journey ceases to follow a straight upward line and turns into a self-renewing cycle of ingoing and outflowing with God's own life. Ruus-

---

1. *The Spiritual Espousals*, book three, part one. Further references to this treatise in the Preface will be given in the text according to the following format: *Esp*. II.2/3.C, indicating a quotation from the *Espousals*, book two, parts two and three (combined), section C. *The Sparkling Stone*, abbreviated *Stone*, will be referred to by part and section.

broec has described this divine rhythm of contemplation in what must surely be one of the most beautiful passages in all mystical literature:

> There the spirit is caught up in the embrace of the Holy Trinity and eternally abides within the superessential Unity in a state of rest and blissful enjoyment. In this same Unity, considered now as regards its fruitfulness, the Father is in the Son and the Son in the Father, while all creatures are in them both. This is beyond the distinction of Persons, for here we can only make distinctions of reason between fatherhood and sonship in the living fecundity of the divine nature.
>
> This is the origin and beginning of an eternal going forth and an eternal activity which is without beginning, for it is a beginning without beginning. Since the almighty Father has perfectly comprehended himself in the ground of his fruitfulness, the Son, who is the Father's eternal Word, goes forth as another Person within the Godhead. Through this eternal birth all creatures have gone forth eternally before their creation in time. (*Esp*. III.3.A)

A striking facet of this soaring speculation is its eminently practical quality. The soul is granted no permanent rest in passive contemplation. The same dynamic movement that led into the divine darkness propels the spirit into the clarity of God's personal image and the multiplicity of the entire creation established in that image. The contemplative, then, never abandons the active pursuit of good works and the practice of virtue with which the spiritual journey began. Externally not much seems to have changed in the process. Yet internally all has become different, for those who have been raised up above their created being are internally "transformed and become one with that same light with which they see and which they see" (*Esp*. III.3.B). Creatures now appear in their divine foundation as well as in their divinely created otherness. They are to be respected and cherished for both.

Ruusbroec's theology of the Trinity thus lays a firm foundation for a spiritual morality as well as for a mysticism of creation. Finitude itself, however different from God, is never separate. His ideal is not uninterrupted contemplation, but a "common life," the *ghemeyne leven*, which, constantly moving back and forth between ingoing and outflowing, hides the deepest interiority under the practice of everyday virtue. The balance of this ideal has never been surpassed: It retains the Dominican ideal of *contemplata tradere* and anticipates the later, Jesuit model, *in actione contemplativus*. Ruusbroec does not present this ideal as a practical compromise for

PREFACE

the sake of charity: It follows directly from the dynamic Trinitarian character of his mysticism itself.

Here lies the secret of Ruusbroec's lasting appeal to spiritual men and women. The cyclical character of his mystical theory allows them, at whatever level they may find themselves, to join an upward movement that returns even the lowliest earthly reality to its divine origin, and a downward movement that grants that reality a divine attention.

The study of Ruusbroec owes much, if not all, to the admirable work of three generations of the Antwerp *Ruusbroecgenootschap* (Ruusbroec Society). What started with the text editions and early monographs of those pioneers of Flemish medieval spirituality—Reypens, Stracke, Van Mierlo, Poukens, Moereels—reached a synthesis in Albert Ampe's unsurpassed systematic exposition and, under the inspiring impulse of Albert Deblaere, a remarkable harvest of fresh, impressively competent work by the new generation of Alaerts, de Baere, Mommaers, and Verdeyen. The new, critical edition now being published in the Low Countries, with its bilingual translation and its excellent introductions, stands as an admirable witness of their common labors.

FOREWORD

John Ruusbroec (1293–1381) is universally regarded as the most important of the Flemish mystics and as one of the most outstanding of all the mystical writers who made the fourteenth century unique: Meister Eckhart, John Tauler, Henry Suso, Catherine of Siena, Bridget of Sweden, Julian of Norwich, Walter Hilton, Richard Rolle, and the author of *The Cloud of Unknowing*. A keen sensitivity to the needs of all the members of the Church of his day, a profound appropriation of the main lines of both Western and Eastern Christian theology, and a rare gift for describing the highest levels of mystical experience—these are among the qualities that have led to his being called "Ruusbroec the Admirable" and "perhaps the very greatest of the mystics of the Church."

With this present edition, four of the most important of Ruusbroec's eleven treatises become available for the first time within a single volume in English translation. It is to be hoped that these translations, together with the information provided in the Preface, Introduction, and Bibliography, will significantly increase the interest in and knowledge of Ruusbroec that have been growing in the English-speaking world since the publication of Evelyn Underhill's two books, *Mysticism* and *Ruysbroeck*, in the second decade of the twentieth century.

The translator here wishes gratefully to acknowledge the generous assistance he has received from many persons in the course of his work. These include five Belgian Jesuits connected with the *Ruusbroecgenootschap* in Antwerp: Fathers Joseph Alaerts, Albert Ampe, Jozef Andriessen, Paul Mommaers, and Paul Verdeyen; Father Albert Deblaere of the Pontifical Gregorian University; Sister Helen Rolfson of St. John's University in Collegeville, Minnesota; Professor Louis Dupré of Yale University; Mrs. Elizabeth Gerrety of the Lauinger Library at Georgetown University; and Dr. John Farina, editor-in-chief of the Classics of Western Spirituality.

INTRODUCTION

In an early account of Ruusbroec's life, written about forty years after his death, Henry Pomerius noted that during the mystic's lifetime people would come from many places in northern Europe—"from Strasbourg, Basel, and other places, especially from along the Rhine"—to consult with him at Groenendaal, the Augustinian priory southeast of Brussels where he spent the final thirty-eight years of his life.[1] Many others, unable to visit Ruusbroec at Groenendaal, appropriated his teaching by reading manuscripts of his works, which already in his own lifetime began to be frequently copied both in his native Brabantine dialect of Middle Dutch and in translations into other Germanic dialects or Latin. Nearer our own day, persons who have devoted their lives to the study of mystical writings are generally agreed on the preeminent quality of Ruusbroec's work. Early in the twentieth century Evelyn Underhill, in her groundbreaking work *Mysticism*, turned to Ruusbroec more than to any other mystic when treating the culmination of the mystical experience in the final chapter of her book, for she judged his description of what she termed "the unitive life" to be of unparalleled excellence. So, too, Louis Cognet, the respected French historian of Christian spirituality, held Ruusbroec's work to be "one of the most exceptional achievements that Western mysticism has produced."[2] The main purpose of this Introduction will be to show why Ruusbroec's writings are so important and to place them within their religious and cultural context, in order that readers living more than six centuries after the time of their composition may approach them with as much understanding as possible.

---

1. *De origine monasterii Viridisvallis*, in *Analecta Bollandiana* 4 (1885): 296.
2. Louis Cognet, *Introduction aux mystiques rhéno-flamands* (Paris: Desclée, 1968), p. 281.

INTRODUCTION

RUUSBROEC'S LIFE AND WRITINGS

From His Birth through
His Earliest Years in Brussels

The person who was to become the best known of the Flemish mystics was born in 1293 in the village of Ruusbroec and so in later life came to be known as Jan van Ruusbroec ("John of Ruusbroec") or simply as Ruusbroec (frequently spelled Ruysbroeck in modern English). We have practically no biographical information about the first decade of Ruusbroec's life, but when he was eleven he went to Brussels (eight kilometers northeast of his native village) to live with a relative, John Hinckaert, who was a canon of the large collegiate church of St. Gudula. His early biographer Pomerius writes that for the next four years Ruusbroec was a pupil in Brussels. During this time he presumably pursued the trivium—that is, the subjects of grammar, logic, and rhetoric, which in the Middle Ages comprised the first stage of schooling. Nothing at all is said in any early document of Ruusbroec's further education, but we may assume that it was primarily intended to prepare him for the priesthood, for he was ordained in 1317, at the age of twenty-four.

Ruusbroec spent the next twenty-six years of his life serving as a chaplain at St. Gudula. Here, too, all the early sources are rather silent about most details of his priestly life. Pomerius writes that Ruusbroec would seldom go out into the city, inasmuch as he loved the quiet of contemplation more than external activity. The one activity from these years that the biographer does recount at some length concerns Ruusbroec's attempts to combat the heretical teaching of a woman named Bloemardinne, but since no writings of hers have survived it is impossible to say in precisely what her teaching consisted or even to be certain just how accurate Pomerius's account of this episode in Ruusbroec's life is. We do, however, know that during his years in Brussels Ruusbroec was intent on opposing certain heretical teachings of his day, for he vigorously criticizes these at several places in his earliest treatises, which were written during this period of his life. In fact, this seems to have been the main reason he began writing his treatises in the first place. In the earliest account of his life that has come down to us, his friend Brother Gerard, a monk of the Carthusian monastery at Herne in Brabant, says that the mystic began to write because he perceived "a great need for holy and complete teaching written in the

Dutch language . . . because of some insidious and unorthodox teachings which were then current."[3] A more specific reference to the teachings Ruusbroec was opposing is to be found in a long letter written by John of Schoonhoven, who had entered Ruusbroec's own religious community at Groenendaal at the beginning of 1378, almost four years before the mystic's death. In this letter, composed in the first decade of the fifteenth century in response to John Gerson's critique of certain aspects of Ruusbroec's teaching, John of Schoonhoven writes at one point that God had endowed Ruusbroec with special gifts "in order that he might eradicate and expose the errors of the sect of those Free Spirits who during his lifetime had been greatly multiplying in Brabant and neighboring regions."[4] Because of the important role the movement of the Free Spirit thus played in the genesis of Ruusbroec's own writings, the next section of this Introduction will consider the background and nature of this heresy.

The Heresy of the Free Spirit: Its Background and Major Tenets

As the Oxford historian R. W. Southern observes in his survey of the interrelationship between the Church and society in the Middle Ages, a great expansion in all facets of western European life began around the middle of the eleventh century and consolidated itself so rapidly as to make this "the most remarkable fact in medieval history."[5] By the beginning of the twelfth century, new religious orders were beginning to make their appearance, with lay associations of various kinds growing up around their fringes, and by the first quarter of the thirteenth century the last and most important of these new orders—the Dominicans and Franciscans—had come into existence and were beginning to spread rapidly throughout Europe. This was, then, on the whole a time of great vitality and optimism for the Church.

A century later, the picture was very different. By then the mendicant orders had lost much of their initial fervor and were coming under increas-

---

3. "Die prologhe van her Gerardus," ed. Willem de Vreese, *Het Belfort* 10, pt. 2 (1895): 11. Brother Gerard wrote about Ruusbroec in this Prologue, which introduced a collection of five of the mystic's treatises that Gerard had copied.

4. *Epistola responsalis*, in André Combes, *Essai sur la critique de Ruysbroeck par Gerson*, 3 vols. (Paris: J. Vrin, 1945–1959), 1:729.

5. R. W. Southern, *Western Society and the Church in the Middle Ages* (New York: Penguin, 1970), p. 34.

ingly frequent attacks for precisely that accumulation of wealth which their founders, especially St. Francis, had so feared. The words that Ruus-broec's fourteenth-century contemporary, Geoffrey Chaucer, placed on the lips of the summoner in *The Canterbury Tales* could not have been voiced a century earlier:

> Since you have heard this filthy friar lie,
> Let me refute him. I've a tale to tell!
> This friar boasts his knowledge about hell,
> And if he does, God knows it's little wonder;
> Friars and fiends are seldom far asunder.[6]

Nor was this decline in the overall fervor and reputation of the mendicant orders the only, or even the major, reason why the fourteenth century was a period of great turmoil for both the Church and society at large—the kind of turmoil that has led later historians to call the fourteenth century "the age of adversity," "an age of unrest," or simply "not a happy time for humanity."[7] It was in that century that the Hundred Years' War began, that the Black Death caused millions of deaths throughout the European continent, and that large uprisings of peasants took place in France and the Low Countries. The "Babylonian Captivity" of the popes in Avignon lasted for the greater part of the century (from 1309 to 1377) and was followed by the Western Schism, with two and at times three men each claiming to be the lawful pope. Bishops of the period were often criticized for a preoccupation with wealth, a preoccupation seen as diametrically opposed to the attitude of Christ and his Apostles toward riches, while among the lower clergy there was much illiteracy and, consequently, meager or nonexistent preaching. Not surprisingly, such conditions provided fertile soil for the growth of heretical sects, such as that of the Lollards, as well as of less-organized heretical quests for individual perfection, such as the movement of the Free Spirit. As Robert Lerner writes in his study of the Free Spirit, "In an age of incessant war, famine, and plague, as well as sharp economic insecurity, extremist systems become attractive."[8]

---

6. "The Summoner's Tale," lines 6–10, in *The Canterbury Tales*, trans. Nevill Coghill, 2d ed. (Baltimore: Penguin, 1958), p. 319.

7. These three terms are from Robert Lerner of Northwestern University, R. W. Southern of Oxford, and J. C. L. S. de Sismondi, the nineteenth-century Swiss historian.

8. Robert Lerner, *The Heresy of the Free Spirit in the Later Middle Ages* (Berkeley and Los Angeles: University of California Press, 1972), p. 243.

INTRODUCTION

A major source of difficulty in writing about this last-named heresy is the fact that the Free Spirit never constituted a well-defined sect. Gordon Leff, a British historian who has specialized in the study of medieval heresy, writes that the heresy of the Free Spirit was really "a state of mind as much as a settled body of doctrine,"[9] while some of the twentieth century's leading historians of spirituality have gone even further by suggesting that the term "Free Spirit" is best used to refer simply to a number of independent, though similar, phenomena.[10] In any case, the wide range of positions attributed to Free Spirit thought already in the Middle Ages is evident in one of the earliest descriptions of the movement, St. Albert the Great's *Compilatio de novo spiritu*.[11] Written sometime between 1262 and 1280, it contains ninety-seven propositions claimed to be characteristic of the heresy, among them the following: that humans and all other beings are of the same substance as God; that a person can become God; and that such a person is freed from all ecclesiastical obligations and from the observance of fastdays, feasts, confession, and prayer, since these are all obstacles to perfection. However, since we do not know just how Albert obtained these propositions and since his list contains many repetitions and contradictions, it will be more helpful to turn to some of the literature of the movement itself.

One of the most important testimonies of Free Spirit thought is *The Mirror of Simple Souls*, written in Old French around the beginning of the fourteenth century. This work has been known to students of mysticism for many centuries, but only toward the middle of the present century was it correctly identified by Romana Guarnieri as the work of a French beguine, Margaret Porete, who because of it was condemned of heresy at Paris and burned at the stake in 1310.[12] This lengthy treatise is in the form of a dialogue between Love and Reason concerning the conduct of a soul and has as one of its major themes that of extreme passivity in religious conduct. This theme is broached early on in the work, when the liberated

---

9. Gordon Leff, *Heresy in the Later Middle Ages*, 2 vols. (Manchester: Manchester University Press, 1967), 1:400.

10. Jean Orcibal, "Le 'Miroir des simples âmes' et la 'secte' du Libre Esprit," *Revue de l'histoire des religions*, tome 176 (1969): 37; Josephus de Guibert, *Documenta Ecclesiastica Christianae Perfectionis Studium Spectantia* (Rome: Pontificia Universitas Gregoriana, 1931), p. 115.

11. Albert's *Compilatio* is printed in de Guibert's *Documenta* (see previous note), pp. 116–25.

12. Guarnieri first announced her discovery in 1946. She has since edited and published the Old French text of the treatise—*Le mirouer des simples ames*—in the *Archivio italiano per la storia della pieta* 4 (1965): 501–635.

soul exclaims: "Virtues, I take leave of you forever,"[13] a statement repeated a number of times throughout the treatise. At another point Love says of the soul that "this daughter of Zion has no desire for Masses or sermons, for fasting or prayers," and goes on to explain the reason for this lack of desire: "Why should this soul desire the things named above, since God is just as present everywhere without these things as with them?"[14]

This disparaging of the sacramental mediation of the Church is singled out by Robert Lerner as one of the three major points by which the devotees of the Free Spirit skirted orthodoxy.[15] The other two points Lerner advances are the Free Spirits' autotheism, that is, their belief in the possibility of a person's total identification with God on earth, and, closely related to this, the view that this identification can be lasting rather than momentary. No such unqualified claims are to be found in *The Mirror of Simple Souls*, but they do appear in another important Free Spirit tract, *Sister Catherine*.[16] This treatise, probably written in Strasbourg in the first half of the fourteenth century, was originally composed in Alemannic but was soon translated into other Germanic dialects as well as into Latin. It purports to describe the relationship between a beguine named Catherine and her confessor, the famous German mystic Meister Eckhart. At one point Catherine unqualifiedly proclaims, "Sir, rejoice with me. I have become God,"[17] and later assures her confessor that this is a permanent identification:

> "I am confirmed in the bare Godhead, in which there is neither form nor image." "Are you there for good?" he asked. She answered, "Yes. . . . I am as I was before I was created: just God and God. . . . In God there is nothing but God. No soul gets to God until it is God, as it was before it was made."[18]

---

13. Ibid., pp. 525, 544, etc. It should be noted that, in its context, such a statement is not an invitation to libertine behavior; Margaret Porete elsewhere states that a nature transformed by Love is so well ordered that it does not seek anything that is prohibited (527). It was above all the book's quietistic tendency that made it theologically suspect.

14. Ibid., pp. 536, 537. When in 1312 the ecumenical Council of Vienne condemned "errors of the beghards and beguines concerning the state of perfection," several of the condemned articles seem to have been based on Margaret Porete's book. Thus, the second condemned proposition reads: "That it is not necessary to fast or pray after one has attained this degree of perfection, since one's sensual nature is now so perfectly subject to his spiritual and rational nature that such a person can freely grant his body whatever is pleasing to it." For more on this point, see Lerner, *The Heresy of the Free Spirit*, pp. 78–84.

15. Lerner, *The Heresy of the Free Spirit*, p. 227.

16. *Daz ist Swester Katrei*, in *Deutsche Mystiker des vierzehnten Jahrhunderts*, ed. Franz Pfeiffer, 2 vols. (Leipzig, 1845–1857; Aalen: Scientia Verlag, 1962), 2:448–75.

17. Ibid., p. 465.

18. Ibid., pp. 468–69.

INTRODUCTION

Whether or not this treatise was known directly by Ruusbroec, its teaching on the possibility of a person's becoming God had been considered a characteristic of the Free Spirit movement already at the time of Albert's *Compilatio* in the preceding century. Such a teaching was among those denounced by Ruusbroec in his writings, particularly his later ones.

RUUSBROEC'S TWO EARLIEST TREATISES:
THE KINGDOM OF LOVERS AND THE SPIRITUAL ESPOUSALS

The first of Ruusbroec's works, *The Kingdom of Lovers*, was probably written in the early 1330s, while he was still serving as a chaplain at St. Gudula. The longest section of this treatise concerns the seven gifts of the Holy Spirit, which Ruusbroec compares to seven streams by which the Spirit leads a truly righteous person to eternal life. According to Brother Gerard, Ruusbroec was not altogether satisfied with this, his first work, and did not intend it to be published. He was therefore surprised to learn, when he visited Brother Gerard's monastery about 1362, that the monks there possessed a copy of it, for it had been given them without Ruusbroec's knowledge by a priest who had formerly been his secretary. Rather than have them return the copy, however, Ruusbroec said that he would instead write another work in which he would elucidate those points that had seemed of doubtful orthodoxy to Brother Gerard and his confreres. Their difficulties centered above all on Ruusbroec's treatment of the gift of counsel, in particular his claim that in the simple enjoyment of God's being a person will become "one [with God] without difference" (*één sonder differencie*). Ruusbroec's later, explanatory treatise, *The Little Book of Clarification*, treats three modes of union with God, of which the third is precisely this "union without difference."

If Ruusbroec was not completely satisfied with his first work, his attitude toward his second, *The Spiritual Espousals*, was quite different. Brother Gerard writes that Ruusbroec "considered it altogether reliable and good" and adds that it had become widely known and read already in the mystic's lifetime.[19] Ever since, this work has been almost unanimously looked upon as his masterpiece. Leonce Reypens, one of the twentieth century's pioneers in the revival of Ruusbroec studies, even claimed that most of the mystic's subsequent treatises may be regarded primarily as works adapting the teaching of the *Espousals* for different kinds of readers or clar-

---

19. "Die prologhe van her Gerardus," p. 14.

7

ifying one or another aspect of that teaching either in response to a request for clarification or in order to meet some objection.[20] Since this is also the first and longest of the treatises included in the present volume, a number of introductory remarks are in order.

The Prologue and book one of the *Espousals*

Ruusbroec probably wrote *The Spiritual Espousals* not long after finishing *The Kingdom of Lovers*. Its Prologue opens with a quotation from Scripture, taken from the parable of the virgins in Matthew's Gospel: "See, the bridegroom is coming. Go out to meet him" (Mt 25:6). This verse serves as a leitmotiv for the entire treatise, for in the three "books" of the *Espousals* he explains the spiritual import of these words for each of three ways of Christian living: the active life, the interior life, and the contemplative life.

The active life, which by itself characterizes the life of beginners and is the minimum necessary for anyone who wishes to be saved, is discussed by Ruusbroec in the four parts of book one of his treatise, sections that correspond to the fourfold division he makes in his Scriptural leitmotiv: "(1) See, (2) the bridegroom is coming. (3) Go out (4) to meet him." In the relatively short first part, Ruusbroec considers what is necessary for someone in the active life to be able to see in a supernatural sense, while in the second part he discusses three comings of Christ the Bridegroom: in the past through the Incarnation, in the present in our daily lives, and in the future at the Last Judgment. It is in considering the second of these three comings that Ruusbroec presents the first of the many extended similes that characterize key points of his teaching in this work. This first simile consists of a lengthy comparison between Christ and the sun as it sends forth its rays into a deep valley between two mountains. Although some aspects of this and others of Ruusbroec's similes will probably strike modern readers as somewhat forced and artificial, there is no doubt that such literary devices serve to make his teaching more vivid and memorable than purely abstract and general statements would be.

The longest part of book one of the *Espousals* is the third. In it Ruusbroec discusses many of the virtues and virtuous activities that are necessary if a person is to "go out" to God and neighbor in the following of Christ. These virtues include humility (as the foundation of all the virtues), obedience, renunciation of one's own will, patience, meekness, kindness,

---

20. "Le sommet de la contemplation mystique chez le bienheureux Jean de Ruusbroec," *Revue d'ascétique et de mystique* 3 (1922): 253.

compassion, generosity, zeal, moderation, purity, righteousness, and charity, and their treatment by Ruusbroec is intricately and ingeniously correlated with the beatitudes and the overcoming of the capital sins. There may be a tendency on the part of many readers today, eager to get to the more "exalted" aspects of Ruusbroec's mystical doctrine, to pass quickly over such passages. But if Ruusbroec is to be properly understood, any such tendency should be firmly resisted. As noted earlier in this Introduction, one of Ruusbroec's primary motivations in writing his first treatises was to counter that broad, amorphous attitude known as the heresy of the Free Spirit, one of whose major characteristics was precisely the disparaging of what Ruusbroec calls the active life. In fact, some of the most severe language in the *Espousals* is directed against this error:

> Those guilty of this deviation are, in their own estimation, contemplatives. . . . Because of the natural rest which they feel and possess within themselves in a state of emptiness, they conclude that they are free and are united with God without intermediary. They also believe that they are above all the practices of the holy Church, above God's commandments, above the law, and above all virtuous works which might be practiced in any manner, for they consider this state of emptiness to be so great a thing that it must not be disturbed by any works. . . .
>   . . . They accordingly do not observe fastdays or feastdays or any of the commandments except insofar as they do so to be seen by others, for they live without conscience in all things.
>   I hope there are not many such persons to be found, for they are the most wicked and harmful persons alive and can hardly ever be converted.[21]

It should be clear from even these few lines that for Ruusbroec the active life is not some mere preliminary to a mystical way of life proper but rather forms an integral part of *every* truly Christian life. An accurate grasp of his teaching will therefore require close attention to all that he says about the virtues in this section of the *Espousals*.

The fourth and final part of book one, treating three ways of meeting the divine Bridegroom, introduces several important themes that will frequently recur in the treatise: the interrelationship between what is today

---

21. *The Spiritual Espousals*, book two, part four, section C. Henceforth, the source of a quotation from this treatise will be cited in the text according to the following format: II.4.C. For Ruusbroec's other treatises, none of which are divided into "books," the citations will include only the number of the part and the letter of the section.

often called the *via negativa* (or apophatic mysticism) and the *via affirmativa* (or kataphatic mysticism); the roles of knowledge and love in the spiritual life; and the simultaneity of working and resting. The first of these themes appears in Ruusbroec's treatment of the first way of meeting God, namely, by directing the mind to God in everything that concerns our salvation. Like all genuine Christian mystics, Ruusbroec is well aware that God ultimately transcends all the concepts, images, and names we might apply to him: "Although there are many names which we attribute to God, his sublime nature is a simple oneness which no creature can name" (I.4.A). Mystics of the *via negativa* like Pseudo-Dionysius and Meister Eckhart adhere rigorously to this principle and consequently place much emphasis on the need for silence vis-à-vis the divine darkness. That Ruusbroec will not follow their lead in every respect is evident already here in book one of the *Espousals*, for he offers a very positive appreciation of the practice of "naming God" even as he recognizes its partial inadequacy: "In whatever ways or under whatever names a person represents God as the Lord of all creation, he is doing well. . . . Because of his incomprehensible nobility and sublimity, which we can neither name nor fully express, we give him all these names. This is the way and the kind of knowledge by which we should keep God present in our mind" (I.4.A). In our later consideration of book three of the *Espousals*, more will be said about the way in which Ruusbroec distances himself from the strict practitioners of the *via negativa*.

It is likewise in his discussion of the need to direct the mind to God in everything that concerns our salvation that Ruusbroec broaches the theme of the respective roles of knowledge and love in the spiritual life. After noting that such direction of the mind to God is the same as seeing God in a certain way, Ruusbroec immediately adds that "to this activity belong also affection and love, for knowing and seeing God without affection has no savor and does not help us advance" (I.4.A). In making this assertion, which recurs in various formulations throughout the treatise, Ruusbroec is placing himself firmly within the Christian mystical tradition, in which contemplation has most commonly and most concisely been understood as a certain "loving knowledge" of God. And if it is true that for some mystics the aspect of knowing predominates and for others the aspect of loving, for Ruusbroec there is a very evident balance and harmony between both these poles. For him, and for the mystics of the Low Countries in general, the various powers of the soul are experienced not as separate faculties but as one unified dynamism. Neither the understanding nor the will, neither knowledge nor love, can be said to predominate, for

10

the two are inextricably intertwined in an experience of union in which God is both known or "seen" in a new dimension of consciousness and loved in what Ruusbroec, at the very end of the *Espousals*, calls "a blissful embrace of loving immersion."[22]

After very briefly noting that the second way of meeting the Bridegroom in the active life consists in our not directing the mind to any other end considered equal in importance to God, Ruusbroec states that the third and final way is by resting in God above all creatures. Indeed, such resting in God above all gifts, above oneself, and above all creatures brings one to "the highest level of the active life" (I.4.C). At first sight, it may seem very strange to read that the culmination of the active life consists not in some particular kind of activity but rather in rest, but in fact this reflects one of the most characteristic tenets of Ruusbroec's entire doctrine. As already noted by Louis Dupré in his Preface to this volume, Ruusbroec's Trinitarian theology is marked by a twofold movement: At one pole there is the movement inward toward "the dark silence" and toward rest in the "superessential Unity," while at the other pole there is, simultaneously, a movement outward in the generation of the Son and the breathing forth of the Holy Spirit. As was the case with the interrelationship between knowledge and love, this is an understanding Ruusbroec shares with the mystics of the Low Countries in general. In the words of Paul Mommaers of the *Ruusbroecgenootschap*: "When the Flemish mystics speak of God, they emphatically affirm. . . that God is, at one and the same time, repose and activity, essence and persons. He is at all times both these aspects. . . . Repose is not only the 'perfection' of activity; activity is just as much the 'perfection' of repose."[23] This same simultaneous interplay between repose and activity, rest and work, likewise characterizes the lives of all those who have been created in the divine image and who live in accordance with that image. As Ruusbroec writes at one point with all possible clarity: "Anyone who does not possess both rest and activity in one and the same exercise has not attained this righteousness" (II.4.C). This being so, it is only to be expected that Ruusbroec would emphasize not only virtuous activity but also loving repose in God in his treatment of the active life.

---

22. On this point, see Albert Deblaere, "The Netherlands [School of Mysticism]," in *Sacramentum Mundi: An Encyclopedia of Theology*, ed. Karl Rahner, 6 vols. (New York: Herder and Herder, 1969), 4:144.

23. Paul Mommaers, "Bulletin d'histoire de la spiritualité: L'école néerlandaise," *Revue d'histoire de la spiritualité* 49 (1973): 474.

Book two of the *Espousals*

From what has just been said, it should also be clear that the transition from the active life to what Ruusbroec calls the interior life does not in any sense require the abandonment of the works and virtues characteristic of the active life. Rather, it is a matter of becoming free from any distracted or distracting absorption in a multiplicity of works, from what Ruusbroec calls "restlessness of heart" (II.4.B). In place of such restlessness there will occur a deeper and deeper unification of all our powers, which the mystic describes as the supernatural "adorning" of certain unities that are within us already by nature. The highest of these unities is that which creatures have in God himself, a unity that preserves our very being, for without it we would at once fall into nothingness. The next unity is called "the unity of the higher powers," that is, the powers of memory, understanding, and will. Ruusbroec says that this is actually the same unity as the first, only here it is being considered not in its essence but in its activity, as the source of "our entire power of performing spiritual activity" (II.1.B). The third and lowest unity is that of the heart, considered as the source of our sensory activity and all other works of the body.

In part one of the second book of the *Espousals*, corresponding to the word "See" in his scriptural leitmotiv, Ruusbroec briefly describes how these three unities are to be "supernaturally adorned and possessed" in the active life and goes on to describe how they "are more beautifully adorned and more nobly possessed when fervent interior exercises are added to those of the active life" (II.1.B). As the foundation and source of such exercises he names three things: God's working within us through an interior impulse or urging of the Holy Spirit; our stripping of all strange images and creaturely attachments from the heart; and a gathering together of all our powers in such a way that, with our will unencumbered, we might turn to God as often as we wish. All this, he concludes, brings about an enlightenment of our understanding and so enables us to see in a way characteristic of the interior life.

Contrary to the procedure he follows in books one and three of the treatise, here in book two Ruusbroec comments on the scriptural phrases "the Bridegroom is coming" and "go out" together rather than in two separate sections; for that reason, I have followed other modern editors in heading this long section of book two with the title "Parts Two and Three." On the basis of what he has already said about the three unities that exist in every human being, Ruusbroec begins this part by writing that there are three comings of Christ in the interior life: an inward urging or attraction in the heart, an influx of divine gifts into the three higher powers, and "an interior stirring or touch in the unity of the spirit."

The first of these comings occurs, then, in the affective side of our nature and is characterized by four different modes. Of these, the first three consist of increasingly intense experiences of consolation and joy in God, while the fourth is a state of emptiness and desolation. Throughout the treatment of these four modes, Ruusbroec illustrates his meaning through similes drawn from changes in the sun's heat and its varying effects on the earth from late springtime till early autumn, as the sun passes through the zodiacal signs of Gemini, Cancer, Leo, Virgo, and Libra. Here, too, are found two of the best known of all Ruusbroec's extended similes, those of the bee and the ant, which illustrate how a person in the interior life will behave when experiencing a superabundance of consolation (mode two) and a restless "transport of love" (mode three). While the mystic's descriptions of these various degrees of religious consolation and joy are as acute and as beautiful as any in mystical literature, at least as impressive is his sane and judicious treatment of how a person will ideally behave during those periods of emptiness and desolation that are an inevitable part of any authentic spiritual life:

> All the exterior and interior virtues which were ever practiced with delight in the fire of love will now be practiced with diligence and with a good heart insofar as a person knows how and is able, for never before were they so valuable in God's eyes, never before so noble and fine. A person will gladly do without all the consolation which God ever bestowed upon him if that is for God's glory. . . . In this way the virtues come to their perfection, and sadness is changed into eternal wine. (II.2/3.A)

After describing various obstacles to this kind of proper behavior in times of desolation, Ruusbroec concludes his treatment of this first coming of Christ by showing how the latter is himself our model in all four modes. Such references to Christ as the exemplar for our own behavior recur several more times at the conclusion of particular sections of the *Espousals*. The relative frequency of these references, each covering several pages, is an indication of how seriously Ruusbroec took his own admonition: "If we are not to go astray, we must walk in the light and keep our eyes fixed on Christ" (II.2/3.A).

In turning to the second coming of the divine Bridegroom, Ruusbroec employs a different image from that of the sun to help clarify his meaning, for he compares this coming to a spring of water with three streams flowing from it. These are "streams of God's grace," and each flows into one of the three higher powers: The first stream raises the memory to a state of simplicity, above the distractions of sensible images; the second stream enlightens the understanding, so that a person may see and behold something of the nature of the Godhead and the attributes of the three divine Persons; and the third stream enkindles the will and so leads a person to "go out" to God in love and to various categories of human beings in both love and compassion. After once more referring to Christ as our model in this, Ruusbroec depicts in harsh terms the sorry state of the Church's leadership in his own day. Whereas the popes, bishops, and priests of the early Church lived generally exemplary lives, "today the situation is just the opposite," for the leaders of the Church

> have turned completely to worldly concerns and do not have thoroughly at heart the matters and concerns which have been placed in their hands. For this reason they pray with their lips, but their heart does not savor the meaning of their prayers. . . . As a result, they are coarse and dull and are not enlightened with divine truth. Sometimes they seek to eat and drink well and to enjoy bodily comforts without moderation—and would to God that they were chaste of body. As long as they live in this way they will never attain enlightenment. (II.2/3.B)

Obviously Ruusbroec sensed the importance of speaking out not only against the heretics of his day but also against those churchmen whose poor example in positions of leadership had much to do with the rise and spread of heresies.

Ruusbroec retains the imagery of water to describe the third coming of the Bridegroom, likening it to an underground vein that feeds the spring and the three streams of the second coming. The very word he most frequently uses to describe this third coming—*gherinen,* regularly translated into English as "touch"—may even have carried for Ruusbroec connotations of Eckhart's term *rinen* (to flow) and so have referred to the "touch" or "impact" the flowing vein of God's grace produces in the unity of the spirit.[24] Above all, Ruusbroec insists that this touch cannot be brought

---

24. This was first suggested by Helmut Hatzfeld, "The Influence of Ramon Lull and Jan van Ruysbroeck on the Language of the Spanish Mystics," *Traditio* 4 (1946): 383–84. For a lengthier treatment of this mystical *gherinen*, see Leonce Reypens, "Ruusbroec-studiën: I, Het mystieke 'gherinen,' " *Ons Geestelijk Erf* 12 (1938): 158–86.

about through any human agency: "A creature undergoes this touch passively," for "at this level no one is active but God alone" (II.2/3.C).

This terminology of touch, together with Ruusbroec's insistence that it is undergone passively, highlights the two complementary aspects by which Christian mystics have regularly described the special character of their experience: that it is a "direct" or "immediate" experience of God and that it is undergone "passively." There have been numerous ways by which such mystics have tried to convey through words the directness of their experience, but one of the most-favored ways, from the time of the Greek Fathers, has been through the terminology of touch. The reason for this preference is surely that which Albert Deblaere points out in an important article on the essential character of Christian mysticism, namely, the fact that of all the five senses that of touch is "the coarsest [*le plus grossier*] and most sensual, but also the most direct," and so serves in a particularly fitting way "to designate the first mystical 'contact' " with God.[25]

But if the touch itself is passively received, its effect is the awakening of an intense kind of activity on the part of the human spirit, for the latter becomes filled with an insatiable hunger and craving for God. This is what Ruusbroec calls "the storm of love" or "the struggle of love":

> . . . in this most profound meeting, in this most intimate and ardent encounter, each spirit is wounded by love. These two spirits, that is, our spirit and God's Spirit, cast a radiant light upon one another and each reveals to the other its countenance. This makes the two spirits incessantly strive after one another in love. Each demands of the other what it is, and each offers to the other and invites it to accept what it is. This makes these loving spirits lose themselves in one another. (II.2/3.C)

According to Ruusbroec, this experience constitutes the apex of the interior life, "the most interior exercise a person can practice when enlightened by created light" (II.2/3.C). Above this there is only what the mystic calls the contemplative life, for the divine touch that gives rise to the struggle just described is "the last intermediary between God and his creature. Above this touch, in the still being of the spirit, there hovers an incomprehensible resplendence; this is the sublime Trinity, from which this touch proceeds. There God lives and reigns in the spirit, and the spirit in God" (II.2/3.C).

---

25. Albert Deblaere, "Témoinage mystique chrétien," *Studia Missionalia* 26 (1977): 127. In this article, Deblaere also discusses the "direct" and the "passive" character of mystical experience.

INTRODUCTION

From such references to the culmination of the interior life at the conclusion of this section of the *Espousals*, one would almost expect that in the fourth and final part of book two Ruusbroec would turn immediately to the life that follows the interior life in his tripartite scheme, namely, the contemplative life. Such an expectation would be warranted, for in fact part four does serve as a transition to the treatment of the contemplative life in book three and may even be said to constitute its threshold. Moreover, the material in this final part of book two not only points forward to book three but also recapitulates much of what has preceded it, both in book one and in the first three parts of book two. This recapitulation is, however, no mere summary but rather what Paul Mommaers calls "a true rereading" (*une véritable relecture*), in which the virtues of the active life and the mediated experiences of union in the interior life are shown to be organically related to that contemplative "union without intermediary" which is still to be described.[26]

In accordance with his scriptural leitmotiv from the parable of the virgins, Ruusbroec here discusses various ways of "meeting the Bridegroom." He first says that there are two such ways—with intermediary and without intermediary—but at once goes on to show that there are really three ways, since there is both a natural and a supernatural meeting (or union) without intermediary. The natural union without intermediary is the basis or precondition for the other two and is in fact the same as that unity with God which simply preserves us in being and which was already discussed at the beginning of book two of the *Espousals*. Here in the final part of the same book, Ruusbroec notes that this unity renders us neither holy nor blessed, since all persons possess it, good and bad alike; it is, however, "the first principle of all holiness and blessedness" (II.4.A).

In proceeding to his discussion of the union with intermediary, Ruusbroec uses the doctrine of the seven gifts of the Holy Spirit to structure his "rereading" of what has already been said about the active and the interior life. The first three gifts—fear of the Lord, kindness, and knowledge—in particular lead a person to "progress. . . in virtue and in his likeness to God." Such progress, together with that concomitant resting in God which was earlier shown to be an integral part of the active life, is said by Ruusbroec to constitute "the entire active life." The next two gifts—fortitude

---

26. Paul Mommaers, "Une phrase clef des *Noces spirituelles*," in *Jan van Ruusbroec: The Sources, Content and Sequels of His Mysticism*, ed. Paul Mommaers and Norbert De Paepe (Louvain: Leuven University Press, 1984), pp. 102–3.

and counsel—are above all necessary for properly responding to the four modes of the first coming of Christ in the interior life. A careful reading of the mystic's treatment of these two gifts will reveal many correspondences with his earlier descriptions of those four modes—"interior consolation and sweetness" (as in modes one and two), "interior restlessness" (as in mode three), and a sense of being "abandoned by God" (as in mode four). He likewise repeats his admonition not to rest in any experience of consolation but rather to be willing to "forgo all gifts and all consolation for the sake of finding the one whom one loves." Ruusbroec's treatment of the last two gifts—understanding and wisdom—is even more explicit in the correlations made with earlier sections of the *Espousals*. Of the gift of understanding he writes that it "is what we previously likened to a spring with three streams" (that is, the second coming of the Bridegroom in the interior life), while of the gift of wisdom he states unequivocally that "this is a divine stirring or touch in the unity of our spirit" and proceeds to describe once more that "storm of love" earlier portrayed in his treatment of the third coming of the Bridegroom.

Following this recapitulation of all he has said previously about various kinds of union with intermediary, Ruusbroec turns to the supernatural union without intermediary. He here employs some of the same terminology that will appear even more frequently in his consideration of the contemplative life in book three, as when he writes that God's call "makes us lose ourselves and flow forth into the wild darkness of the Godhead. Thus united—one with the Spirit of God, without intermediary—we are able to meet God with God and endlessly possess our eternal blessedness with him and in him" (II.4.C). The proper interpretation of such a passage will be discussed in our consideration of book three; at this point it is first of all important to note that of the three modes Ruusbroec ascribes to this union without intermediary—namely, emptiness, active desire, and the concomitance of both resting and working—the second is explicity said to be "*with* intermediary" while the third is in large measure based on the intermediary of virtuous activity. From all that has been said earlier in this Introduction and in Louis Dupré's Preface about the Ruusbroeckian dialectic of rest and work, emptiness and virtuous activity, it should be clear that Ruusbroec's consideration of a union with intermediary in a section of the treatise devoted to the union without intermediary is not a matter of inconsistency on his part. Rather, it is but one more evidence of the mystic's basic principle that such realities are complementary and concomitant rather than consecutive. As Paul Henry observes in his long and carefully reasoned essay on Ruusbroec's Trinitarian mysticism,

17

INTRODUCTION

The reader familiar with other mystics, such as St. Teresa of Avila, for whom the spirtual "marriage" comes after the "full union" and the latter comes after the state of "quiet," will derive [from Ruusbroec] an impression of confusion and of disorder. But in fact *the concomitance of "intermediary" mystical states* at even the highest level is only a consistent corollary of his doctrine of the complementarity of divine moments [in the Trinity].[27]

It should only be added that Ruusbroec's teaching on the concomitance of these states derives not only from his Trinitarian theology but also, and perhaps more significantly, from the fact that he was above all a superb phenomenologist of the mystical life and therefore realized that such concomitance is truly more in accord with the lived reality of mystical experience. Nowhere is this more perceptively or more beautifully expressed than in the following passage, which comes near the end of his consideration of the union without intermediary:

> [A person in this state] is hungry and thirsty, for he sees angelic food and heavenly drink; he works intensely in love, for he sees his rest; he is a pilgrim and sees his fatherland; he strives for victory in love, for he sees his crown. Consolation, peace, joy, beauty, riches, and everything else that brings delight is revealed in God to the enlightened reason without measure in spiritual likenesses. Through this revelation and God's touch, love remains active, for this righteous person has established for himself a truly spiritual life in both rest and activity. . . .
>
> It is in all this that a person's righteousness consists. He goes toward God with fervent interior love through his eternal activity, enters into God with his blissful inclination toward eternal rest, remains in God, and nevertheless goes out to creatures in virtues and righteousness through a love which is common to all. This is the highest point of the interior life. (II.4.C)

As he nears the conclusion of book two of the *Espousals*, Ruusbroec warns at some length against various heretical deviations from this way of righteousness. These deviations, which could in general be called the quietisms of his day, were already referred to—and in part quoted—in our discussion of the mystic's stringent opposition to the movement of the Free Spirit. After describing these deviations according to three different but interrelated categories, Ruusbroec closes book two with a further reference

---

27. Paul Henry, "La mystique trinitaire du bienheureux Jean Ruusbroec: II," *Recherches de science religieuse* 41 (1953): 62.

18

to Christ as our model in leading the interior life and with a final allusion to the by-now-familiar dialectic of flux, reflux, and eternal rest: "We will eternally abide in God and constantly flow forth and ceaselessly turn back within. . . . May God help us that this might come about. Amen."

Book three of the *Espousals*

Because of its relatively great length and complex structure, book two of the *Espousals* was considered section by section in this Introduction. Book three, only one-eighth as long, does not so clearly call for such an approach. Instead, we will consider only two central points: the nature of the contemplative life according to Ruusbroec and, a related point, how he differs from the mystics of the *via negativa* in this regard.

To begin, an important essay on Ruusbroec's mystical teaching was written by Leonce Reypens in 1931, as part of the *Ruusbroecgenootschap*'s commemoration of the five hundred and fiftieth anniversary of Ruusbroec's death. In this essay Reypens stated that the mystic's teaching rests on "a foundation of exemplarism," a position that has been supported and developed by other scholars.[28] Since this exemplaristic foundation is especially pronounced in book three of the *Espousals*, something should be said here about the meaning of the term.

The scriptural roots of the doctrine of exemplarism are to be found in such texts as Colossians 1:15–16, where Christ is spoken of as the image of the invisible God, the firstborn of all creation, in whom, through whom, and for whom all things have been created, and John 1:1–4, where all things are said to come into being through the Word and (according to the punctuation of these verses still customary in Ruusbroec's time) to be life in the Word. Exemplarism is prominent in the writings of the Greek Fathers and St. Augustine, was given lengthy treatment by St. Anselm in his *Monologion*, and was likewise taught by St. Thomas Aquinas, who writes that in one sense all things "are in God through their own intelligible natures, which in God are the same as the divine essence. Hence things, as they exist in God in that way, are the divine essence."[29] In other words, creatures have not only their created being in the temporal order but also an eternal being in God, a being identical with God himself. Ruusbroec's own

---

28. Leonce Reypens, "Ruusbroec's mystieke leer," in *Jan van Ruusbroec: Leven, Werken*, ed. Ruusbroecgenootschap (Mechelen: Het Kompas, 1931), p. 151. The works by Ampe and Fraling listed in the Bibliography of the present volume also emphasize the exemplaristic element in Ruusbroec's works.

29. *Summa Theologiae* 1.18.4.ad 1.

most succinct statement of this appears in part three of the third book of the *Espousals*: "Through this eternal birth [of the Son] all creatures have gone forth eternally before their creation in time. God has thus seen and known them in himself—as distinct in his living ideas and as different from himself, though not different in every respect, for all that is in God is God" (III.3.A). Accordingly, "in this divine image all creatures have an eternal life apart from themselves, as in their eternal Exemplar" (III.3.A).

This doctrine is truly fundamental for Ruusbroec's understanding of the contemplative life, for he goes on to say that "it is to this eternal image and likeness that the Holy Trinity has created us. God therefore wills that we go out from ourselves into this divine light, supernaturally pursuing this image which is our own life and possessing it with him both actively and blissfully in a state of eternal blessedness" (III.3.B). Those who, through their generous cooperation with God's grace, have been raised up to attain this image are precisely those whom Ruusbroec calls contemplatives: Even though all creatures have this eternal life in God, contemplatives alone are able to "behold" or experience it. For this reason, book three of the *Espousals* may be regarded as being primarily a description of what this experience is like.

There is no doubt but that many of Ruusbroec's ways of trying to express this experience sound daring and even questionably orthodox. He himself realized the risks involved, for he writes in the introductory section of book three that only "a person who is united with God and enlightened in this truth can understand it. . . . I therefore beseech everyone who does not understand this or feel it in the blissful unity of his spirit not to take offense at it but simply to let it be as it is." What, then, does he say about this contemplative experience? Among his statements are the following: that it is "to be God with God, without intermediary or any element of otherness which could constitute an obstacle or impediment" (III.Intro.); that one becomes able "to contemplate God with God without intermediary in this divine light" (III.1); that a person's spirit "ceaselessly becomes the very resplendence which it receives" (III.1)—a resplendence he later identifies with the Son; that "the spirit's capacity for comprehending is opened so wide for the coming of the Bridegroom that the spirit itself becomes the very breadth which it comprehends" (III.2); that contemplatives "are transformed and become one with that same light with which they see and which they see" (III.3.B); and that a contemplative's spirit is "made one with the Spirit of God" (III.4).

It was these and similar statements that provoked the attack on Ruusbroec's teaching by John Gerson toward the end of the fourteenth century, something alluded to earlier in this Introduction. If taken as individual statements, divorced from their context, they might indeed sound auto-theistic, but the first principle for their proper interpretation is to see how they relate to the rest of book three. When this principle is followed, it becomes altogether clear that these statements are to be understood as expressions of mystical consciousness and not as claims of identity with God on the level of being. Thus, Ruusbroec writes at one point that "the loving contemplative neither sees nor feels in the ground of his being, in which he is at rest, anything other than an incomprehensible light" (III.1). He goes on to say that such a person "feels and finds himself to be nothing other than the same light with which he sees" (III.1), and a few pages later writes that contemplatives "see, feel, and find themselves to be the same simple ground from out of which the resplendence shines without measure in a divine way" (III.3.B). In all three statements the word "feel" is prominent: The mystic "feels" himself so caught up into God that he is at that time unaware of any difference between himself and God. As Albert Deblaere writes in reference to the literature of the Flemish mystics in general, "As a being it [the soul] remains distinct from God. But as consciousness it is caught up into the blissful enjoyment of God through God. . . . The terms which designate this mystical experience and contemplation—'above created mode,' 'superessential,' 'with the Light in the Light,' 'of God with God'—seem to point to this significance and could otherwise scarcely have an intelligible content."[30] Or in the even more concise phrasing of another Ruusbroec scholar, Joseph Alaerts, "there is not a fusion, but a communion of love."[31]

The final point to be considered regarding book three of the *Espousals* is the way in which Ruusbroec differs from those mystics like Pseudo-Dionysius and Meister Eckhart who closely follow the *via negativa* through their strong emphasis on the darkness, silence, and ineffability of God. The final paragraphs of the *Espousals* are, in themselves, within this tradition, for Ruusbroec here writes that a contemplative will enter "a state of essential bareness, where all the divine names and modes and all the living ideas which are reflected in the mirror of divine truth all pass away into simple ineffability." Even the divine Persons "must give way" before the essential Unity, "for here there is nothing other than an eternal state of rest

---

30. Albert Deblaere, *De mystieke schrijfster Maria Petyt (1623–1677)* (Ghent: Koninklijke Vlaamse Academie voor Taal- en Letterkunde, 1962), pp.80–81.
31. Joseph Alaerts, "La terminologie 'essentielle' dans *Die gheestelike brulocht*," *Ons Geestelijk Erf* 49 (1975): 328. See also A. Van de Walle, "Is Ruusbroec pantheïst?" parts 1–2, *Ons Geestelijk Erf* 12 (1938): 359–91; 13 (1939): 66–105.

in a blissful embrace of loving immersion." Similarly, in part one of the same third book he says that a contemplative "must lose himself in a state devoid of particular form or measure, a state of darkness in which all contemplatives blissfully lose their way."

Once more, however, such statements can only be understood in the light of their entire context. The state of darkness is in no sense absolute or all-encompassing, for "in this darkness an incomprehensible light is born and shines forth; this is the Son of God, in whom a person becomes able to see and to contemplate eternal life" (III.1). So, too, "the eternal state of rest" in which even the divine Persons give way before the essential Unity is not utterly divorced from all activity, for it is at all times the very ground of what Ruusbroec calls "the active meeting of the Father and the Son, in which we are lovingly embraced by means of the Holy Spirit in eternal love" (III.4). In sum, even if the notes of ineffability, modelessness, rest, and Unity predominate in the final paragraphs of the *Espousals*, they always remain in dialectical relationship with the notes of effability, distinctness, activity, and Trinity. This could hardly be more beautifully expressed than by the words with which Ruusbroec concludes his entire treatise: "That we might blissfully possess the essential Unity and clearly contemplate the Unity in the Trinity—may the divine love grant us this, for it turns no beggar away. Amen. Amen."[32]

OTHER TREATISES FROM
RUUSBROEC'S YEARS IN BRUSSELS

The third of Ruusbroec's treatises (and the second translated for the present volume) has most commonly been entitled *The Sparkling Stone*, a title taken from his extended use of that scriptural symbol (Rv 2:17) at the beginning of part two of the treatise. According to the mystic's Carthusian friend Brother Gerard, the *Stone* was written in response to a request from a hermit with whom Ruusbroec had discussed spiritual matters and who wished to have the mystic's teaching set down in writing so that he and others could profit from it; an echo of the two men's conversation seems to have been preserved in the bit of dialogue that begins section C of the sec-

---

32. Two works are particularly helpful regarding the differences between Ruusbroec and Eckhart: Louis Cognet, *Introduction* (see n. 2), esp. pp. 254–60 and 279–81; and Louis Dupré, *The Common Life: The Origins of Trinitarian Mysticism and Its Development by Jan Ruusbroec* (New York: Crossroad, 1984).

ond part of the treatise. The *Stone* was probably written not long after *The Spiritual Espousals* and is certainly reminiscent of it. Both works treat of the active, the interior, and the contemplative lives; the emphasis in the *Stone*, however, is decidedly on questions concerning the contemplative life, including some that may well have been raised by the hermit as a result of having read book three of the *Espousals* (such as the question of how contemplative union with God differs from actual identification with God, a matter discussed by Ruusbroec in part two, section D).

Limitations of space here preclude a full-scale introduction to *The Sparkling Stone*. One point in particular should, however, be noted, especially because it points to a certain development in Ruusbroec's thinking from the time he completed the *Espousals*. The very way in which Ruusbroec begins the *Stone* is indicative of this evolution, for whereas in the earlier treatise he speaks simply of a threefold division in the Christian life (the active, interior, and contemplative lives), in the *Stone* he speaks of *four* characteristics of the most perfect kind of Christian: "A person who wishes to live in the most perfect state within the holy Church must be someone who is zealous and good, who is interiorly fervent and spiritual, who is lifted up to the contemplation of God, and who goes forth to all in common. When these four things are found together in a person, then his state is perfect." Ruusbroec returns to this theme at the very end of the treatise, for after discussing the highest levels of the contemplative life in terms reminiscent of the *Espousals* (such as his statement that a contemplative will feel "that he has died and lost his way and that he has become one with God, without difference"), he proceeds to show how such a person will simultaneously be zealous in good works:

> The person who has been sent down by God from these heights into the world is full of truth and rich in all the virtues. . . . He stands ready and willing to do all that God commands and is strong and courageous in suffering and enduring all that God sends him. He therefore leads a common life, for he is equally ready for contemplation or for action and is perfect in both.

Two comments on these passages are in order. First, this common life is certainly not some fourth life added onto the contemplative life; one of Ruusbroec's main points is that such readiness "for contemplation or for action" is an intrinsic aspect of the contemplative life itself. Secondly, what Ruusbroec writes at the beginning and end of the *Stone* is certainly not contrary to anything in the *Espousals;* that earlier treatise has several even more extensive passages on going out to all "in common." It is, however, true that in book three of the *Espousals*, the one that treats the contemplative life as such, there is no explicit reference to the fact that contemplatives lead this common life. The prominence of such references in *The Sparkling Stone* may well be an implicit admission on Ruusbroec's part that his description of the contemplative life in the final book of the *Espousals* was too liable to misinterpretation in a one-sided, quietistic sense.

Ruusbroec's fourth and fifth treatises—*The Four Temptations* and *The Christian Faith*—are works of a primarily ascetical and catechetical nature. They too seem to have been written in Brussels, while a sixth—*The Spiritual Tabernacle*—was undoubtedly begun in Brussels but completed only at a later period of Ruusbroec's life. The *Tabernacle* is a long, allegorical work in which many ritual details from the Book of Exodus and other parts of the Old Testament are given Christian interpretations. Although its heavily allegorical character may not be attractive to modern readers, it contains many fine passages on the contemplative life and seems to have been very popular in Ruusbroec's own day, at least if we may deduce this from the fact that more manuscripts of this treatise are extant than those of any other of his writings.

RUUSBROEC'S MOVE TO GROENENDAAL

In accordance with Pomerius's description of Ruusbroec as quiet and retiring, it is not surprising that in 1343, after twenty-six years of priestly ministry in Brussels, Ruusbroec and two like-minded confreres—his relative John Hinckaert and Frank of Coudenberg—left St. Gudula in order to lead a more solitary religious life at Groenendaal, "the green valley," about ten kilometers from the city itself. A succession of hermits had been living at Groenendaal since 1304. The one residing there in 1343 was a certain Lambert, who willingly moved to a different location, while the duke of Brabant agreed to give the three men the site and some surrounding property if they would build a house for five religious, at least two of whom would always be priests. This grant of land took place on Wednesday of Easter Week in 1343. With the consent of the bishop of Cambrai, in whose territory Groenendaal lay, Ruusbroec and his companions began constructing a chapel, which was consecrated two years later.

While the new location was in many respects more satisfactory to the three men than was St. Gudula, there were still problems to be overcome, above all the fact that a number of other persons, both clergy and laity, considered it most improper for these men—who by now had been joined by several others—to be living as religious even though they did not belong to any religious order or wear a religious habit. After a few years, and with the encouragement of the bishop of Cambrai, the group therefore decided to become canons regular of St. Augustine. The bishop clothed them in the habit on March 10, 1349, and on the next day appointed Frank of Coudenberg provost, Ruusbroec serving under him as prior.

It was in this setting that Ruusbroec spent the remaining thirty-two years of his life. Outwardly these years were quite uneventful. Pomerius makes a point of how good an example Ruusbroec set for the younger members of the community by taking upon himself many of the most humble and laborious tasks during the periods of manual labor. He also taught his confreres by word, for Pomerius writes that Ruusbroec would often speak with them about religious matters after evening prayer and adds that these conversations occasionally lasted until it was time for the office of vigils in the early hours of the morning.

Persons from outside Ruusbroec's own religious community also benefited from his words. As mentioned at the beginning of this Introduction, during these years at Groenendaal he was often visited by persons who wished to speak with him about the spiritual life. One visitor, named Canclaer in Pomerius's manuscript and described by him as "a doctor of theology, of the Order of Preachers, a man of great and excellent reputation," may in fact have been the Rhenish mystic John Tauler, the difference in spelling then being due to an error in transcription, something quite possible given the similarity between "Tauelaer" and "Canclaer" in gothic script. There is nothing improbable in such a visit between these two mystics, who did not live that far from one another, but it is most unlikely that the identity of this "Canclaer" will ever be firmly established. We do, however, know that one of Ruusbroec's most important visitors was Gerard Groote, commonly considered the father of the Devotio Moderna. Groote first visited Groenendaal in 1377 in order to speak with the man whose mystical treatises he had already read. Groote undertook the translation of several of these into Latin and was also so impressed by the ideal of the religious life as practiced at Groenendaal that he saw it as a model for the congregation that he wished to found and that, after his untimely death in 1384, came into being as the Congregation of Windesheim.

INTRODUCTION

The Treatises of the Groenendaal Years

During the years at Groenendaal, Ruusbroec continued his literary activity. Pomerius writes that when the mystic was not occupied with community duties, he would go out alone into the forest and there compose his treatises on wax tablets, which he would then bring back to the monastery to be copied by others. As he grew older and became unable to use the stylus himself, he would take a confrere with him into the forest and dictate to him the texts of his final works.

The first of the treatises Ruusbroec began at Groenendaal was *The Seven Enclosures*. According to one early manuscript, it was written in particular for Margaret of Meerbeke, a member of the Poor Clare community in Brussels. Since the first sisters of that convent made their profession on April 19, 1346, this treatise was probably written not long afterward in order to provide the young community with a description of how they should lead the religious life within their cloister. Louis Cognet's observation that the whole of Ruusbroec's work "unites in an unbroken line the humblest ascetic strivings and the highest manifestations of the theopathic state"[33] is almost perfectly exemplified in this treatise: On the one hand it describes the way the sisters are to take their meals and tend the sick; on the other hand it portrays at some length a state of mystical union in which a person becomes "one spirit and one life with God."

A Mirror of Eternal Blessedness was likewise written for a Poor Clare, quite possibly the same one for whom Ruusbroec wrote the *Enclosures*. Finished in 1359, it contains a long section on the Eucharist and for that reason has sometimes been called *The Blessed Sacrament*, whereas the title commonly used today derives from a later section in which Ruusbroec calls the soul's inner vision of God's resplendence "a living mirror on which God has impressed the image of his nature" (3.B). Although this treatise is not as coherently developed as the *Espousals*, it has long been recognized as containing some of Ruusbroec's most mature reflections on mystical union with God. It is above all for this reason that the *Mirror* is among the treatises translated for the present volume.

Two points in particular should be made by way of introduction to the *Mirror*. First, although many medieval authors make prominent use of the image of a mirror in their writings, they often develop this imagery in the moralistic or devotional sense of offering their readers a means of seeing how they ought to live. Ruusbroec's use of the image is more strictly the-

---

33. Cognet, *Introduction*, p. 281.

ological, being really but a corollary of that exemplarism which was discussed earlier in this Introduction; in fact, the *Mirror* probably contains Ruusbroec's most lucid presentation of that doctrine. He writes that the image of God which we have received in the depth of our being is God's Son, in whom we all live and are eternally imaged forth. So intimate is this union that God's image "fills the mirror of our soul to overflowing, so that no other light or image can enter there" (3.B). But the mystic immediately adds that, however intimate the union, there is nevertheless no strict identity: "The image is not the mirror, for God does not become a creature."

This distinction between union and identity leads to a second point. Various scholars have noted that there was a certain evolution in Ruusbroec's opposition to heresy over the years. The earliest treatises are particularly focused on that disparaging of virtuous activity and of the Church's sacramental mediation which later came to be called quietism. In the later treatises, Ruusbroec is additionally intent on attacking what could be called pantheism but is more properly termed autotheism—the claim that an individual can, in the strictest and fullest sense, become God. For example, at one point in his lengthy consideration of the Eucharist in the *Mirror*, Ruusbroec singles out those "who say that they themselves are Christ or God, that their hand created heaven and earth, that heaven and earth and all things depend on their hand, and that they have been raised above all the sacraments of the holy Church, so that they neither need nor desire them" (2.B). This, he goes on to say, "is probably the most foolish and perverse opinion that has ever been heard since the creation of the world." Later in the treatise he returns to the same point.

We may never know exactly where Ruusbroec read or heard such statements, but Jozef Van Mierlo's careful study of Ruusbroec's struggle against heresy led that scholar to the conclusion that in such passages the mystic was referring to the teaching of Meister Eckhart or to derivatives of that teaching.[34] Statements drawn from Eckhart's writings or sermons and condemned in Pope John XXII's bull *In agro dominico* in 1329 do indeed sound similar to some of the statements listed by Ruusbroec (for example, article ten of the bull, stating that "I am so changed into him [God] that he makes me his one existence, and not just similar," or article thirteen, stating that "the just and divine man. . . performs whatever God performs, and he created heaven and earth together with God"). Ruusbroec's knowledge of those "who say that they themselves are Christ or God" may also have

---

34. Jozef Van Mierlo, "Ruusbroec's bestrijding van de ketterij," *Ons Geestelijk Erf* 6 (1932): 340.

come from an acquaintance with works of extreme Eckhartian mysticism such as the anonymously composed *Sister Catherine*, with its already-quoted exclamation, "Sir, rejoice with me. I have become God." In any case, it is certain that Eckhart's theology was known at Groenendaal to at least some extent by the time Ruusbroec wrote the *Mirror*, for some years earlier Ruusbroec's disciple and confrere John van Leeuwen published a short treatise attacking Eckhart in a most abusive way.[35] It was, then, very likely Ruusbroec's concern over Meister Eckhart's teaching that led to the above-mentioned development in his opposition to heresy.

Shortly after writing the *Mirror* Ruusbroec composed *The Seven Rungs in the Ladder of Spiritual Love*. In its opening lines he writes that "a holy life is a seven-runged ladder of love on which we climb up to the kingdom of God." These rungs, which he proceeds to describe in the body of the work, are good will, voluntary poverty, purity, humility, zeal in God's service, contemplative union with the Trinity, and contemplative immersion in the simple being of the Godhead. Not unexpectedly, at the conclusion of the work he uses the imagery of the ladder to emphasize a point he had been insisting on from the time of his very first treatises: The ascent up this ladder toward the "eternal rest" of the seventh rung must not be understood as though there comes a time when the "good works" of earlier rungs may be left behind; rather, it is a matter of "entering into a state of emptiness and blissful enjoyment, going out in good works, and constantly remaining united to the Spirit of God." In other words, "we must constantly be ascending and descending the rungs of our heavenly ladder."

The next of Ruusbroec's treatises—*The Little Book of Clarification*—has already been referred to. Although this treatise has been known under various titles—for example, *Samuel* (from the reference to that prophet in the first sentence of the work), *The Book of Supreme Truth*, and *The Little Book of Enlightenment*—the present title is the one that seems to accord best with the nature and purpose of the work. As noted earlier, Ruusbroec wrote it because Brother Gerard and other Carthusians at Herne were puzzled and even disturbed by passages in *The Kingdom of Lovers* that did not sound orthodox. In the mystic's own words, "Some of my friends desire and have asked me to show and explain—in a few words and as accurately and clearly as I can—the truth which I understand and feel concerning all the

---

35. This treatise was entitled *Boexken van Meester Eckaerts leere*. John van Leeuwen's references to Eckhart in this and other treatises of his may be found in C. G. N. de Vooys, "Meister Eckart en de Nederlandse mystiek," *Nederlandsch archief voor kerkgeschiedenis*, n.s. 3 (1905): 182–94.

most sublime doctrine which I have written, in order that no one might be harmed by my words but that everyone might be improved" (Prologue). This is, then, a work of explanation or clarification, centering above all on the meaning of the terms "union with intermediary," "union without intermediary," and "union without difference." It was probably written sometime in the early 1360s and has understandably been regarded by many Ruusbroec scholars as the mystic's spiritual testament. Inasmuch as it is the last of the treatises translated for the present volume, a few additional comments should be made.

Perhaps the most helpful advice for a proper understanding of *The Little Book of Clarification* is that one should note how Ruusbroec's threefold dialectic of going out, turning back within, and resting in a state of enjoyment underlies all that he writes in this treatise. It will be recalled that these three elements are simultaneous, not consecutive, and that they characterize both the life of the Trinity and that of a genuine contemplative. The connection between this dialectic and the three kinds of union Ruusbroec wishes to discuss is made altogether explicit in part three, section B, of *The Little Book*, where he writes that

> as they [contemplatives] turn inward, God's love reveals itself as flowing out with all that is good, as attracting inward into unity, and as being superessential and devoid of mode in eternal rest. They are therefore united with God through an intermediary and without intermediary and also without difference.

The union with intermediary is accordingly characterized by a "flowing out with all that is good," in other words, by what Ruusbroec elsewhere calls the active life, with its emphasis on "the sacraments of the holy Church, the divine virtues of faith, hope, and love, and a virtuous life in accordance with God's commandments" (1.A). It is through such intermediaries that a person "goes out" to God and to all who stand in need of his help. The union without intermediary, in its turn, is marked by an inward movement toward God, who is experienced as dwelling in the depth of one's being. In this treatise, such union is described above all in terms of a person's renouncing his own will and adhering to God's, a renunciation that brings with it a deep sense of peace and well-being: "Because he is of one mind and one will with God, he feels God within him in the fullness of his grace, as the life-giving health of his entire being and of all his works" (2.A). Such peace and unity is not static or final, however, for "there is nevertheless an essential inclination to go onward, and that is an essential distinction between the soul's being and God's being" (3.B).

INTRODUCTION

That last phrase itself implies that the third union—that which is without difference or distinction—will *not* be characterized by such an "inclination to go onward" but rather by what the mystic describes as "eternal rest." Such rest—unlike the union without intermediary—is no longer in the contemplative's own deepest or "essential" being but rather in God's own being (*wesen*), which is the superessential being (*overwesen*) of all his creatures:

> All enlightened spirits are there raised up above themselves into a modeless state of blissful enjoyment which overflows whatever fullness any creature has ever received or ever could receive. There all exalted spirits are, in their superessential being, one enjoyment and one beatitude with God, without difference. This is what Christ desired when he prayed to his heavenly Father that all his beloved might be made perfectly one, even as he is one with the Father in blissful enjoyment through the Holy Spirit. . . . I consider this the most loving prayer which Christ ever prayed for our salvation. (3.B)

It need hardly be noted that this "union without difference" is far removed from that kind of autotheism which Ruusbroec attacks so forcefully in his later treatises (including part one and the Conclusion of *The Little Book*). As he states in another work, "whenever I write that we are one with God, this is to be understood as a oneness in love and not in being or nature" (*Mirror* 3.D). Moreover, it is here not a matter of loving God with "our love" but rather of allowing ourselves to be embraced in God's own love, which is in fact the Holy Spirit enfolding the contemplative in the same divine bond of love that unites Father and Son in the Spirit. Such union, according to Ruusbroec, is not even a matter of being united with God for the first time but rather of being reunited with that loving being from whom we once came forth. Josef Pieper, paraphrasing Paul Tillich, once wrote that "love is not so much the union of those who are strangers to one another as the *re*union of those who have been alienated from one another. But alienation can exist only on the basis of a pre-existing original oneness."[36] That preexisting oneness lies at the heart of Ruusbroec's exemplarism, and those who once more attain it are precisely the genuine contemplatives, those who not only "go out and enter in and find their nourishment both without and within," but who also "are drunk with love and sleep with God in a dark resplendence" (*Little Book* 3.B).

---

36. Josef Pieper, *About Love*, trans. Richard Winston and Clara Winston (Chicago: Franciscan Herald Press, 1974), p. 15.

INTRODUCTION

The last of Ruusbroec's eleven treatises is called *The Twelve Beguines*, a title based not on its entire content but on a verse prologue in which twelve beguines each speak by turn. The work actually seems to be a composite of three or four separate treatises that were later and somewhat artificially combined into one, perhaps by Ruusbroec's confreres at a time when he himself was too old and feeble for further literary activity. Parts of this treatise are as readable today as anything Ruusbroec ever wrote, whereas other sections are devoted to reflections on medieval astronomy and astrology, which, already in Ruusbroec's lifetime, Gerard Groote felt should have been deleted before publication.

RUUSBROEC'S DEATH AND BEATIFICATION

In November of 1381, when he was eighty-eight years old, Ruusbroec fell so ill that he asked to be moved from his room to the community's infirmary. He had been in the infirmary about two weeks when, in the presence of the rest of the community, he died peacefully and devoutly on December 2. He was buried in the monastery chapel, but in 1783, at the time of the suppression of the monastery under Emperor Joseph II, his remains were moved to St. Gudula, the church at which he had long served as a chaplain (and which in 1961 was raised to the rank of a cathedral church under the new title of St. Michael). Early in 1909 the Vatican published a decree confirming the longstanding cult of this holy man and approving a Mass and Office for Blessed John Ruusbroec, to be observed in the archdiocese of Mechelen (now that of Mechelen-Brussels) and also by the canons regular of the Lateran, the spiritual descendants of the foundations of Groenendaal and Windesheim. His feastday is observed on the anniversary of his death, December 2.

THE INFLUENCE OF RUUSBROEC

Any attempt to determine the exact influence of a writer like Ruusbroec on subsequent Christian spirituality is particularly difficult inasmuch as that influence may have been very real even apart from verifiable, direct literary dependence. As Robert Ricard writes concerning the problems of determining "sources" in the transmission of any spiritual teaching, "The more one studies spiritual writings, the more one sees that this im-

31

mense literature rests on diverse traditions whose elements, sometimes very ancient, are all the more difficult to isolate and to trace as their transmission was accomplished in large measure orally."[37] With this in mind, I will concentrate in this part of the Introduction simply on a few instances in which the direct literary influence of Ruusbroec is quite firmly established, without in any sense implying that his influence was limited to—or even most powerfully exercised in—such cases.

As would only be expected, Ruusbroec's influence was particularly strong among other writers in his own community at Groenendaal. Of these, the most important were John van Leeuwen (d. 1378), author of the earlier-mentioned book against Eckhart and of a number of other treatises; William Jordaens (d. 1372), who translated four of Ruusbroec's treatises into Latin so that they might acquire a larger readership and who himself wrote several religious works in Dutch; Godfrey of Wevel (d. 1396), author of *The Twelve Virtues*, a work long attributed to Ruusbroec himself; and John of Schoonhoven (d. 1432), who wrote the defense of Ruusbroec's orthodoxy in response to John Gerson's critique.

However able and successful John of Schoonhoven himself may have considered his defense of his master, there is no doubt but that Gerson's adverse reaction to the third book of *The Spiritual Espousals* and the subsequent publication of his critique of Ruusbroec harmed the latter's reputation as a reliable mystical writer.[38] This was particularly so in France, where Gerson enjoyed a favorable reputation as chancellor of the University of Paris and as a theologian in his own right. On the other hand, in the Low Countries the effects of Gerson's critique were less pronounced. From these lands, three fifteenth-century authors are worthy of special notice: Gerlach Peters, Henry Herp, and Denis of Rijckel.

Gerlach Peters, who died in 1411 at the age of thirty-three, was a canon regular at Windesheim. His best-known work is the *Soliloquium*, consisting of reflections on the contemplative life that were collected and published after his death by his friend John Scutken. Peters's dependence on Ruusbroec is very clear in this work, especially in the teaching that spiritual progress consists in the realization of our likeness to God, who has

---

37. Robert Ricard, " 'La fonte' de saint Jean de la Croix et un chapitre de Laredo: I," *Bulletin hispanique* 58 (1956): 271, n. 12.

38. On this point, see Albert Ampe, "Les rédactions successives de l'apologie schoonhovienne pour Ruusbroec contre Gerson," *Revue d'histoire ecclésiastique* 55 (1960): 402. Ampe here speaks of Gerson's attack as casting "discredit on the works of Ruusbroec and, indirectly, on those of his German and Flemish congeners and on mysticism itself."

impressed his image in the depth of our being. Peters likewise emphasizes what Ruusbroec had called the common life: "We must continually flow forth with Jesus to every Christian. It is not possible not to flow forth and not to love" (*Sol.*, ch. 36).

Even more pronounced is the influence of Ruusbroec in the writings of Henry Herp (d. 1478), a Dutch Franciscan whose reliance on the thought of the Groenendaal mystic led to his becoming known as "the herald of Ruusbroec." His most important work, *The Mirror of Perfection*, was translated from Dutch into Latin by the Carthusian Peter Bloemeveen in 1509 and had, as will be seen, considerable influence in sixteenth-century Spain.

Another Carthusian, Denis of Rijckel (d. 1471), commonly referred to as Denis the Carthusian, spent most of his life at the charterhouse at Roermond and there became one of the most prolific Christian writers of any century. He drew often on Ruusbroec's works in his own writings and considered him a mystic of the highest order, "a second Dionysius the Areopagite." It was also he who was responsible for the epithet "admirable" by which Ruusbroec frequently came to be known: Ruusbroec the Admirable.

Peter Bloemeveen and Denis the Carthusian were by no means the only members of that religious order responsible for spreading the influence of Ruusbroec and other representatives of Flemish and Rhenish spirituality. During the early years of the Reformation and Counter-Reformation, a number of Carthusians were important mediators of the thought of Ruusbroec and of his contemporaries and disciples.[39] This was particularly true of the monks at the charterhouse in Cologne. Among many other published works, they produced Latin translations of the works of Tauler (1548), Ruusbroec (1552), and Suso (1555), all with the aim of encouraging adherence to the Roman Church, especially in Germany, by making available works that would provide sound moral teaching and an introduction to the life of contemplative union with God. Events in Germany, especially the Peace of Augsburg (which in 1555 gave official recognition to Lutheranism and allowed princes and cities to determine the religion of their territories), prevented the Carthusian undertaking from having its full, desired effect in that part of Europe, but these and other

---

39. On their role, see Kent Emery, Jr., "The Carthusians, Intermediaries for the Teaching of John Ruysbroeck during the Period of Early Reform and the Counter- Reformation," *Analecta Cartusiana* 43 (1979): 100–129.

translations had much to do with making Ruusbroec and other medieval mystics known throughout the continent.[40]

In Spain, the Franciscan author Francis of Osuna (d. ca.1540) knew and utilized the works of both Ruusbroec and Suso, while his confrere Bernardine of Laredo (d. 1540) borrowed heavily from Herp's *Mirror* in the second edition of his own *Ascent of Mount Zion*, a work certainly read by St. Teresa of Avila (d. 1582). It is also quite possible that at least some of the clear similarities between the thought of St. John of the Cross (d. 1591) and the great Rhenish-Flemish mystics were due to the influence of Herp, "the herald of Ruusbroec," either through John's having read Herp's *Mirror* in its Latin translation or through the mediation of Bernardine of Laredo's *Ascent*.[41] Another Spanish spiritual writer, the Franciscan John of the Angels (d. 1609), relied heavily on Ruusbroec, even to the point of reproducing whole passages word for word and frequently singling him out for special praise.

By the late sixteenth century, French writers had become more receptive to the works of Ruusbroec than they had been closer to the time of Gerson's critique. Benet of Canfield (d. 1610), an English convert from Puritanism who took refuge in France and there became a Capuchin, was directly and strongly influenced by Ruusbroec, as was the Carmelite John of St. Samson (d. 1636).

Within Protestant circles, it was above all in seventeenth-century Germany that Ruusbroec's works exercised a notable influence. Gottfried Arnold, a Lutheran Pietist poet, historian, and theologian, was responsible for the first complete translation of Ruusbroec into German and used these works extensively in his own more popular writings, thereby transmitting the works of the Flemish mystic to Protestantism.[42]

Until the second half of the nineteenth century, the only one of Ruusbroec's treatises to be printed in its entirety in the original Middle Dutch was *The Spiritual Espousals*, published in Brussels in 1624, and even this edition contained some modernization of spelling and other changes from the original text. This significant gap in Ruusbroec scholarship began to be

---

40. This paragraph is based on Gérald Chaix, "L'édition de 1552 et la réception de Ruusbroec au XVIe siècle," in Mommaers and De Paepe, *Jan van Ruusbroec* (see n. 26), pp. 142–52.

41. Helmut Hatzfeld, "Influence" (see n. 24), argues that St. John of the Cross even read Ruusbroec's own work, in a Latin translation of the *Espousals*. But note Robert Ricard's critique of Hatzfeld in " 'La fonte' de saint Jean de la Croix" (see n. 37), pp. 265–74.

42. Peter C. Erb, "The Use of Ruusbroec among German Protestants," in Mommaers and De Paepe, *Jan van Ruusbroec* (see n. 26), p. 154.

filled in 1858, when Professor Jan Baptist David of the University of Louvain published the first of six volumes giving the entire text of Ruusbroec's works in their original language, a project he completed in 1868. Despite the fact that fewer than two hundred copies of this edition were published, David's work fostered a revival of interest in Ruusbroec, especially in the Low Countries. In 1892 Alfred Auger published at Louvain an important theological study of Ruusbroec's mysticism, and three years later Willem de Vreese began publishing a number of early documents contributing to our knowledge of the mystic's life and works.[43]

Such interest and activity continued into the twentieth century. In the second decade of this century the two Jesuits Jozef Van Mierlo and Leonce Reypens each published the first of what would come to be many subsequent studies of Ruusbroec and other spiritual writers of the Low Countries.[44] In 1927, the two of them numbered among the contributors to the first issue of *Ons Geestelijk Erf* (Our spiritual heritage), a quarterly devoted to the study of Netherlandic spirituality. Van Mierlo and Reypens, together with several other Belgian Jesuits, were also the founders of the *Ruusbroecgenootschap*, a center headquartered at St. Ignatius University in Antwerp for the purpose of scholarly research and publication in the field of Low Countries spirituality. In the 1930s, members of the *genootschap* published the complete works of Ruusbroec in the original Middle Dutch and in the following decade produced a revised edition of those four volumes. Younger members of the group are currently engaged in producing a definitive critical edition of the mystic's works. This edition, whose first two volumes appeared in 1981, will also include a modern English translation of each of Ruusbroec's works as well as the sixteenth-century Latin translation of the Carthusian Lawrence Surius.

The twentieth century has also seen a revived interest in the writings of Ruusbroec in other countries. The prominent place given him by Evelyn Underhill in her *Mysticism* was mentioned at the beginning of this Introduction. She also wrote a biography of the mystic (1915) as well as the Introduction to Dom C. A. Wynschenk's English translation of three of Ruusbroec's treatises (1916). The Benedictine monks of the Abbey of Wis-

43. Alfred Auger, *De Doctrina et Meritis Joannis van Ruysbroeck* (Louvain: J. van Linthout, 1892); Willem de Vreese, "Bijdragen tot de kennis van het leven en de werken van Jan van Ruusbroec," *Het Belfort* 10, pt. 2 (1895): 5–20, 102–13, 169–81, 253–62; 11, pt. 1 (1896): 57–67, 95–101.

44. Jozef Van Mierlo, "Het leven van Jan van Ruysbroeck door Pomerius en Surius," *Dietsche Warande en Belfort* 11, pt. 1 (1910): 109–30; Leonce Reypens, "Voor de geschiedenis van Jan van Ruusbroec: I," *Dietsche Warande en Belfort* 15 (1914): 405–16, 505–22.

ques (later Oosterhout) produced a complete French translation of Ruusbroec's works between 1912 and 1938, while in 1946 J.-A. Bizet published
a highly praised French translation of *The Kingdom of Lovers* and *The Spiritual Espousals;* Bizet's long Introduction to that volume is also proving to
be of enduring value.

All of these projects and studies, and a number of similar ones, are
evidence of a greater interest in the writings of John Ruusbroec than at any
other time in the past few centuries. It is hoped that the present volume
will in its turn contribute to a deeper understanding and appreciation of
the mystic of whom Abbot Cuthbert Butler once wrote that "in all prob-
ability . . . there has been no greater contemplative; and certainly there has
been no greater mystical writer."[45]

A NOTE ON THE TRANSLATION

In the most general terms, one of two basic philosophies will underlie
the translation of any ancient text. One is that of formal correspondence,
which is characterized by considerable respect for the sentence structures
and patterns of expression of the original text. This entails a concomitant
willingness to allow the resulting translation to reflect the ambiguities of
the original text, thereby leaving the reader the possibility of exploring
how best to resolve such ambiguities. The other philosophy is that of dynamic equivalence, which places a greater emphasis on transforming the
constructions and speech patterns of the original language into those of the
receptor language, so as to present in a contemporary idiom what the author is deemed to have been saying in his. No translation will ever be a
pure representative of either philosophy, but the differences are real
enough. As regards English translations of Scripture, the Revised Stan-
dard Version represents a formal-correspondence approach, while the no-
ticeably different Jerusalem Bible represents the philosophy of dynamic
equivalence.[46]

In terms of this distinction, the present translation of Ruusbroec goes
considerably farther in the direction of dynamic equivalence than, say,

---

45. Cuthbert Butler, *Western Mysticism* (New York: E. P. Dutton, 1923), pp. 272–73.

46. On this distinction between philosophies of translation, see Daniel Harrington, *In-
terpreting the New Testament* (Wilmington, Del.: Michael Glazier, 1979), pp. 25–41. On the
translation of Ruusbroec in particular, see Helen Rolfson, "Ruusbroec in American English,"
in Mommaers and De Paepe, *Jan van Ruusbroec* (see n. 26), pp. 187–95.

INTRODUCTION

Wynschenk's English translation of 1916 or the English translations included in the critical edition of the mystic's works now being published by the *Ruusbroecgenootschap*. There are advantages and disadvantages with both approaches, but as long as the extremes of stodgy literalness and mere paraphrase are avoided, readers may approach either type with a basic confidence that they will thereby be enabled to understand at least the major lines of an author's thought.

It should also be pointed out that the various headings and subheadings found throughout the text of Ruusbroec's treatises in the present volume do not come from the mystic himself (with the exception of the division of *The Spiritual Espousals* into books one, two, and three). Headings were, however, included in even very early manuscripts as an aid to the reader. For centuries, these were for the most part simply chapter headings, numbered consecutively, but in the *Ruusbroecgenootschap*'s edition of the 1930s a more coherent system was devised. It is this system that, with some modifications, has been used here. Scriptural references have also been incorporated into the text, with references to the Psalms following the numeration of the New American Bible.

The translations of the *Espousals* and *A Mirror of Eternal Blessedness* were made from the revised edition of Ruusbroec's works published by the *Ruusbroecgenootschap* in the 1940s, while the translation of *The Little Book of Clarification* was made from the critical text published in 1981 and the translation of *The Sparkling Stone* from a copy of the critical text that has been prepared for future publication in that same series.

THE SPIRITUAL
ESPOUSALS

PROLOGUE

"See, the bridegroom is coming. Go out to meet him" (Mt 25:6). These words, written for us by St. Matthew the Evangelist, were spoken by Christ to his disciples and to all persons in the parable of the virgins. The Bridegroom is Christ and human nature is the bride, whom God created according to his own image and likeness. In the beginning he placed his bride in the noblest and most beautiful, the richest and most luxuriant place on earth, that is, in Paradise. He subordinated all other creatures to her, adorned her with grace, and gave her a commandment so that through obedience to it she might deserve to be made firm and steadfast with her Bridegroom in eternal faithfulness and so never fall into any adversity or any sin. But then came an evildoer, the enemy from hell, who in his jealousy assumed the form of a cunning serpent and deceived the woman. They both then deceived the man, in whom human nature existed in its entirety. Thus did the enemy seduce human nature, God's bride, through deceitful counsel. Poor and wretched, she was banished to a strange land and was there captured and oppressed and beset by her enemies in such a way that it seemed she would never be able to return to her homeland or attain reconciliation.

But when it seemed to God that the right time had come and he took pity on his beloved in her suffering, he sent his only-begotten Son to earth into a magnificent palace and a glorious temple, that is, into the body of the glorious Virgin Mary. There the Son wedded this bride, our nature, and united her with his own person through the purest blood of the noble Virgin. The priest who witnessed the bride's marriage was the Holy Spirit. The angel Gabriel brought the message. The glorious Virgin gave her consent. Thus did Christ, our faithful Bridegroom, unite our nature with himself. He came to us in a strange land and taught us through a heavenly way of life and with perfect fidelity. He worked and struggled as our champion against our enemies, broke open the bars of our prison, won the struggle, vanquished our death through his own, redeemed us through his blood, freed us through his water in baptism, and made us rich through his sacraments and his gifts, so that, as he says, we might "go out" with all

41

virtues, "meet him" in the palace of glory, and enjoy him forever in eternity.

Therefore Christ, the Master of truth, says: "See, the bridegroom is coming. Go out to meet him." Through these words Christ our Lover teaches us four things. First of all he gives a command, when he says, "See." Those who remain blind and ignore this command are all damned. Secondly, he reveals to us what we are to see, namely, the coming of the Bridegroom. Thirdly, he tells us what we are to do, when he says, "Go out." Fourthly, when he says "to meet him," he reveals to us the reward and end of our entire activity and our entire life, namely, a loving meeting with the Bridegroom.

We wish to clarify and explain these words in three ways. First, in a way applicable to everyone (since it is necessary for all who wish to be saved), we will speak of the life of beginners, which is called an active life. Secondly, we wish to explain the same words as regards an interior, exalted life of desire, which many persons attain through the practice of virtue and the grace of God. Thirdly, we wish to clarify these words as regards a superessential, contemplative life, which few persons are able to attain or savor because of the high and noble nature of this life.

BOOK ONE: THE ACTIVE LIFE

PART ONE: "SEE."

A. THE THREE THINGS NECESSARY FOR SEEING MATERIAL OBJECTS

Now as regards the first life, Christ, the wisdom of the Father, has from the time of Adam spoken to all persons in an interior manner according to his divinity, addressing them with the word "See." Such seeing is necessary for us. Note carefully, too, that for anyone who wishes to see something either in a material or spiritual way, three things are required. If one wishes to see an exterior, material object, the first thing that is required is the exterior light of the sun or some other material light, so that the medium through which one sees, namely, the air, may be made bright. The second thing that is required is willingness on the part of the viewer to let the things he wishes to see be reflected in his eyes. The third requirement is that the instruments of sight, the eyes, be healthy and without blemish, so that coarse, material objects may be able to be reflected in them in a subtle way. If any one of these three requirements is lacking, then one's bodily vision will be faulty. We do not intend to say anything further about this kind of vision but shall turn instead to that spiritual, supernatural way of seeing in which all our blessedness consists.

B. THE THREE THINGS NECESSARY FOR SEEING SPIRITUAL REALITIES

If anyone is to see in a supernatural way, there are also three things that are required: the light of God's grace, a will that is freely turned toward God, and a conscience free of mortal sin. Note first of all that because God is a good common to all and because his fathomless love is offered to

43

all alike, he bestows his grace in two ways: as prevenient grace, and as the grace whereby one merits eternal life. All persons receive prevenient grace, whether they be pagans or Jews, good or bad. Because of the love which God has toward all persons in common, he has had his name and his redemption of human nature preached and revealed to the ends of the earth. Whoever wishes to be converted can be converted. All the sacraments— baptism and all the other sacraments—are available to anyone who wishes to receive them, according as each one has need, for God wishes everyone to be saved and no one to be lost. On the Day of Judgment no one will be able to complain that not enough was done for him even though he wished to be converted. God is a radiant light that is common to all and that sheds its brightness upon heaven and earth and upon each person according to his need and his deserts.

Even though God is common to all, and even though the sun shines upon all trees alike, nevertheless many trees do not bear fruit, while other trees bear only wild fruit, which is of little use to us. For this reason, people are accustomed to pruning trees and to grafting onto them branches from fruit-bearing trees, so as to obtain fruit that tastes good and is useful. Now in a spiritual sense, the light of God's grace is a fruit-bearing branch that comes from the life-giving Paradise of the eternal kingdom. No human activity can be savory and useful unless it grows from this branch. This branch of God's grace, which makes a person pleasing to God and worthy of eternal life, is offered to everyone but is not grafted onto everyone, for some do not wish to have their tree's wild branches pruned away, that is, their unbelief or their perverse disobedience to God's commandments.

Prevenient grace

If this branch of God's grace is to be grafted onto our soul, then three things are necessary: God's prevenient grace, a will that is freely turned toward God, and a purified conscience. Prevenient grace touches everyone, for it is given by God, but not everyone responds with a free conversion of his will and a purification of his conscience, and for this reason such a person lacks that grace of God whereby one merits eternal life.

Prevenient grace touches a person either from without or from within. From without, this may occur through periods of sickness or through the loss of material goods or of relatives or friends. It may also occur through having to suffer public humiliations, through being moved by someone's preaching, or through the good example given us by the saints or other good persons in their words or in their works. In all these ways a person can come to know himself as he is, and this is what it means to be touched by God from without.

Sometimes a person is also touched from within, as when he reflects on the sufferings of our Lord and on the good that God has done for him and for all persons. Or again, this may occur through a person's consideration of his sins and of the shortness of life, through the fear of death and of hell, through reflection on the eternal pains of hell and the eternal joy of heaven, or through the knowledge that God has spared him in his sins and is awaiting his conversion. Or one might observe all the wonderful things that God has created in heaven and on earth in all his creatures.

All these are works of prevenient grace, which move a person from without or from within in many different ways. Moreover, a person has a natural and fundamental inclination toward God through the spark of the soul and through the higher reason, which always desires what is good and hates what is evil.[1] In these ways God touches everyone in the requisite manner, each according to his need, with the result that at times a person will feel cast down, accused, and beset by fear and dread, and so will remain turned inward, reflecting upon himself. All this is still prevenient grace, not meritorious grace.

It is thus that prevenient grace creates in a person a readiness to receive this other kind of grace, through which one merits eternal life. When the soul is thus void of any evil will and evil works, and feels accused and cast down and fearful about what it ought to do as it looks upon God and upon itself and its evil works, then there comes about a natural sorrow for sin and a natural good will. This is the highest state to which prevenient grace can bring a person.

Cooperation between God and ourselves

When a person has done all that he can and is able to proceed no further because of his own weakness, then it falls to the fathomless goodness of God to bring the work to completion. Thus there arises a higher light of God's grace which, like a ray of sunlight, is cast upon the soul without

---

1. "The spark of the soul" (*die vonke der zielen*), a term common in the Rhenish and Flemish mystics, designates the soul's fundamental inclination toward its origin, God. For further details, see Hieronymus Wilms, "Das Seelenfünklein in der deutschen Mystik," *Zeitschrift für Aszese und Mystik* 12 (1937): 157–66. "The higher reason" (*die overste redene*) refers to an Augustinian distinction (*De Trinitate 12.4*) taken over by medieval thinkers: The higher reason and the lower (*ratio superior* and *ratio inferior*) are two functions of the mind; by the former we contemplate eternal truths, by the latter we come to the knowledge of temporal things.

its being merited or desired in a way commensurate with its worth. In this light God gives himself to us out of his gratuitous goodness and beneficence, a gift which no creature can merit in advance. This is a mysterious work of God acting within the soul above the temporal order and moving the soul and all its powers. It is here that prevenient grace ends and the other kind begins, namely, this supernatural light.

This light is the first thing that is required if one is to see in a supernatural way, and from it there arises the second thing, this time on the part of the soul, namely, a free conversion of the will in a moment of time. From this, charity issues forth in the union between God and the soul. These two things—the supernatural light and the free turning of the will toward God—are so closely related to one another that one cannot be brought to completion without the other. Wherever God and the soul come together in the unity of love, there God gives the light of his grace above the temporal order and the soul responds through the power of grace with its free conversion in a brief moment of time. From this, charity is born in the soul out of both God and the soul, for charity is a bond of love between God and the loving soul.

From this grace of God and this free conversion of a will that has been enlightened by grace, charity is born, that is, divine love, and from divine love there arises the third thing that is required if a person is to see in a supernatural way, namely, a purification of his conscience. These three things are so intimately related to one another that one of them cannot last long at all without the others, for whoever has divine love necessarily has perfect sorrow for his sins. Still, it is permissible to understand the sequential ordering of the things of God and of creatures as it has here been described: God bestows his light, and through that light a person responds with a free and perfect conversion; from these two there arises a perfect love toward God, and from this love there issues a perfect sorrow for sin and a purification of one's conscience; this last occurs when one reflects upon his offenses and upon the way these have disfigured the soul. Because he loves God, a person becomes displeased with himself and all his works. This is the sequence of events in the process of conversion. There follows genuine sorrow and perfect contrition for all the offenses that a person has ever committed, together with a firm resolve never to sin again and always to serve God in humble obedience. Such a person will make a good confession, without concealing, obscuring, or dissimulating any of his sins. Afterward he will make complete satisfaction in accordance with the counsel of a wise confessor and will begin the practice of virtue and of all good works.

These three things, as you have heard, are required if a person is to see in a divine way. If you already possess them, then Christ is saying within you, "See," and you are indeed seeing. This is the first of the four main points that Christ our Lord addresses to us: "See."

PART TWO: "THE BRIDEGROOM IS COMING."

Christ next shows what one is to see when he says, "The bridegroom is coming." Christ our Bridegroom speaks this word in Latin: *venit*. This word could be in either the present or the perfect tense and so contains within itself two different times: the time which is past and that which is present. In addition, Christ means the time which is still to come. For this reason we shall have to consider three comings of our Bridegroom Jesus Christ. In the first of these comings he became a human being out of love for us. The second coming takes place daily in many and various ways in every loving heart, for he comes with new gifts and new graces according to the measure in which each person is able to receive them. The third coming is that on the Day of Judgment or at the hour of death. In all three comings of our Lord and in all his works, three things are to be considered: the motive or reason, the interior mode or state, and the exterior works or effects.

A. THE FIRST COMING OF OUR LORD, IN THE INCARNATION

The reason God created angels and human beings was his fathomless goodness and nobility. He wished the blessedness and richness that he is in himself to be revealed to rational creatures so that they might savor him in this temporal world and enjoy him beyond the temporal order in eternity. The reason God became a human being was his incomprehensible love and the need of all persons, for they had been corrupted through original sin and could do nothing of themselves to change their condition. But there were four reasons why Christ, according to both his divinity and his humanity, performed all his works on earth: first, his divine love, which is immeasurable; secondly, that created love which is called charity and which he had in his soul through his union with the eternal Word and through the perfect gifts which he received from his Father; thirdly, the

great need of human nature; and fourthly, the honor of his Father. These
are the reasons for the coming of Christ our Bridegroom and for all that he
did, whether exteriorly or interiorly.

Now in order that we might follow Christ our Bridegroom in the practice of virtue as best we can, we should consider the mode or state of his
interior life as well as the exterior works that he performed, namely, virtues
and virtuous works. As regards the state of his interior life in respect to his
divinity, that is something incomprehensible and inaccessible to us. It consists in the fact that he is constantly being born of the Father and that
through him and in him the Father knows, creates, orders, and rules all
things in heaven and on earth, for Christ is the wisdom of the Father. The
Father and the Son breathe forth a Spirit, that is, a love, which is a bond
joining them to one another and to all the saints and all good persons both
in heaven and on earth. We shall say nothing further about this state, but
turn instead to that interior state or condition which Christ had as a result
of divine gifts and in respect to his created human nature. There are actually very many such states, for Christ had just as many interior states as
he had interior virtues, since each virtue has its own corresponding state.
These virtues and their states were in Christ's soul in such a way as to be
beyond the understanding and comprehension of all creatures. Still, we
shall say something about three of them, namely, humility, charity, and
the patient endurance of interior and exterior suffering. These are the three
principal roots which lie at the beginning of all virtue and all perfection.

Christ's humility

You should understand that there are two kinds of humility in Christ
as regards his divinity. The first is that he willed to become a human being
and so took upon himself that same human nature which had been banished
and condemned to the depths of hell. He willed to become one with this
nature in the unity of his person, with the result that everyone, whether
good or evil, can say, "Christ, the Son of God, is my brother." The other
kind of humility as regards Christ's divinity is that he chose a poor maiden
and not the daughter of a king to be his mother. Thus it was that that poor
maiden became the mother of God, of him who is Lord of heaven and earth
and of all creatures. Moreover, of all the works of humility which Christ
ever did it can truly be said that God did them.

Let us next consider the humility which, by means of grace and divine
gifts, was in Christ as regards his humanity. His soul with all its powers
bowed down in reverence and homage before the exalted might of the Fa-

ther, and a heart thus bowed down is a humble heart. As a result, Christ performed all his works for the honor and praise of his Father and in no way sought glory for himself as regards his humanity. He was humble and subject to the Old Law and to its commandments, and sometimes even to its customs when that was fitting. For that reason he was circumcised and was taken to the Temple to be redeemed, as was the custom, and he paid the tribute money to Caesar just like the other Jews. He was also humble and submissive to his mother and to Joseph, serving them with genuine humility in all their needs. He chose poor and insignificant persons as his companions, to go about with him and convert the world. These were the Apostles, and he was lowly and humble among them and among everyone else. He was thus at the disposal of all persons whatever their needs, whether interior or exterior ones, just as if he were the servant of all the world. This humility which was in Christ our Bridegroom is the first point of which I wished to speak.

Christ's charity

The second point is charity, the beginning and fountainhead of all virtues. This charity held the higher powers of Christ's soul in stillness and in an enjoyment of the same bliss which he now enjoys. This same charity kept him constantly raised up to his Father in reverence, love, praise, and veneration, leading him to pray fervently for the needs of all persons and to offer up all his works for the honor of his Father. This same charity made Christ bend low with loving fidelity and kindness to every human need, whether bodily or spiritual. In this he gave an example to all human beings, showing them through his own life how they ought to live. He gave food to all, inwardly nourishing with true spiritual teaching those who were able to receive it and feeding others outwardly through the senses with signs and wonders. Sometimes he also fed the people with bodily food, as when they followed him into the desert and were in need of it. He made the deaf hear and the blind see, he made the dumb speak and the enemy flee out of the possessed, he made the dead rise and the lame walk: All of which is to be understood in both a corporeal and a spiritual sense.

Christ our Lover labored for us both exteriorly and interiorly with true fidelity. We cannot thoroughly understand his charity, for it flowed forth from the fathomless spring of the Holy Spirit in a way that transcends the experience of all creatures who ever received charity, since Christ was both God and a human being in one person. This charity is the second point of which I wished to speak.

Christ's patient endurance of suffering

The third point is to bear suffering patiently. We should consider this point very carefully, for it adorned Christ our Bridegroom throughout his life. He began to suffer at the time of his birth, for he was born in poverty and in cold. He was circumcised and so shed his blood. He was forced to flee to a strange land. He served his mother and Joseph. He suffered hunger and thirst, disgrace and contempt, and the slanderous words and deeds of the Jews. He fasted, kept vigils, and was tempted by the devil. He was subject to everyone. He went from country to country and from city to city with much labor and zeal in order to preach the Good News.

Finally he was arrested by the Jews, who were his enemies even though he was a friend to them. He was betrayed, mocked, and insulted; scourged and beaten; and condemned on the basis of false testimony. In great pain he carried his cross to the highest place on earth and was there stripped naked. No man or woman has ever seen so beautiful a body so cruelly treated. He suffered disgrace, pain, and cold before all the world, for he was naked and it was cold, with a sharp wind cutting into his wounds. He was nailed to the wood of the cross with blunt nails and was so stretched out that his veins were ruptured. He was raised up on the cross, which was then dropped down into its hole with such force that his wounds began bleeding. His head was crowned with thorns. His ears heard the Jews cruelly shouting, "Crucify him! Crucify him!" and many other abusive words. His eyes saw the obstinacy and malice of the Jews and the misery of his mother, and his eyes lost their power of sight in the bitterness of pain and death. His nose smelled the foulness which those standing by spat out of their mouths into his face. His mouth and his sense of taste were drenched with vinegar and gall. Every sensitive part of his body was pervaded with the pain of the scourging. Thus was Christ our Bridegroom wounded unto death, abandoned by God and all creatures; he hung dying on the cross like a piece of wood for which no one cared except Mary his mother, who could do nothing to help him.

Christ also suffered spiritually, in his soul, because of the obdurate willfulness of the Jews and of those who put him to death, for however many signs and wonders they saw, they persisted in their evil ways. He suffered because of the ruin and retribution which would come upon them on account of his death, for God would inflict retribution upon them in both soul and body. He also suffered because of the distress and misery of his mother and his disciples, who were sorely afflicted. He suffered because his death would be of no avail for so many persons and because many would be ungrateful and even swear false oaths in order to ridicule and revile him who had died out of love for us. His human nature and his lower reason suffered because God withdrew from them the influx of his gifts and consolation and left them to themselves in such distress. For this reason, Christ said in complaint, "My God, my God, why have you forsaken me?" (Mk 15:34). But our Lover was silent about all his sufferings and cried out to his Father, "Father, forgive them, for they do not know what they are doing" (Lk 23:34). Christ was heard by his Father because of his reverence (cf. Heb 5:7), for those who acted out of ignorance were afterward probably all converted.

These, then, were interior virtues of Christ: humility, charity, and the patient endurance of suffering. Christ practiced them throughout his life, died with them, and so redeemed us through his righteousness. Out of his generosity he opened his side, from which flowed forth abundant streams, the sacraments of salvation. He ascended in power and sits at the right hand of his Father, where he reigns eternally. This is the first coming of our Bridegroom, one which is entirely past.

B. The Second Coming of Our Lord,
Which Takes Place Daily with New Graces

The second coming of Christ our Bridegroom takes place daily in good persons; indeed, it takes place frequently and repeatedly, with new gifts and graces, in all those who prepare themselves for it to the best of their ability. We do not intend to speak here of a person's initial conversion or of the graces which were first bestowed when he turned from sin to virtue. Rather, we wish to speak of a day-to-day increase in new gifts and new virtues and of a present, daily coming of Christ our Bridegroom into our soul. To do this properly, we have to consider the cause or reasons, the manner, and the effects of this coming.

There are four reasons for this coming: God's mercy and our great need, God's generosity and our desire. These four bring about our growth in virtue and in nobility, as can be understood through the following comparison: When the sun sends forth its rays and its light into a deep valley located between two high mountains, if the sun is then standing in the highest point of the heavens so that it can cast its light on the very floor of the valley, then there is a threefold effect: Through light reflected from the mountains, the valley becomes brighter and warmer and more fruitful than plain and level land. In the same way, when a good person rests only on

51

his littleness in the most lowly part of his being and admits that he has nothing and is nothing and can do nothing of himself—being able neither to persevere nor to progress in virtue—and when he confesses that he often fails to practice the virtues and good works, then he is admitting his poverty and need and is thereby forming a valley of humility. Because he is humble and in need and because he admits his need, he manifests and laments his need before the goodness and mercy of God. In this way he becomes aware of God's sublimity and his own lowliness, and in this sense he becomes a deep valley. Now Christ is a righteous and merciful sun who stands in the highest point of the heavens, that is, at the right hand of his Father. From there he sheds his light on the valley floor of humble hearts, for Christ is always moved by a person's need when that person humbly manifests and laments it. Then there arise two mountains, that is, two desires: one to serve and praise God as he deserves, and another to acquire virtues to a high degree. These two mountains are higher than the heavens, for these desires touch God without intermediary and yearn for his magnanimous generosity. This generosity cannot then hold itself back but must flow forth, for the soul is now capable of receiving more gifts.

These are the reasons for this new coming with new virtues. This valley, the humble heart, then receives three things: It becomes brighter and more radiant with graces, and warmer in charity, and more fruitful in perfect virtues and good works. These are the reasons, the manner, and the effects of this second coming.

Another form of this second coming

There is another coming of Christ our Bridegroom which takes place daily with an increase in graces and new gifts, for when a person receives any of the sacraments with a humble heart and without placing any obstacle in the way of the sacrament's effects, then he receives new gifts and an increase of grace because of his humility and because of the mysterious working of Christ in the sacraments. Obstacles that impede the sacraments' effects include being baptized in a state of unbelief, confessing one's sins without contrition for them, receiving the Sacrament of the Altar in a state of mortal sin or with an evil intention, and so on for the other sacraments. Those who do such things receive no new graces but rather sin all the more.

This, then, is another coming of Christ our Bridegroom which is present to us every day. We should reflect on it with a heart full of desire so that it might take place in ourselves, for this coming is necessary if we are to remain steadfast or go forward into eternal life.

C. THE THIRD COMING OF OUR LORD,
AT THE JUDGMENT

The third coming of Christ, which is still in the future, is that which will occur at the Judgment or at the hour of death. The reasons for this coming lie in the appropriateness of the time, the rightness of there being a trial, and the justice of the Judge. The appropriate time for this coming is the hour of death and the Last Judgment of the entire human race. When God created the soul out of nothing and joined it to a body, he set for it a fixed day and hour, known only to himself, when it would have to leave the temporal order and appear in his presence. The rightness of the soul's being tried consists in the fact that it must give an account before the eternal Truth of all the words it ever spoke and all the deeds it ever performed. The justice of the Judge lies in the fact that it is Christ to whom the judgment and the verdict belong, for he is the Son of Man and the wisdom of the Father, a wisdom to whom all judgment belongs (cf. Jn 5:27). To this wisdom all hearts are open and manifest, whether they are in heaven, on earth, or in hell. These three points are, then, the reasons for Christ's general coming on the Last Day as well as for his particular coming to each person at the hour of his death.

The five kinds of persons who will be judged

Five kinds of persons have to appear before this Judge. The first and worst group are those Christians who die in a state of mortal sin, without contrition and sorrow for their sins, for they scorned Christ's death and his sacraments or else received them unworthily and in vain. They did not practice the works of mercy in charity toward their neighbor, as God has commanded, and for this reason will be condemned to the deepest part of hell.

The second group are the unbelievers, whether pagans or Jews. All of these have to appear before Christ, even though they were already damned during their lifetime since they had within themselves neither grace nor divine love and therefore lived constantly in the death of eternal damnation. But they will be less severely punished than evil Christians since they received fewer gifts from God and owed him less allegiance.

The third group are those good Christians who at times fell into sin and who rose again through contrition and works of penance, but without having done all the penance that justice required. These will go to purgatory.

The fourth group are those persons who kept God's commandments or, if they ever broke them, turned back to God with contrition and penance and works of charity and of mercy. Having made full satisfaction for their sins, at their last breath they will go directly to heaven without passing through purgatory.

The fifth group are those who, over and above all exterior works of charity, have their citizenship in heaven (cf. Phil 3:20) and are united with and immersed in God and God in them, so that nothing intervenes between God and themselves except time and their condition of mortality. At the very moment that these persons are released from the body they come into the enjoyment of their eternal bliss. They will not be judged but, with Christ, they will judge all the others on the Last Day.

At that time all mortal life and all temporal suffering, whether on earth or in purgatory, will come to an end. All the damned, together with the devil and all his company, will sink and be buried in the depths of hell in an eternally endless state of perdition and horror. The blessed, however, will be transported at once into eternal glory with Christ their Bridegroom and will see, savor, and enjoy the fathomless richness of the divine being forever and ever. This is the third coming of Christ, which we all await and which is still to come.

The first coming, namely, when God became a human being, lived humbly, and died out of love for us, is one which we should imitate exteriorly through the perfect practice of the virtues and interiorly through charity and genuine humility. The second coming, which is in the present and which takes place when Christ comes with his graces into every loving heart, is one which we should desire and pray for every day, so that we might persevere and progress in new virtues. The third coming, at the Judgment or at the hour of our death, is one which we should await with longing, confidence, and awe, so that we might be released from this present misery and enter the palace of glory.

This threefold coming is the second of the four main points which we wish to treat.

PART THREE: "GO OUT."

Recall that at the beginning of his parable Christ says, "See," by which he means that we should see by means of charity and a purified conscience, as you have already heard at the beginning of this treatise. Next he shows us what we are to see, namely, these three comings. Now he tells us what we are to do, when he says, "Go out." If you possess the first point and so are able to see by means of grace and charity, and if you have attentively observed your model, Christ, and his own going out, then from this charity and this loving observation of your Bridegroom there arises in you a righteousness which makes you desire to follow him in the practice of virtue. Then Christ will be saying within you, "Go out."

This going out is to be done in three ways: We must go out to God and to ourselves and to our neighbor, and this must be done with charity and righteousness. Charity constantly strives upward toward the kingdom of God, that is, to God himself, for he is the source from which charity has flowed forth without intermediary and in which it abides by means of union. Righteousness, which arises from charity, desires the perfection of all those virtues and forms of behavior which are honorable and proper to the kingdom of God, which is the soul. These two, charity and righteousness, lay a foundation in the kingdom of the soul in which God is to dwell; this foundation is humility.

These three virtues bear the entire weight of the edifice of all the virtues and of all nobility. Charity keeps a person constantly facing the fathomless goodness of God from which charity flows forth, in order that the person might live honorably for God and persevere and grow in all the virtues and in genuine humility. Righteousness keeps a person facing the eternal truth of God, in order that he might be open to the truth and become enlightened and fulfill all the virtues without going astray. Humility keeps a person facing the great majesty of God, in order that he might remain small and lowly and surrender himself to God and not rely on himself. This is the way a person should act before God so as constantly to grow in new virtues.

A. HUMILITY AS THE FOUNDATION AND MOTHER OF THE VIRTUES

Because we have laid down humility as a foundation, we will speak of it first of all. Humility, which is also called lowliness or self-abasement, is an interior bowing of the heart and mind before the transcendent majesty of God. Righteousness requires this, and because of charity the loving heart cannot leave this undone. When a humble, loving person observes that God has served him in so humble, loving, and faithful a way, and that God is so powerful, high, and noble, whereas a human being is so poor, small, and lowly, then there arises in his humble heart a feeling of great reverence and veneration toward God. To honor God in all one's works, whether exterior or interior, becomes the first and dearest work of humility, the sweetest work of charity, and the most fitting work of righteousness. The loving, humble heart cannot pay enough homage either to God or to Christ's noble humanity and cannot set itself as low as it would like. For this reason it seems to the humble person that he is always falling short in the homage he pays to God and in his own humble service.

Such a person is also humble and reverent toward the holy Church and the sacraments. He is temperate in all things: in his eating and drinking, in his words and in the way he answers others, in his bearing and dress, in his performance of lowly duties and in his humble appearance; in all this he is without hypocrisy or pretense. He is also humble in his interior and exterior devotions before God and other persons, so that no one is offended because of him. In this way he overcomes and drives away pride, the root and beginning of all sin. By means of humility the bonds of the devil, of sin, and of the world are broken, and a person becomes well ordered within himself and firmly established in the ways of virtue. Heaven is opened to such a person and God is disposed to hear his prayer. He is filled with grace and has Christ, the firm rock, as his foundation. Whoever builds the life of virtue on the foundation of humility cannot go astray.

Obedience

This humility gives rise to obedience, for only a humble person can be interiorly obedient. Obedience is a humble, submissive, docile attitude of mind and an openness of the will to all good things. Obedience makes a person submissive to everything which God commands, forbids, or wills. It makes a person's external senses and the powers he has in common with the animals submissive to the higher reason, so that he may live in a fitting and reasonable way. It makes a person submissive and obedient to the holy Church and to the sacraments, to the Church's prelates and to whatever they teach, command, or advise, and to all the good customs practiced within Christianity. It also makes a person open and docile toward everyone else in matters of advice, activity, or service, whether corporal or spiritual, in accordance with what each person needs and discretion requires. It dispels disobedience, that daughter of pride which is more to be avoided than venom or poison. Obedience in will and in deed adorns and expands a person's humility and makes it manifest. It makes for peace in community life: If it is found in the superior in the way in which it ought to be, then it draws to him those who are his subjects; it preserves peace and tranquillity among those who are equals; and a person who is obedient is loved by those who are set over him as his superiors, while he is also exalted and enriched by God with his eternal gifts.

Renunciation of one's own will

This obedience leads to the renunciation of one's own will and opinion, for only an obedient person can submit his own will to that of another in all things, although anyone might perform external works and yet remain self-willed. Renunciation of one's own will makes a person live without particular preferences, whether regarding things to be done or left undone, in matters which are strange or which deviate from the teaching and example of the saints. Such a person will rather live in accordance with the honor and commandments of God, the will of his superiors, and whatever makes for peace with those with whom he lives—all as discretion requires. By means of the renunciation of one's own will regarding things to be done or left undone or endured, all matter and occasion for pride are entirely driven out and humility is perfected to the highest degree. God becomes the master of a person's entire will, which becomes so united with God's that the person can neither will nor desire anything else. Such persons have put off the old self and put on the new (cf. Col 3:9–10), which is made and renewed according to the most beloved will of God. Of such as these Christ says, "Blessed are the poor in spirit" (that is, those who have renounced their own will) "for the kingdom of heaven is theirs" (Mt 5:3).

Patience

Renunciation of one's will gives rise to patience, for no one can be perfectly patient in all things except a person who has submitted his own will to the will of God and of all other persons in everything that is useful and proper. Patience is the tranquil endurance of everything which might befall a person from God or from creatures. Nothing can perturb a patient person: neither the loss of earthly possessions nor the loss of friends and relatives, neither sickness nor disgrace, neither death nor life, neither purgatory nor the devil nor hell. The reason for his calm is that he has abandoned himself in true charity to the will of God. Since he is not burdened by mortal sin, he finds it easy to bear everything which God requires of him in time and in eternity. Through this patience a person is also adorned and armed against anger, sudden wrath, and impatience in suffering, things which often unsettle a person both interiorly and exteriorly and make him prone to many kinds of temptations.

Meekness

This patience gives rise to meekness and kindness, for only a patient person can be meek in times of adversity. Meekness makes a person peaceful and tranquil in all circumstances. A meek person can suffer harsh words and manners, harsh gestures and deeds, and all kinds of injustice against himself and his friends, and through it all remain at peace, for meekness means bearing everything in peace. By means of meekness the irascible power remains unmoved in a state of quiet, the concupiscible power is raised up in virtues, and the rational power, observing this, is filled with joy, while the conscience savors it and remains at peace.[2] The second capital sin, which is anger, rage, and wrath, is driven away through meekness, for the Spirit of God abides in a humble, meek person, and Christ says, "Blessed are the meek, for they shall possess the earth" (Mt 5:5), by which he means that they will possess their own nature and all earthly things in tranquillity.

Kindness

From the same source which gives rise to meekness there also arises kindness, for only a meek person can be kind. This kindness makes a person present a loving appearance and give affable responses and do all kinds of benevolent deeds for those who are quarrelsome, in the hope that they will come to see themselves as they are and amend their ways. Through graciousness and kindness, charity remains living and fruitful in a person, for a heart full of kindness is like a lamp full of precious oil. This oil of kindness enlightens erring sinners through good example, and it salves and heals through comforting words and deeds those whose hearts are

---

2. Ruusbroec here uses terminology common in scholastic philosophy. "The irascible power" and "the concupiscible power" are the two sensitive appetites, that is, those aroused by objects perceived through the senses: The concupiscible strives toward pleasure and away from pain, while the irascible is aroused to overcome obstacles that prevent movement toward a sensible good or away from a sensible evil. "The rational power," the will, is on a higher level, being the appetite that seeks goods as they are perceived by the intellect rather than by the senses. This tripartite understanding of the human soul may be found already in Plato; see, for example, book four of the *Republic*.

wounded, grieved, or embittered. Through the fire of charity it provides a flame and bright light for those who are living virtuous lives, and neither jealousy nor disfavor can harm it.

Compassion

This kindness gives rise to compassion and to a general sympathy with everyone, for only a kind person can share the sorrows of all others. This compassion is an interior movement of a heart filled with pity for the material and spiritual needs of all persons. Compassion makes a person suffer with Christ in his passion as one considers all that it entailed: the causes and nature of his suffering, his resignation, his love, his wounds, his tenderness, his grief, his shame, his nobility, his misery, his disgrace, the way he was despised, his crown of thorns, the nails, his kindness, his patient languishing and death. The many unheard-of sufferings of Christ, our Savior and Bridegroom, move a kind person to pity and compassion for Christ.

Compassion also makes a person look to himself and recognize his faults and failings in the practice of virtue and the worship of God, his lukewarmness and laziness, the multiplicity of his failings, the way he has wasted time and the way he presently falls short in the practice of virtues and of a perfect way of life. This makes a person have pity on himself in true compassion.

Compassion likewise makes a person aware of the way others have erred and gone astray: their negligence of God and of their eternal salvation; their ingratitude for all the good that God has done for them and all the sufferings that he endured for them; the fact that they are inexperienced, ignorant, and unpracticed in the ways of virtue but clever and adroit in the ways of evil and wickedness; and the way they pay close attention to the loss and gain of earthly goods but are negligent and careless of God, of eternal realities, and of their eternal salvation. Such observations arouse in a good person great compassion and concern for the salvation of all.

A person should also observe with pity the bodily needs of his neighbor and the manifold sufferings of human nature: hunger, thirst, cold, nakedness, sickness, poverty, scorn, the oppression of the poor in so many ways, the grief caused by the loss of relatives, friends, possessions, honor, and peace, and the countless afflictions which weigh upon human nature. All this moves a good person to compassion and makes him suffer with all others. But such a person suffers most of all because people are so impatient in their sufferings and thereby lose their reward, often to the point of even deserving hell. Such is the work of compassion and pity.

JOHN RUUSBROEC

This work of compassion and of a love common to all overcomes and drives away the third capital sin, which is hatred or envy, for compassion is a wounding of the heart which love extends to all without distinction. This wound cannot be healed as long as anyone still suffers, for to compassion alone, above all other virtues, God has commended sorrow and suffering. For this reason Christ says, "Blessed are the sorrowing, for they shall be consoled" (Mt 5:4). That will take place when they reap in joy what they now, through compassion and sympathy, sow in sorrow (cf. Ps 126:5).

Generosity

This compassion gives rise to generosity, for only a compassionate person can be supernaturally generous with fidelity and affection toward all, although one might give generously to particular persons of one's own choosing without doing so out of charity and supernatural generosity. Generosity is the bountiful flowing forth of a heart which is moved by charity and compassion. When a person considers with compassion the sufferings and passion of Christ, there arises within him the virtue of generosity. This leads him to praise, thank, honor, and revere Christ for his sufferings and for his love for us and to surrender joyfully and humbly his body and soul to Christ in time and in eternity. When a person observes himself with compassion and has pity on himself, and when he reflects on the good which God has done for him and on his own failings, then he must take refuge in the generosity, graciousness, faithfulness, and trustworthiness of God and intend with a perfectly free will to serve him forevermore. When a generous person observes the errors, deviations, and unrighteousness of others, he earnestly implores God with ardent faith to let his divine gifts flow forth and to manifest his generosity toward all persons, so that they might acknowledge him and turn to the truth. This generous person also observes compassionately the material needs of everyone: He serves, he gives, he lends, and he consoles others according to their need and his ability, with prudent discretion. This generosity leads persons to practice the seven works of mercy; the rich do so through their opportunities for service and their possessions, the poor through their good will and their sincere desire to do as much as the rich if they could. In this way the virtue of generosity is practiced to perfection.

When generosity is a fundamental disposition of a person's being, then all the other virtues are increased and all the powers of the soul adorned, for a generous person is always joyful in spirit and carefree of heart, filled to overflowing with desires and dedicated to all persons without distinction in the practice of virtue. However poor a person might be, if he is generous and not enamored of the things of this world, he is like God. All that lies within him and all that he feels flow forth as a gift, and in this way he drives away the fourth capital sin, which is avarice or miserliness. Of such a person Christ says, "Blessed are the merciful, for they shall obtain mercy" (Mt 5:7), namely, on that day when they hear the words: "Come, you blessed of my Father, take possession of the kingdom which, because of your mercy, has been prepared for you from the creation of the world" (cf. Mt 25:34).

Zeal

This generosity gives rise to a supernatural zeal and devotion to every kind of virtuous and proper behavior. Only a person overflowing with generosity can experience this zeal, which is an insistent impulse from within toward the practice of virtue and conformity with Christ and his saints. Through such zeal a person desires to dedicate his heart and senses, his soul and body, and all that he is or has or might obtain to the honor and praise of God. Such zeal makes a person vigilant in both reasoning and discretion and leads him to practice virtue with both body and soul as righteousness requires. By means of this supernatural zeal all the powers of the soul are laid open to God and made ready for the performance of every virtue. A person's conscience is filled with joy and God's grace is increased. The virtues are practiced with gladness and joy, and the exterior works a person performs receive a certain graceful embellishment. Whoever has received this living zeal from God has had the fifth capital sin driven away from him, namely, spiritual sloth and a feeling of repugnance toward the practice of the virtues which are necessary for salvation. This living zeal also at times drives away bodily sluggishness and sloth. Of the zealous Christ says, "Blessed are they who hunger and thirst for righteousness, for they shall be satisfied" (Mt 5:6), namely, when God's glory is revealed and fills each person according to the measure of his love and righteousness.

Moderation and sobriety

This zeal gives rise to moderation and sobriety, both interior and exterior, for only a person who is especially diligent and zealous for maintaining his soul and body in righteousness can hold to the proper measure in matters of sobriety. Sobriety preserves the higher powers as well as the

61

powers we have in common with the animals from intemperance and excess. Sobriety wishes neither to experience nor even to know of things
which are forbidden.

The incomprehensible nature of God transcends all creatures in
heaven and on earth, for everything that a creature can comprehend is creaturely; because God is above all creatures and is both without and within
them, every created concept is too narrow to comprehend him. If a creature
were to comprehend, understand, and experience God, he would have to
be drawn beyond himself into God and so comprehend God with God.
Whoever, then, might wish to know what God is and to inquire into this
would be doing something forbidden and would go mad. The light of every
creaturely understanding thus falls short in the knowledge of what God is,
for what God is transcends all creatures, although nature and Scripture and
all creatures testify that he is. It is the part of sobriety to believe the articles
of faith and not to try to fathom them, for that is impossible in this life.
One should neither interpret nor understand the mysterious and subtle
teachings of Scripture, which the Holy Spirit has composed, in any way
that is not in accord with the life of Christ and of his saints. A person should
observe nature and Scripture and all creatures and draw from them whatever is beneficial, but nothing more. This is the meaning of spiritual sobriety.

A person should also maintain sobriety in the realm of the senses and
control his animal powers through the power of reason. In this way the
sensual appetite will not exert too much influence over a person's taste for
food and drink, but he will instead take his food and drink in the way a
sick person takes medicine—out of the need to maintain his strength for
the purpose of serving God. A person should be moderate and temperate
in word and deed, in silence and speaking, in food and drink, in what he
does and what he leaves undone, all according to the practice of the holy
Church and the example of the saints.

By means of spiritual sobriety and moderation from within himself, a
person maintains a firm and stable faith, a pure understanding, a power of
reason calm enough to understand the truth, an inclination to virtue according to God's will, a peaceful heart, and a serene conscience; he thereby
comes to possess a lasting peace with God and with himself. By means of
sobriety and moderation of the exterior, bodily senses, a person often preserves the health and tranquillity of his bodily nature, the probity of his
outward behavior, and the honor of his name. In this way he enjoys peace
with himself and with his neighbor, for through his moderation and sobriety he draws to himself in a pleasing way all persons of good will. He

also drives away the sixth capital sin, which is intemperance, excess, and gluttony. Of such persons Christ says, "Blessed are the peacemakers, for they shall be called sons of God" (Mt 5:9), for they are like the Son, who established peace for every creature that desired it. With all those who make peace by means of moderation and sobriety Christ will share the inheritance of his Father, and they will possess it with him for all eternity.

Purity

This sobriety gives rise to purity of soul and body, for only a person who is sober in body and soul can be perfectly pure in these same respects. Purity consists in not clinging to any creature with passionate desire but only to God alone, for all creatures are to be used by us, while God is to be enjoyed.[3]

Purity of spirit makes a person cleave to God beyond understanding, beyond feeling, and beyond all the gifts which God might shower upon the soul, for purity desires to pass beyond everything which a creature receives in his understanding or feeling and to find its rest in God. A person should approach the Sacrament of the Altar not for the sake of refreshment or because of desire, and not because he seeks pleasure or peace or satisfaction or consolation or anything else except the honor of God and growth in all the virtues. This is purity of spirit. Purity of heart means that in every instance of bodily temptation or natural inclination a person turns to God freely and unhesitatingly, with renewed confidence and trust and a firm intention to remain with God forever. Consenting to the sins or passions which our lower nature lusts after like a beast separates a person from God. Purity of body means that a person withdraws from and guards himself against impure deeds of whatever kind when his conscience attests and declares them to be impure and contrary to the commandments and the honor and will of God.

These three kinds of purity overcome and drive away the seventh capital sin. This sin consists first in a turning of the spirit away from God to seek its pleasure in some created thing, secondly in impure acts of the body beyond those acts which the holy Church permits, and finally in a carnal

---

3. This distinction between use (*orboren*) and enjoyment (*ghebruken*) goes back to St. Augustine, who from the time of his *De beata vita* had regularly written of the *fruitio Dei*—the "enjoyment of God," loving God for his own sake—as the true end of human life. In later parts of the *Espousals*, Ruusbroec makes frequent use of the terms *ghebruken* (here regularly translated as "blissful enjoyment") and *ghebrukelijk* (blissful) to describe that resting in God which is an essential aspect of mystical experience.

dwelling of the heart upon any creature with relish and desire, whatever that creature may be. I do not, however, mean those sudden inclinations of pleasure or desire which no one can avoid.

Now you should know that purity of spirit keeps a person in a certain likeness to God—undisturbed by creatures, inclined toward God, and united with him. Purity of body is to be likened to the whiteness of the lily and the purity of the angels; when it withstands temptation, it is to be likened to the redness of the rose and the nobility of the martyrs; when it is practiced out of love and for the glory of God, it is to be likened to the sunflower, for then it is one of the highest adornments of nature. Purity of heart brings about a renewal and increase of the grace of God. Through such purity all the virtues are inspired, practiced, and preserved. It guards and protects the external senses, subdues and restrains the lustful desires that arise within a person, adorns the entire interior life, and serves as a lock for the heart by keeping out earthly things and everything deceitful, even as it opens up the heart to heavenly realities and to all truth. For this reason Christ says, "Blessed are the pure of heart, for they shall see God" (Mt 5:8). Our eternal joy, our entire reward, and our entrance into salvation consist in this vision. A person should therefore be sober and moderate in all things, and in his behavior should avoid all occasions in which purity of soul or body could be defiled.

B. Righteousness as a Weapon in the Practice of the Virtues

Now if we wish to possess these virtues and drive away their opposites, we must have righteousness and must practice and preserve it in purity of heart right up to the time of our death, for there are three powerful adversaries which tempt and attack us at all times, in all places, and in many different ways. If we make peace with any one of these three and become its follower, then we are vanquished, for they concur and collaborate in every kind of spiritual disorder. These three adversaries are the devil, the world, and our own flesh. Of these, the last is closest to us and is often the most deceitful and harmful, for our lustful desires are the weapons with which our enemies attack us. Idleness and the neglect of virtue and of God's honor are the cause and occasion of this struggle, while the weakness of our nature, carelessness, and ignorance of the truth are the sword with which our enemies sometimes wound or even overcome us.

For this reason we should divide ourselves into two parts. The lower part is like a brute animal, opposed to the virtues and wishing to be separate from God; this part we must detest, persecute, and chastise through penance and austerity of life. In this way it will always be kept subordinate and subject to reason, and righteousness and purity of heart will constantly hold the upper hand in all virtuous activities. All the pain, suffering, and persecution which God allows to come upon us through the adversaries of virtue are things which we should gladly suffer for the honor of God, out of esteem for virtue, and in order to obtain and possess righteousness in purity of heart. Christ says, "Blessed are they who suffer persecution for righteousness' sake, for theirs is the kingdom of heaven" (Mt 5:10), for where righteousness is held fast in suffering and in the practice of virtue, there is found the coin which weighs as much as the kingdom of God and which enables a person to obtain eternal life.

Through all these virtues a person goes out to God and to himself and to his neighbor in a worthy manner of life, in virtuous activity, and in righteousness.

C. The Soul as a Kingdom under the Crown of Charity

Whoever wishes to obtain and preserve these virtues must adorn, possess, and give order to his soul just as if it were a kingdom. The free will, which is king in the soul, is free by nature and still more free by grace. It must wear a crown which is called charity. A person must receive this crown and kingdom from the emperor, who is our Lord and Master and the King of Kings, and must possess, rule, and preserve the kingdom in his name. This king, the free will, must reside in the principal city of the kingdom, that is, in the concupiscible power of the soul, and must be adorned and vested with a robe of two parts. Its right side is to be adorned with a divine gift called fortitude, in order that the king might be strong and powerful enough to overcome all obstacles and enter the heavenly palace of the supreme Emperor, where he might lovingly incline his crowned head before that supreme King with affectionate devotion. All this is the proper work of charity, whereby a person receives and adorns the crown and preserves and possesses the kingdom for all eternity. The left side of the robe is to be a cardinal virtue called moral fortitude. Through it this king, the free will, must vanquish all immorality, bring all virtues to their perfection, and possess his kingdom in power until the time of his death.

This king must choose councillors in his kingdom, the wisest persons of the realm. These are to be the two divine virtues of knowledge and discretion, both of them enlightened by the light of God's grace. These must reside near the king in a palace called the rational power of the soul, and they must be adorned and clothed with a moral virtue called temperance, so that the king might always have counsel in acting or refraining from acting. By means of knowledge a person must purify his conscience of all his failings and adorn it with every virtue, while by means of discretion he must give and take, do and leave undone, be silent and speak, fast and eat, listen and answer, and do all things according to knowledge and discretion, clad in the moral virtue known as temperance or moderation.

This king, the free will, must also set up in his kingdom a judge, who is to be righteousness or justice. This is a divine virtue when it arises from love, and it is also the highest of the moral virtues. This judge must reside in the very middle of the kingdom, that is, in the heart or in the irascible power, and must be adorned with a moral virtue called prudence, for justice cannot reach its perfection without prudence. This judge, justice, must travel through the kingdom with the power and authority of the king, with the wisdom of the king's councillors, and with his own prudence. He is to appoint and depose, to judge and condemn, to put to death and allow to live, to amputate, to make blind and restore to sight, to raise up and put down, and to dispose all things justly. So, too, he is to scourge, punish, and extirpate all vice.

The common folk of this king, namely, all the powers of the soul, must be grounded in humility and in the fear of God and must be subject to God and to all the virtues, each power in its own proper way.

Whoever possesses, preserves, and orders the kingdom of his soul in this way has gone out with love and virtues to God and to himself and to his neighbor. This is the third of the four main points which we wish to treat.

PART FOUR: "TO MEET HIM."

When a person through the grace of God is able to see and has a purified conscience, and when he has observed the three comings of Christ our Bridegroom, and when he has gone out in virtuous activity, there then follows a meeting with our Bridegroom, which is the fourth and last point. In this meeting lies our entire salvation. It is the beginning and end of all the virtues, and without this meeting no virtue has ever been practiced.

THE SPIRITUAL ESPOUSALS

Whoever wishes to meet Christ as his beloved Bridegroom and to possess eternal life with him and in him must in this present life meet Christ in three ways. The first of these is that a person must direct his mind to God in all those things whereby he is to merit eternal life. The second is that he neither think about nor love anything more than God or as much as God. The third is that he rest in God with great ardor above all creatures, above all God's gifts, above all virtuous activities, and above all those feelings which God might infuse into his soul or body.

A. THE FIRST WAY: DIRECTING THE MIND TO GOD IN ALL THAT CONCERNS OUR SALVATION

You should understand that whoever wishes to direct his mind to God must have God present to him under some divine attribute, that is, he must direct his mind to him alone who is Lord of heaven and earth and all creation, who died for us, and who is able and willing to grant eternal salvation. In whatever ways or under whatever names a person represents God as the Lord of all creation, he is doing well; if he singles out for his consideration a particular divine Person in the ground and majesty of the divine nature, he is doing well; and if he conceives of God as Conserver, Savior, Creator, or Ruler, or as bliss, power, wisdom, truth, or goodness, all in respect to the fathomless character of the divine nature, he is doing well. Although there are many names which we attribute to God, his sublime nature is a simple oneness which no creature can name. Because of his incomprehensible nobility and sublimity, which we can neither name nor fully express, we give him all these names. This is the way and the kind of knowledge by which we should keep God present in our mind. Directing one's mind to God is the same as seeing God in a spiritual way. To this activity belong also affection and love, for knowing and seeing God without affection has no savor and does not help us advance. For this reason a person should always incline lovingly toward God in all his works, directing his mind to him and loving him above all things. To do this is to meet God in intention and in love.

If a sinner wishes to turn from his sins with true and fitting repentance, he must meet God in a state of freely willed conversion and contrition and must have a genuine intention of serving God forevermore and never again sinning. Then in this meeting he will receive from God's mercy a sure hope of eternal salvation and the forgiveness of his sins; he will also receive the foundation of all the virtues: faith, hope, and love, together with a will that is disposed toward the practice of all the virtues.

If a person wishes to advance in the light of faith and observe all Christ's works, all his suffering, all that he has promised us and done for us, and all that he will do up to the Day of Judgment and on into eternity, and if such a person wishes his observations to be conducive to his salvation, then he must meet Christ anew and keep him present in his mind through thanksgiving, praise, and fitting veneration for all his gifts and for all that he has done or will do in eternity. Then will a person's faith be strengthened and he will be more ardently moved toward all the virtues.

If he then wishes to advance in virtuous activity, he must also meet Christ through self-renunciation. This means that he must not seek himself or set up any alien goal, but must rather perform all his works with discretion, direct his mind to God and to his praise and glory in all things, and persevere in this until death. In this way his reason will be enlightened, his charity will be increased, and he will become more devout and more readily inclined toward all the virtues.

B. The Second Way: Not Directing the Mind to Any Other End Equal to God

A person should direct his mind to God in all good works; in evil works this cannot be done. A person must not direct his mind toward two ends, toward both God and something else in addition. Rather, everything to which a person's mind is also directed should be beneath God—not contrary to God but subordinate to him and serving as a help and aid in coming to God. If this is so, then all is in order.

C. The Third Way: Resting in God above All Creatures

A person should also rest upon and in him whom one intends and loves more than upon all the messengers he sends, namely, his gifts. The soul should likewise rest in God above all the adornments and gifts which it might send through its own messengers. These messengers are intention, love, and desire, for they carry to God all our good works and virtues. Above all these things and above all multiplicity, the soul should rest in its Beloved.

This is the manner and way in which we should meet Christ through-out our entire life, in all our works and virtues performed with an upright intention, so that we might also meet him in the light of glory at the hour of our death.[4] This manner and way, as you have heard it described, is called the active life. This life is necessary for all persons, at least in the sense that they not live contrary to any virtue even though they may not possess all the virtues to this degree of perfection. To live contrary to the virtues is to live in sin, for as Christ says, "Whoever is not with me is against me" (Lk 11:23). Whoever is not humble is proud, and whoever is proud and not humble does not belong to God. It is the same with all the other sins and virtues: a person must either possess the virtue and be in the state of grace or possess the contrary of the virtue and be in the state of sin. Let everyone examine himself and live in the way that has here been de-scribed.

D. THE TRANSITION FROM THE ACTIVE LIFE TO THE INTERIOR LIFE

A person who lives as perfectly as has here been described and who offers his entire life and all his activities to the glory and praise of God, directing his mind to God and loving him above all things, will often be moved by the desire to see, to know, and to experience who this Bride-groom is, this Christ who for his sake became a human being and labored in love unto death, who has forgiven him his sins and driven away the devil, who has given him himself and his grace and left him his sacraments, and who has promised him his kingdom and himself as his eternal reward and given bodily sustenance, interior consolation and sweetness, and countless other gifts according to each person's need.

When such a person considers all this, he is moved by an extremely strong desire to see and to know Christ his Bridegroom as he is in himself, for although he knows Christ in his works, this is not enough. He must therefore do as the publican Zacchaeus did when he desired to see Jesus as he was (cf. Lk 19:1–10). He must run ahead of the crowd, that is, ahead of all the multiplicity of the created order, since this makes a person short of

---

4. The phrase "in the light of glory" (*in lichte der glorien*) refers to a supernatural aid en-abling the blessed in heaven to behold God in the beatific vision. The later theological elab-oration of this doctrine of the *lumen gloriae* was based primarily on the commentaries of the Fathers of the Church on Psalm 36:9: "and in your light we see light."

stature and so unable to see God. He must then climb the tree of faith, which grows downward from above, since its roots are in the Godhead.[5] This tree has twelve branches, which are the twelve articles of the creed. The lowest of these speak of God's humanity and of those matters which concern the salvation of our body and soul. The highest branches of this tree speak of the Godhead—of the Trinity of Persons and of the Unity of the divine nature. A person must cling to this Unity in the highest part of the tree, for it is there that Christ is to pass by with all his gifts.

Here comes Jesus, who sees this person and speaks to him in the light of glory, saying that according to his divinity he is infinite, incomprehensible, inaccessible, and fathomless, transcending all created light and every finite concept. This is the highest knowledge of God that a person can acquire in the active life, namely, that he acknowledge in the light of faith that God is incomprehensible and unknowable. In this light Christ says to this person's desire, "Come down quickly, for I must stay at your house today" (Lk 19:5). This quick descent is nothing other than a desirous and loving immersion into the abyss of the Godhead, where no understanding which requires created light can reach. But where understanding remains without, desire and love enter within.

When the soul thus inclines toward God with love and intent above all that it understands, then it abides in God and God in it. When the soul ascends with desire above the multiplicity of the created order, above the activity of the senses and above all natural light, then it meets Christ in the light of faith; it becomes enlightened and confesses that God is unknowable and incomprehensible. When the soul inclines with desire toward this incomprehensible God, then it meets Christ and is filled with his gifts. When it loves and is at rest above all gifts, above itself, and above all creatures, then it abides in God and God in it. This is how we are to meet Christ at the highest level of the active life.

If you possess righteousness in charity, if you have laid down humility as a foundation and built upon it a dwelling, namely, the virtues which have here been described, and if you have met Christ through faith and through directing your mind and your love to him, then you abide in God and God in you, and you have come into possession of the active life. This is the first life of which we wished to speak.

---

5. This unusual image of a tree growing downward from above is also found in the first Vision of Ruusbroec's Flemish predecessor, the thirteenth-century beguine Hadewijch of Antwerp, although she describes it as "the tree of the knowledge of God." See Hadewijch, *Hadewijch: The Complete Works*, trans. Mother Columba Hart (New York: Paulist Press, 1980), p. 266.

BOOK TWO: THE INTERIOR LIFE

The wise virgin, that is, the pure soul which has abandoned earthly things and which lives for God through the virtues, has taken into the vessel of her heart the oil of charity and of virtuous works, together with the lamp of a spotless conscience. But whenever Christ the Bridegroom delays his coming with consolation and a new influx of gifts, the soul becomes drowsy, sleepy, and indolent. In the middle of the night, that is, when it is least expected, a spiritual cry resounds within the soul: "See, the bridegroom is coming. Go out to meet him." We now wish to speak of this seeing, and of an interior coming of Christ, and of a person's going out spiritually to meet him. We will clarify and explain these four points with respect to an interior exercise full of desire—the kind of life which many persons attain through the practice of moral virtues and interior zeal.

In these words of the parable, Christ teaches us four things. First, he wishes our understanding to be enlightened with a supernatural brightness; this we learn when he says "See." Secondly, he shows us what we are to see, namely, the interior coming of our Bridegroom, the eternal truth; this is what we are to understand when he says "The bridegroom is coming." Thirdly, he commands us to go out in interior exercises practiced in the way righteousness requires, and for this reason he says "Go out." Fourthly, he shows us the end and purpose of all this work, namely, a meeting with Christ our Bridegroom in the blissful Unity of the Godhead.

PART ONE: "SEE."

A. The Three Things Necessary for Seeing

The first word which Christ says is "See." If a person wishes to see in a supernatural way in the interior life, three things are necessary. The first of these is the light of God's grace in a higher way than that which can be experienced in a life of exterior works without fervent interior zeal. The second is the stripping of all strange images and solicitude from the heart, so that a person may be free and imageless, delivered from attachments and empty of all creatures. The third thing which is necessary is a free turning of the will and a gathering together of all the bodily and spiritual powers in such a way that the will, unencumbered by any inordinate affection, might flow into the Unity of God and of the mind. This allows the rational creature to attain the sublime Unity of God and to possess it in a supernatural way. It is for this reason that God created heaven and earth and all that is in them, and it is likewise for this reason that he became a human being, taught us, lived for us, and himself became the way to this Unity. He died in the bond of love, ascended into heaven, and has opened up for us the same Unity through which we might possess eternal bliss.

B. The Threefold Unity Which Is in Us Naturally and Supernaturally

The natural possession of the three unities

Now note carefully: There is a threefold unity which is in everyone naturally and which is in good persons supernaturally as well. The first and highest unity is that which we have in God, for all creatures depend on this unity for their being, their life, and their preservation. If they were separated from God at this level, they would fall into nothingness and become nothing. This unity is in us essentially, by nature, whether we are good or evil, and without our cooperation it neither sanctifies nor saves us. We possess this unity within ourselves and yet above ourselves, for it both grounds and preserves our very being and life.

The second unity is also in us by nature. This is the unity of the higher powers, a unity from which they arise naturally as active powers; this is the unity of the spirit or of the mind. This is the same unity as the first, which is in God and depends on him, but here we are considering it as regards its activity and there as regards its essence; in each case the spirit is whole and entire according to the totality of its substance. We possess this unity within ourselves above the activity of the senses. From it arise the powers of the memory, the understanding, and the will—our entire power of performing spiritual activity.[6] In this unity the soul is called spirit.

---

6. For Ruusbroec, as for St. Augustine, the memory is no mere power of recollection but rather the power by which the human spirit comes to awareness of itself and of the divine ground from which it arises.

The third unity which is in us by nature is the ground of the bodily powers, that is, the unity of the heart, which is the beginning and source of our corporeal life. The soul possesses this unity in the body and in the life-giving center of the heart; from it flow all the works of the body and of the five senses. Here the soul is simply called soul, for it is the form of the body and animates the flesh by giving it life and keeping it alive.

These three unities exist naturally in a person and constitute a single life and kingdom. In the lowest unity are located a person's power of feeling and the powers he shares with the animals; in the second a person is constituted as a rational and spiritual being; in the highest a person is preserved in being in an essential way. All this is in everyone by nature.

The supernatural possession of these unities in the active life

The kingdom and eternal dwelling place of these three unities can also be supernaturally adorned and possessed, first of all through moral virtues practiced in charity in the active life. This kingdom is still more beautifully adorned and more nobly possessed when the fervent exercises of the interior life are added to the active life, and it is most nobly and blissfully adorned through a supernatural, contemplative life.

In the active life, the lowest or bodily unity is supernaturally adorned and possessed through exterior exercises of moral perfection after the manner of Christ and his saints. This means carrying the cross together with Christ and subordinating human nature to the commandments of the holy Church and to the teaching of the saints, with prudent discretion and according to what human nature can bear. The second unity, which is in the spirit and is entirely spiritual, is supernaturally adorned and possessed through the three divine virtues of faith, hope, and love, together with the influx of God's grace and gifts and our ready willingness to practice all the virtues according to the example of Christ and holy Christianity. The third and highest unity transcends our powers of conceptual understanding and is yet within us essentially. It is supernaturally possessed by us when in all our virtuous activities we intend God's praise and glory and when we rest in him above all intention, above ourselves, and above all things. This is the unity from which we have flowed forth in a creaturely way, in which we abide essentially, and to which we are lovingly returning through charity. These are the virtues which adorn the three unities in the active life.

The preparation for the supernatural possession of these unities in the interior life

We now wish to go on and show how these three unities are more beautifully adorned and more nobly possessed when fervent interior exercises are added to those of the active life. When through charity and an upright intention a person offers himself in all his works and in his entire life to the glory and praise of God, and when he seeks rest in God above all things, then he should humbly and patiently, with self-surrender and firm confidence, await new riches and gifts—but always without anxiety as to whether God will bestow them or not. This is the way a person makes himself ready and capable of receiving an interior life full of desire. When the vessel is ready, the precious liquid is poured in. There is no more precious vessel than a loving soul and no more beneficial drink than the grace of God. It is in this way that a person will offer to God all his works and his entire life with a simple and upright intention and will also, above that intention, above himself, and above all things, rest in that sublime unity where God and the loving spirit are united without intermediary.

C. The Enlightenment Which Occurs in the Highest Unity

From out of this unity where the spirit is united with God without intermediary, grace and all gifts flow forth. From out of this same unity where the spirit rests above itself in God, Christ, the eternal truth, says, "See, the bridegroom is coming. Go out to meet him." It is Christ, the light of truth, who says "See," and it is through him that we are able to see, for he is the light of the Father, without which there is no light in heaven or on earth. Christ's speaking within us is nothing other than an influx of his light and grace. This grace descends upon us in the unity of our higher powers and of our spirit. From this unity the higher powers actively flow forth in all the virtues by means of the power of grace, and to it they return in the bond of love. In this unity lie the power and the beginning and end of all creaturely activity, both natural and supernatural, insofar as it is performed in a creaturely way by means of grace, divine gifts, and the power proper to creatures. God bestows his grace upon the unity of the higher powers so that a person may constantly practice the virtues by means of the power, richness, and impulse of grace, for God gives his grace for the sake of works, whereas he gives himself above all grace for the sake of enjoyment and rest. This unity of the spirit is where we are to dwell in the peace of God and in the richness of charity. Here all the multiplicity of the virtues comes to an end, and they live together in the simplicity of the spirit.

Now the grace which flows forth from God is an interior impulse or urging of the Holy Spirit which drives our own spirit from within and urges it out toward all the virtues. This grace flows from within, not from without, for God is more interior to us than we are to ourselves,[7] and his interior urging and working within us, whether done naturally or super-naturally, is nearer and more intimate to us than are our own works. For this reason God works in us from within outward, whereas all creatures work from without inward. Grace and all God's gifts and inspirations thus come from within, in the unity of our spirit, and not from without, in the imagination by means of sensible images.

D. THE REQUISITE CONDITIONS
FOR OBTAINING THIS ENLIGHTENMENT

Christ now speaks in a spiritual way within a person who is devoted to him: "See." There are three things, as I said earlier, which make a person able to see in interior exercises. The first of these is the illumination of divine grace. This grace within a soul is like a candle in a lantern or other glass vessel, for it warms and brightens and shines through the vessel, that is, through a person who is good. It also reveals itself to a person who has it within himself, provided that he is careful in observing himself, and it reveals itself to others through him by means of his virtues and good example. This radiation of God's grace touches and moves a person promptly from within; this quick movement is the first thing which makes us able to see. This same quick movement of God gives rise to the second prerequisite. This is from the person's side and consists in a gathering together of all his powers, from within and from without, in the unity of the spirit and the bond of love. The third thing which is necessary is freedom, so that without hindrance from sensible images a person can turn within as often as he wishes and as often as he thinks of his God. In other words, a person must be unattached to pleasure and pain, gain and loss, exaltation and hu-

---

7. The expression "more interior to us than we are to ourselves" is reminiscent of St. Augustine's well-known phrase *interior intimo meo:* God is "deeper within me than my own inmost being" (*Confessions 3.6*).

miliation, strange anxieties, and joy and fear, just as he must also not be bound to any creature.

These three things make a person able to see in interior exercises. If you possess them, then you have the foundation and the beginning of such exercises and of the interior life.

PARTS TWO AND THREE:
"THE BRIDEGROOM IS COMING. GO OUT."

Even if a person's eyes are sound and his power of vision sharp, if there is no lovable and desirable object present to be seen, then his soundness of vision will bring him little or no pleasure and profit. For this reason Christ reveals to the eyes of the enlightened understanding what they are to see, namely, an interior coming of Christ their Bridegroom. This particular coming occurs in three different manners in persons who are given to the devout practice of exercises in the interior life. Each of these three comings raises a person to a higher level and a more fervent practice.

The first coming of Christ in interior exercises drives and urges on a person sensibly from within, drawing him with all his powers upward to heaven and pressing him to attain unity with God. A person feels this urging and this attraction in the heart and in the unity of all the corporeal powers, especially in the concupiscible power, for this coming stirs and works in the lower part of a person, since that part must be purified, adorned, enflamed, and drawn inward. This insistent urging of God from within both gives and takes, makes rich and poor, brings happiness and sorrow, causes hope and despair, and makes hot and cold. No tongue can express the gifts and works which occur here with all their opposites. This coming, with all the exercises proper to it, can be divided into four modes, each higher than the previous one, as we will later explain. Through this coming the lower part of a person's being is adorned in the interior life.

The second manner of the interior coming of Christ is nobler than the first, bears a greater likeness to Christ as he is in himself, and brings with it more gifts and greater resplendence. It consists in an influx of the riches of divine gifts into the higher powers of the soul, and these gifts strengthen, enlighten, and enrich the spirit in many different ways. This flowing of God into the spirit requires that it, with all these riches, flow out in return, back into that very ground in which the flowing had its source. God bestows and reveals marvelous things in this influx, but he requires of the soul all his gifts back again, multiplied beyond anything that a creature can accomplish. This exercise and this state of being are nobler and more like God than the first. Through them the three higher powers of the soul are adorned.

The third manner of the interior coming of our Lord is an interior stirring or touch in the unity of the spirit, where the higher powers of the soul have their abode. From here they flow forth, to here they return, and here they constantly remain, united by the bond of love and the natural unity of the spirit. Through this coming the interior life attains its inmost and highest state, and the unity of the spirit is adorned in many different ways.

Now in each of these comings Christ demands of us a particular way of going out of ourselves—a way of living that is in accordance with the manner of his coming. For this reason he speaks spiritually within our heart at each coming, saying: "Go out through your exercises and your whole life in accordance with the way in which my grace and gifts impel you." This means that if we wish to be perfect, we must go out and live in interior exercises according to the way in which the Spirit of God urges, drives, draws, flows into, and touches us. If we withstand God's Spirit through a contrary manner of life, then we will lose this interior urge and the virtues will remain far from us.

These are the three comings of Christ in interior exercises. We now wish to explain and clarify each coming individually. Here you must pay careful attention, for anyone who has never experienced this will not easily understand it.

A. THE FIRST COMING, INTO THE HEART, OCCURRING IN FOUR DIFFERENT MODES

The first mode: sensible fervor and consolation

Christ's coming likened to the sun in mountainous country

The first coming of Christ in exercises full of desire is an interiorly felt impulse of the Holy Spirit which urges and impels us toward all the virtues. We wish to compare this coming to the powerful shining of the sun which, from the moment of its rising, gives light to the entire world and pervades it with its radiance and warmth. In the same way Christ, the eternal sun who dwells in the highest part of the spirit, sends forth his beams and radiance and light. He also enlightens and enkindles the lower part of a person, that is, the corporeal heart and the powers of sensation. All this happens more quickly than the twinkling of an eye, for God's work is fast. But this can happen only to a person who is able to see interiorly with the eyes of his understanding.

In mountainous country, in the central part of the earth, the sun shines upon the mountains and brings about an early summer, with much good fruit, strong wine, and a land full of joy. The same sun also shines in flat country, near the outer reaches of the earth. Here the land is colder and the power of the sun's heat less, yet even here the sun produces much good fruit, though not so much wine. In the same way, persons who dwell in the lower part of their being, among the external senses, but who in God's grace practice the moral virtues through exterior exercises performed with an upright intention, bring forth much good fruit of virtue in many different ways. However, they experience little of the wine of interior joy and spiritual consolation.

A person who wishes to experience the radiance of the eternal sun, which is Christ himself, must have the power of sight and must make his abode in mountainous country by gathering together all his powers. Free and unencumbered by attachments to pleasure or pain or any creature, he must be raised up to God with all his heart. There Christ, the sun of righteousness, will shine into his free and uplifted heart. This is the mountainous country that I mean.

In his interior coming and through the power of his Spirit, Christ, the glorious sun and divine resplendence, enlightens, shines through, and enkindles the heart which is free, together with all the powers of the soul. This is the first effect of his interior coming in exercises full of desire. Just as the power and nature of fire enkindle material which is ready to be set aflame, so does Christ with the ardent heat of his interior coming enkindle the heart which is ready, free, and uplifted. At this coming he says, "Go out, through exercises which are in accordance with this coming."

The effects of this coming and our response to it

This heat gives rise to unity in our heart, for we can attain true unity only if the Spirit of God enkindles his fire in our heart. This fire unifies all the things that it can master and transform, making them like itself. Unity means that a person feels interiorly gathered together with all his powers in the unity of his heart. Unity produces interior peace and restfulness of heart, and is a bond which draws together body and soul, heart and senses, and all the exterior and interior powers, enveloping them in the unity of love.

This unity produces interior fervor, for only a person who has been gathered together in unity can be interiorly fervent. Interior fervor means that a person is turned within to his own heart, so that he might understand and experience the interior working and inspirations of God. Interior fervor is a perceptible fire of love which God's Spirit has enkindled and fanned to a flame. Such fervor burns, drives, and urges a person from within in such a way that he does not know whence it comes or what is happening to him.

Interior fervor gives rise to a felt affection which penetrates a person's heart and the concupiscible power of the soul. Only a person who is interiorly fervent can have this affection, which is characterized by desire and by the perceptible savor which it produces in the heart. Felt affection and love consist in a desire, a taste, and a yearning which a person feels for God as an eternal good which includes all other goods. Felt affection lets go of all creatures as regards enjoying them, though not as regards making use of them to the degree necessary. Fervent affection feels itself touched from within by an eternal love to which it must always be devoted. Fervent affection easily renounces and disdains all things so that it might obtain what it loves.

This felt affection gives rise to devotion to God and to his glory, for only a person who has a felt affection and love for God can have within his heart devotion which is full of desire. Devotion means that the fire of love and of affection has sent its flame of desire up to heaven. Devotion stirs and urges a person both exteriorly and interiorly to the service of God. Devotion makes both body and soul blossom out in showing reverence and respect to God and to all persons. God requires devotion of us in all the acts of service which we are to do for him. Devotion purifies both body and soul of everything which can be an obstacle or hindrance, and it points out and leads a person to the right way to salvation.

This fervent devotion gives rise to thanksgiving, for no one can thank and praise God so well as a person who is fervent and devout. It is right that we should thank and praise God, for he has created us as rational beings and has ordained that heaven and earth and the angels should serve us. Because of our sins he became a human being, teaching us, living for us, and showing us the way. He served us in a humble form, suffered an ignominious death for our sake, and promised us his eternal kingdom, where he himself will be our reward and our servant. He spared us in our sins and has fully forgiven us, even as he will forgive us in the future. He has poured his grace and his love into our souls and wishes to abide in us and with us for eternity. He has visited us with his noble sacraments in accordance with our needs and will continue to do so all the days of our lives. He has left us his body and blood to be our food and drink according to the hunger and desire of each of us. He has placed before us nature, Scripture, and all creatures to be a mirror and example in which we might observe and learn how to turn all our works into virtues. He has given us health, strength, and power, and has sometimes sent us sickness for our own good. He has provided for our exterior necessities and has laid within us the foundation of interior peace and tranquillity. He has seen to it that we bear Christian names and that we have been born of Christian parents. For all these things we should thank God here on earth, so that we might eternally thank him in heaven.

We should also praise God to the fullest extent of our ability. The praise of God means that a person offers honor, reverence, and veneration to the divine majesty throughout his life. Such praise of God is the most proper and fitting work of the angels and saints in heaven and of all loving persons on earth. A person should praise God with his heart, his desire, and his powers as these strive upward toward God; so, too, he should praise God with his words and deeds, his body and soul, and all his possessions as he uses them in humble service both exteriorly and interiorly. Those who do not praise God here on earth will remain without the power of speech in eternity. The praise of God is the most pleasant and delightful activity of a loving heart. Such a heart, full of praise itself, desires that all creatures praise God. There will be no end to this praise of God, for that is our bliss: rightly will we praise him for all eternity.

Fervent thanksgiving and praise give rise to a twofold pain of heart and torment of desire. The first of these is that a person realizes that he is deficient in thanking, praising, honoring, and serving God, and the other is that he does not advance as much as he would like in charity, virtue, fidelity, and perfect behavior so as to be worthy of thanking, praising, and serving God as he deserves. This is the second pain. Together they are both the root and fruit, the beginning and end of all interior virtues. The interior sorrow and pain which arise from our deficiencies in virtue and in praise of God constitute the highest activity in this first mode of interior exercise, and hereby this mode comes to its perfection.

THE SPIRITUAL ESPOUSALS

Two explanatory similes

Boiling water. Consider now a comparison which will show what this exercise is like. When natural fire has, by means of its heat and its power, brought water or some other liquid to a boil, that is its highest activity. The water then reverses direction and falls back down to the bottom, where it is again raised up to the same boiling activity through the power of the fire, in such a way that the fire is constantly exerting its force and the water is constantly boiling. The interior fire of the Holy Spirit works in the same way. It drives, urges, and impels the heart and all the powers of the soul up to the boiling point, that is, up to the giving of thanks and praise to God in the way I have already described. Then a person falls back down to the same ground where the Spirit of God is aflame, so that the fire of love is constantly burning and a person's heart is constantly thanking and praising in word and deed and yet constantly remaining in humble lowliness, for such a person considers what he should do and would like to do to be something great and what he actually does to be something small.

The sun in late springtime. When summer draws near and the sun rises higher in the sky, it draws moisture out of the earth through the roots and trunk of a tree into its branches, and as a result leaves, blossoms, and fruit appear. In the same way, when Christ, the eternal sun, rises higher in our hearts and it becomes summer in the rich flowering of virtues, then he sheds his light and heat onto our desires so as to draw the heart from the multiplicity of earthly things to unity and interior fervor. He makes the heart grow and bring forth the leaves of fervent affection, the blossoms of a devotion that is full of desire, and the fruit of thanksgiving and praise, and he preserves this fruit eternally in the humble pain that arises from our constant awareness of our deficiencies.

Here ends our treatment of the first of the four principal modes of interior exercises which adorn the lower part of a person's being.

The second mode: a superabundance of consolation

Christ's coming likened to the sun in the sign of Gemini

Since we are comparing the four modes of Christ's coming to the light and power of the sun, we now come upon another power and activity of the sun which speeds the ripening and the multiplication of fruit. When in mid-May the sun rises very high and enters the sign of Gemini (the Twins), that is, a twofold reality having but a single nature, then the sun exerts a

81

double force over trees and plants and everything which grows from the earth. If at that time the planets which govern nature are well ordered in the way which that time of year requires, then the sun will shed its light upon the earth and draw moisture up into the air. This produces dew and rain and the growth and multiplication of fruit. In the same way, when Christ, the resplendent sun, has risen high in our hearts above all things, when the demands of our corporeal nature which are contrary to the spirit have been subdued and discreetly set in order, when the virtues have been possessed in the way described in the previous mode, and when through the heat of charity all the savor and restfulness which a person experiences in the virtues have been borne up to God in an offering of thanksgiving and praise, then as a result there sometimes falls a soothing rain of new interior consolation and a heavenly dew of divine sweetness. This makes the virtues grow and increases them twofold if a person places no obstacle in the way. This is a new and special working and a new coming of Christ into the loving heart. A person is hereby raised to a higher state than he possessed earlier. In this sweetness Christ says, "Go out, in accordance with the mode of this coming."

The effects of this coming and our response to it

This sweetness gives rise to a feeling of delight in the heart and all the corporeal powers, so that a person thinks he is enveloped from within by a divine embrace of affection. This delight and consolation is greater and more pleasant for both soul and body than all the delight which earthly things could produce, even if a single person could enjoy them all together. In this delight God enters the depths of the heart by means of his gifts and does so with so much savor, consolation, and joy that the heart overflows from within. This makes a person realize how miserable are those who live apart from love. This delight causes a melting of the heart, so that a person cannot contain himself out of the fullness of his interior joy.

This delight gives rise to spiritual inebriation. Spiritual inebriation means that a person receives more perceptible savor and delight than his heart or desire could long for or contain. Spiritual inebriation produces much strange behavior in a person. It makes one person sing and praise God out of the fullness of his joy, and it makes another shed many tears because of the delight he feels within his heart. In one it produces restlessness in all his limbs, causing him to run and jump and dance about, and in another the force of this inebriation is so great that he must clap his hands in jubilation. One person cries out in a loud voice and so makes manifest the fullness which he feels within, and another becomes silent and seems to melt away out of the delight he feels in all his senses. Sometimes it seems to such a person that the entire world is experiencing what he is experiencing, and at other times it seems that no one else enjoys the savor which he has attained. It often seems to him that he neither could nor ever will lose this feeling of delight. At times it seems amazing that not everyone has become filled with God, and at other times it seems that God belongs entirely to him alone or to no one else as much as to him. Sometimes he wonders just what this delight is or where it comes from or what is happening to him. On the level of our corporeal sensibility, this is the most delightful kind of life that a person can have on earth. At times this delight becomes so intense that it seems to such a person that his heart will break because of all these manifold gifts and wonderful works.

Such a person should therefore with humble heart glorify and praise the Lord who is able to do all this, and with fervent devotion he should thank him for willing to do it. He should constantly hold in his heart and speak sincerely with his tongue these words: "Lord, I am not worthy of this, but I have great need of your fathomless goodness and support." Through such humility he will be able to grow and increase in higher virtues.

Obstacles to our response

Because Christ's coming in this mode is given to such persons when they begin to turn from the world—at least if they turn completely and give up all worldly consolation in order to belong entirely to God and live entirely for him—they are still weak and need milk and sweet foods, not the strong fare of great temptations and abandonment by God. Hoarfrost and fog often prove obstacles to persons at these times, that is, when they are in this state, for in terms of the interior life it is right in the middle of May. Hoarfrost refers to a person's desiring to be something or thinking that he is something already, or to his ascribing something to himself or thinking that he has earned the feeling of consolation and is worthy of it. This is the hoarfrost that can destroy the blossoms and fruit of every virtue. Fog refers to a person's willingness to rest in interior consolation and sweetness. This darkens the air of reason and closes the powers which should be blossoming open and bearing fruit. As a result, a person loses his knowledge of the truth, even though he may for a time preserve a false sweetness, which is given by the devil and which in the end seduces a person.

JOHN RUUSBROEC

The simile of the bee

I now wish to present a short simile so that you may not go astray but may govern yourself well in this state. You should, then, observe and follow the example of the wise bee. It lives in unity with the rest of the colony gathered together in the hive, and it ventures out not when it is stormy but when the weather is calm and still and the sun is shining. It lands on all the flowers in which sweetness may be found, but it does not remain on any one of them or on any other sweet and beautiful thing. Rather, it draws out of the flowers both honey and wax, that is, sweetness and material that can be used to provide light, and it brings this back to the assembled unity of the hive so that the latter may become fruitful in a very beneficial way. Now when Christ, the eternal sun, shines upon a heart which is open to him, he makes the heart and all the interior powers grow and blossom and overflow with joy and sweetness. At such times a wise person will act like the bee. Observantly, rationally, and discreetly he will fly out to all the gifts and all the sweetness which he has ever felt and to all the good which God has ever done for him; with the sting of charity and interior attentiveness he will examine all the multiplicity of consolations and good things without remaining on the flower of any one gift; and then, laden with thanksgiving and praise, he will fly back to the state of unity where he wishes to rest and abide in God for all eternity.

This is the second mode of the interior exercises which adorn the lower part of a person's being in many different ways.

The third mode: a powerful attraction to God

Christ's coming likened to the sun in the sign of Cancer

When the sun rises as high as possible in the heavens, that is, when it enters the sign of Cancer (which means the Crab, because the sun cannot rise any higher but begins to move backwards, like a crab), then the heat is the most intense of the entire year. The sun draws up all the moisture, the earth becomes dry, and fruit ripens the best. In the same way, when Christ, the divine sun, has risen as high as possible in our hearts, that is, above all gifts, consolation, and sweetness that we might receive from him, in such a way that we—at least if we have mastered ourselves—do not rest in any savor which God might pour into our souls, however great that savor might be, but rather by means of humble praise and fervent thanksgiving constantly turn inward, as described previously, to that same ground from which all gifts flow forth according to the need and merit of each creature—when all this occurs, then Christ has risen as high as possible in our hearts and from there wishes to draw all things to himself, namely, all our powers. When neither savor nor consolation can overcome or prove an obstacle to the loving heart, but the latter is willing to forgo every consolation and every gift in order to find the one whom it loves (cf. Sg 3:4), then arises the third mode of interior exercises through which a person has his powers of feeling and the lower part of his being raised up and adorned.

The first work of Christ and the beginning of this third mode is that God draws the heart, the desires, and all the powers of the soul upward to heaven, calling them to be united with himself and saying spiritually within the heart: "Go out from yourself to me, in accordance with the way in which I am drawing and inviting you." I cannot easily explain this attraction and invitation to coarse, unfeeling persons, but it consists in the fact that God is inviting and calling the heart to its higher unity with him. This interior invitation is more pleasant to the heart than anything else it has ever experienced. This gives rise to a new mode and a higher kind of exercise.

The effects of this coming and our response to it

Here the heart opens wide in joy and desire, all the veins dilate, and the powers of the soul stand ready in their desire to fulfill what is called for by God and by the invitation to unity with him. This invitation consists in the shining of Christ, the eternal sun, upon the heart. This causes so much pleasure and joy within the heart and makes the heart open so wide that it can scarcely be closed again.

A person is thereby wounded in his heart from within and feels the wound of love. Being wounded by love is both the sweetest feeling and the sharpest pain that anyone can experience and is a sure sign that he will be healed. This spiritual wound causes pleasure and pain at one and the same time. Christ, the true sun, again casts his light and rays upon the wounded, open heart and invites it once more to unity. This renews the wound and all its pangs.

This interior call and invitation, together with the fact that the creature lifts himself up in readiness to offer himself and all that he can do and nevertheless finds himself unable to reach or obtain this unity, causes a spiritual pain. In other words, when the inmost depths of the heart and the very source of life have been wounded by love and when a person finds himself unable to obtain what he most desires but must ever remain where he does not wish to be, then from this twofold source arises the pain. Here Christ is raised above the topmost part of the mind and casts his divine rays upon the avid desires of the longing heart. This burning radiance dries up and consumes all the moisture, that is, all the powers and forces of human nature. An open and longing heart and the influx of divine rays give rise to an enduring pain.

When a person cannot attain God and yet cannot do without him, then from these two things there arises a transport of restlessness in some persons, both from within and from without. As long as a person is experiencing this transport, no creature in heaven or on earth can bring him rest or help him in any other way. In this transport, sublime and salutary words and special teachings and wisdom are sometimes prompted or spoken from within. In this interior transport a person is ready to suffer everything that can be suffered in order to obtain what he loves. The transport of love is an interior restlessness which will scarcely practice or heed the dictates of reason unless it obtains what it loves. This interior transport consumes a person's heart and drinks his blood. The heat which is here felt from within is the most intense of a person's entire life. His corporeal nature is secretly wounded and consumed without being acted upon from outside, and the fruit of the virtues ripens more quickly than in all the modes which have previously been described.

Christ's coming and its effects further likened to the sun in the sign of Leo

In the same time of year the sun enters the sign of Leo (the Lion), which has a fierce nature since the lion is king of the beasts. In the same way, when a person enters this state, Christ, the resplendent sun, is in the sign of Leo, for the rays of his heat are so intense that they bring to a boil the heart's blood of a person experiencing the transport of love. When this passionate state prevails, it masters and overpowers all modes, for it wishes to be devoid of mode, that is, devoid of particular form or measure.[8] Sometimes a person in this state falls into a restless longing and desire to be freed from the prison of his body in order to be united with the one whom he

---

8. "Devoid of mode" (*wiseloes*) and "devoid of particular form or measure" (*sonder maniere*) are common expressions in medieval Christian mysticism and appear frequently in Ruusbroec. They derive, at least in part, from the exordium of St. Bernard's *De diligendo Deo*: "Do you wish to hear from me why and in what manner God is to be loved? I reply: The reason for loving God is God himself, and the manner is that it be without manner (*sine modo*)." In his final work, *The Twelve Beguines*, Ruusbroec defines *wiseloes* as meaning "without manner, neither thus nor so, neither here nor there," in other words, without limitation or definition.

loves. He therefore opens his interior eyes and contemplates the heavenly palace full of glory and joy, where his Beloved is crowned in its midst and flows forth to his saints in the abundance of his riches—while such a person must forgo this. This often causes him real tears and a great yearning. He looks down and observes the wretched condition in which he is imprisoned and from which he cannot escape, and from this flow tears of sadness and misery. These natural tears soothe and cool his heart and are useful for preserving the power and strength of his corporeal being and for helping him survive this passionate state. It is beneficial for a person in this state to give himself to various kinds of reflections and particular exercises, so as to preserve his strength and live long in virtue.

From this transport of restlessness a person is sometimes caught up in the spirit above the senses. There he is told in words or shown in images and representations some truth which he or others need to know or some event which is still to come. This is what is called revelations or visions. If it is a matter of corporeal images, a person receives them in his imagination; an angel may bring this about in him through the power of God. If it is a matter of intellectual truths or spiritual representations in which God reveals himself in his fathomless being, then a person receives them in his understanding and may formulate them in words insofar as they are expressible in this way.

Sometimes a person is caught up above himself and above the spirit—though without being outside himself in every respect—into an incomprehensible good which he could never express or describe in the way in which he heard and saw it, for in this simple activity and simple vision, hearing and seeing are one and the same. No one but God alone, without intermediary and without the cooperation of any creature, can bring this about in a person. It is called rapture, which means that one has been seized or carried off.

Sometimes God gives such persons short flashes of spiritual insight, just like flashes of lightning in the sky. These are short flashes of singular resplendence which shine forth from out of a simple bareness. In an instant the spirit is raised above itself, but at once the light is past and the person comes to himself again. God causes this himself and it is something very exalted, for those who experience it often become enlightened persons.

These persons who live in the transport of love sometimes have still another kind of experience, for a certain light may shine upon them, one which God causes through an intermediary. In this light, the heart and the concupiscible power are raised toward the light. In meeting the light, the heart experiences so much delight and pleasure that it cannot contain itself

87

but bursts out in a cry of joy. This is called jubilee or jubilation, that is, a joy which cannot be expressed in words. This cry cannot be contained: If a person wishes to meet the light with an open and uplifted heart, then this cry of jubilation must follow as long as this particular exercise lasts.

Some interior persons are at times instructed in dreams through their guardian angels or other angels about many different things of which they have need. There are also to be found some persons who have many inspirations—words or thoughts that come into their minds—and yet they continue living according to the external senses. Or they may dream of miraculous things, but they know nothing of the transport of love, for they are absorbed by many things and have not been wounded by love. Such experiences may be natural, or they may come from the devil or from the good angel. For this reason, they should be relied on only insofar as they are in accord with Holy Scripture and with the truth, and no more than that; if still more reliance is placed in them, a person may easily be deceived.[9]

Two similes explanatory of obstacles in this third mode

The dog days. I now wish to point out to you some things which can hinder or harm a person who is experiencing this transport. As you have heard, at this time of year the sun enters the sign of Leo, which is the most unhealthy time of the year even though it is fruitful, for here begin the dog days, which bring many evils with them. During this period the weather sometimes becomes so abnormally hot that in certain regions plants and trees wither away and in certain bodies of water fish languish and die, while on earth some human beings become sick and die. This is not caused simply by the sun, for if that were so the situation would be the same in all regions, in all bodies of water, and among all peoples. Rather, it is sometimes caused by something unnatural or excessive in the objects on which the sun's power acts. In the same way, when a person is in this state of restlessness he comes directly into the dog days. Then the rays of the divine light burn so very hot from above and the heart wounded by love is so enflamed from within—when the ardor of the feelings and the restlessness of the desires are very intensely enkindled—that such a person falls into a state of restless agitation, just like a woman in labor who cannot be delivered of her child. If a person then wishes to look ceaselessly into his own

---

9. Because of the inescapable ambiguity of such experiences, Ruusbroec is here at one with the mainstream of the Christian mystical tradition in minimizing their importance. Several centuries later, St. John of the Cross will be even more insistent on this point.

wounded heart and at the one whom he loves, his pain constantly increases. The torment increases for so long a time that the person withers away in his body, just like the trees in hot lands; he dies in the transport of love and goes to heaven without passing through purgatory. Although a person who dies of love dies a good death, as long as a tree bears good fruit it should not be killed.

Sometimes God flows with great sweetness into a heart which is undergoing this transport. Then the heart swims in a state of bliss, just like a fish in water. The inmost depths of the heart are enkindled in fiery restlessness and in charity because of this blissful swimming in the gifts of God and because of the blissful, restless ardor of the loving heart. To remain long in this condition ravages the body. All who undergo this transport must grow weak in this state, but not all die, provided they can govern themselves well.

Honeydew. I also want to warn you about something which can cause much harm. Honeydew sometimes falls during these periods of heat. This is a certain kind of false sweetness which contaminates or even completely spoils fruit. It usually falls in big drops in the middle of the day, when the sun is shining brightly, and it is difficult to distinguish it from rain. In the same way, some persons can be deprived of their external senses by means of a certain kind of light which is produced by the devil and which surrounds and envelops them. They sometimes have various kinds of images shown to them, both false and true ones, or they hear different kinds of locutions. All this is seen or received by them with much satisfaction. On such occasions there sometimes fall honeydrops of false sweetness, in which a person takes delight. Whoever makes much of this receives a great amount of it and in this way becomes easily contaminated. If he judges things which are contrary to the truth to be true—because they have been shown to him or spoken to him—then he falls into error and loses the fruit of virtue. On the other hand, those who follow the paths which have here been previously pointed out will not be harmed even if they are tempted by such a spirit and such a light.

The simile of the ant

I now wish to provide a short simile for those who are living in the state of transport so that they may undergo it in a noble and fitting way and advance to higher virtues. There is a small insect known as the ant. It is strong and wise and does not easily die. It likes to live together with the rest of its community in hot, dry ground. It works during the summer gathering grain and other food for the winter. It splits the kernels of grain into two, lest they germinate and become spoiled; in this way the grain will be of use when no other food can be obtained. The ant also does not follow strange paths, but all of them follow a single path. If it awaits the proper time, it becomes able to fly.

These persons should act in the same way. They should be strong in awaiting the coming of Christ and wise in warding off whatever the devil shows them or says to them. They should not choose to die but instead should always desire God's glory and the acquisition of new virtues for themselves. They should live in the unity of their heart and of all their powers and follow the call and invitation to unity with God. They should live in hot and dry country, that is, in the strong transport of love and in great restlessness, and they should work in the summer of this time, gathering the fruit of virtue for eternity. They should break this fruit into two parts. One part is that they should constantly yearn for the sublime and blissful state of unity with God, and the other part is that through the power of reason they should control themselves as much as they can and await the time which God has ordained. In this way the fruit of virtue will be preserved for eternity. They should also not follow strange paths or unusual ways but rather the way of love, passing through all storms to the place where love leads them. If they await the proper time and persevere in all the virtues, then they will be able to contemplate the mystery of God and fly toward it.

The fourth mode: a state of abandonment

Christ's withdrawal likened to the sun in the sign of Virgo

We now wish to proceed to a consideration of the fourth mode of Christ's coming. This coming uplifts and perfects a person in the lower part of his being by means of interior exercises. Since we have been comparing this interior coming with the power and radiance of the sun throughout the course of the year, we will continue this comparison by speaking of other works and operations of the sun in the passing of the seasons.

When the sun begins to descend a great deal from its highest point in the heavens toward its lowest, it enters the sign of Virgo (the Virgin), for this time of year, like a virgin, is unfruitful. It was at this time of year that the glorious Virgin Mary, the mother of Christ, was assumed into heaven full of joy and rich in all the virtues.[10] At this season the heat begins to lessen and people begin to harvest for yearlong use and consumption their ripe and long-lasting crops, such as grain and wine and nonperishable fruits. People are also accustomed to sow some of the grain so that it might be multiplied for their use. In this way the entire work of the sun throughout the year is brought to its fulfillment and perfection. In the same way, when Christ, the glorious sun, has risen to the highest point in a person's heart—as I taught when treating the third mode of his coming—and when he then begins to descend and so hide the brightness of his divine rays and withdraw from the person, then the heat and restlessness of love begin to lessen. This hiding of Christ and this withdrawal of the radiance of his light and heat comprise his first activity and a new manner of his coming in this fourth mode. Christ now says spiritually within such a person, "Go out, in accordance with the way I am now showing you."

The effects of this withdrawal and our response to it

This person therefore goes out, finding himself poor, wretched, and forsaken. All the stormy transport and restlessness of love have been cooled. The hot summer has turned to autumn and all a person's riches have turned to poverty, so that he begins to lament and complain about his state: Where have all the warmth of love, all the fervor, thanksgiving, and delightful praise gone? How have the interior consolations, interior joy, and perceptible savor escaped him? How have the strong transport of love and all the gifts which he formerly experienced become lifeless in him? He is thus just like a person who has forgotten everything he ever learned and has lost his livelihood and the fruit of his labor. A person's corporeal nature will often fall prey to disorders because of such losses.

Sometimes these poor persons are also deprived of earthly goods, of friends and family, and are abandoned by all creatures. Whatever holiness they have attained is neither recognized nor esteemed, and their entire lives and activities are interpreted by others as the opposite of what they really are. They are scorned and rejected by everyone around them and sometimes fall into various kinds of sickness or into bodily or spiritual temptations; these last are the worst of all. This poverty gives rise to a fear of falling and a certain kind of half-doubt, which is the outermost point on which a person can stand without falling into despair.

---

10. The reference is, of course, to the feast of Mary's Assumption, celebrated on August 15. This feast originated in the East and began to be celebrated in Rome around the middle of the seventh century; from there it spread gradually throughout Europe.

A person in this state likes to find good persons to whom he can lament and reveal his misery. He also desires the help and prayers of the holy Church, the saints, and all who are good. At such times a person will consider with humble heart that of himself he has nothing and will say with patience and self-resignation these words of holy Job: "God gave and God has taken away. As the Lord judged best, so has it come to pass. Blessed be the name of the Lord" (cf. Jb 1:21). He will also abandon himself in all things, saying and meaning from the depths of his heart: "Lord, I will just as gladly be poor as rich and will do without all the things of which I have been deprived if that is according to your will and for your glory, Lord. Let not my natural will be done, Lord, but rather your will and my will according to the spirit, for I am yours, Lord, and would just as gladly be in hell as in heaven if that were for your glory. Lord, deal with me according to your most noble will."

Such a person will turn all his virtues and his entire state of abandonment into an interior joy and will place himself in the hands of God, rejoicing that he is able to suffer for God's glory. If he does this properly, he will savor more interior joy than ever before, for nothing is more pleasant to one who loves God than the feeling that he belongs entirely to his Beloved. If he has properly followed the path of virtue as far as this point, then even if he does not possess all the forms of virtue which have previously been described, that will not prevent him from experiencing within himself the foundation of all the virtues, namely, humble obedience in what he does and patient resignation in what he suffers. On this twofold foundation this mode is set firm forever.

Christ's further action and our response likened to the sun in the sign of Libra

At this time of year the sun enters the sign of Libra (the Balance), for day and night are now evenly balanced, the sun making the time of daylight equal to that of darkness. In the same way, Christ stands on a balance over against the person who is resigned. It does not matter whether Christ gives sweetness or bitterness, darkness or light, for whatever he lays on the scale such a person balances evenly. All things are the same to him, with the single exception of sin, which should be completely driven away.

When these self-composed persons have been thus deprived of all consolation and think that they are devoid of all virtue and abandoned by God and by all creatures, then it is clear that all kinds of fruit, grain, and wine are now ripe and ready for the harvest, provided only that such persons are able to gather them in. Everything which the body can suffer in any way will now be freely and gladly offered to God without resistance on the part of the higher will. All the exterior and interior virtues which were ever practiced with delight in the fire of love will now be practiced with diligence and with a good heart insofar as a person knows how and is able, for never before were they so valuable in God's eyes, never before so noble and fine. A person will gladly do without all the consolation which God ever bestowed upon him if that is for God's glory. All this is a harvest of grain and of all kinds of ripe fruit, off of which we are to live eternally and through which we become rich with God. In this way the virtues come to their perfection, and sadness is changed into eternal wine. Those who know such persons or live around them are taught and changed for the better through them and through their lives and the example of their patience. The grain of their virtues is thus sown and multiplied for the benefit of all good persons.

This is the fourth mode of Christ's coming, which adorns and perfects a person's corporeal powers and the lower part of his being through interior exercises, though this does not mean that he cannot constantly advance still further in the way of perfection. But because such persons have been subjected to harsh trials, tribulations, temptations, and conflicts by God, by themselves, and by all creatures, the virtue of resignation is perfected with special excellence in their case, even though resignation and the renunciation of one's own will for the will of God are absolutely necessary for everyone who wishes to be saved.

Similes explanatory of obstacles in this fourth mode

Noxious humors and dropsy. Since the equinox occurs at this time of year, the sun does not rise as high as formerly and the weather grows cooler. Some imprudent persons now suffer noxious humors which fill the stomach and cause ill health and various kinds of sickness. These humors destroy the appetite and the taste for good food and cause some persons to die. Because of these noxious humors the health of some persons degenerates and they contract dropsy, from which they suffer a long time or even die. A superabundance of these humors brings about diseases and fevers, from which many persons suffer and sometimes die. In the same way, those persons of goodwill who once savored the things of God and afterward fell away from him and strayed from the truth all grow sick along the way of righteousness or die to virtue or suffer eternal death because of one or another of these sicknesses or because of all three.

It is especially in the state of abandonment that a person must have

93

great fortitude and must act in the way I have just taught. In that case he will not be deceived. The foolish person, however, who governs himself poorly, easily falls prey to such sickness. In him the weather has become cool, and for this reason his nature becomes slack in the practice of virtue and good works and seeks comforts and conveniences for the body, sometimes without discretion and in a measure greater than is necessary. Some such persons would like to receive consolation from God if it could be theirs without cost or effort, and others seek solace in creatures, which is often a source of grave harm. Still others think that they are sick, delicate, and feeble, and that they stand in need of all that they can acquire or of all that they can provide for their bodies in the way of rest and comfort. When a person is thus inclined to follow after material things and bodily comforts without discretion, this is a case of noxious humors which fill his stomach, that is, his heart, and which prevent him from savoring and delighting in good food, that is, in all the virtues.

When a person thus falls into sickness and cold, he sometimes contracts dropsy, that is, he becomes inclined toward the external possession of material things. The more such persons acquire, the more they desire, for they are suffering from dropsy. Their body, that is, their appetites and desires, becomes very swollen, and their thirst cannot be assuaged, whereas their face, that is, their conscience and their power of discretion, becomes thin and wan, for it forms an obstacle and hindrance to the influx of God's grace. If these persons amass the water of earthly possessions around their heart, that is, if they rest in such things with delighted affection, then they will not be able to walk along the way of charitable works, for they are sick. They are short of breath and of an interior spirit; in other words, the grace of God and fervent charity are lacking to them. For this reason they are not able to rid themselves of the water of earthly riches, but on the contrary their heart is enveloped by these, often to the point that they waste away in an eternal death. But whoever keeps the water of earthly things far beneath his heart, so that he is master of his possessions and able to be rid of them whenever necessary, can certainly be cured, even if he suffers a long time from disordered inclinations.

Four kinds of fever. Sometimes these persons who are filled with noxious humors, that is, with a disordered inclination toward bodily comfort and toward illicit consolation from creatures, fall prey to four kinds of fever. The first kind is called quotidian or daily fever and occurs when the heart is ensnared by manifold attachments. Persons so afflicted want to know and talk about everything, to criticize and pass judgment on everything, while they are often unmindful of themselves. They are burdened with many cares about things which do not concern them. Often they have to hear things which are unpleasant to their ears. The most trivial matter is enough to disturb them. Their thoughts range everywhere, just like the wind: first this way, then that; first here, then there. This is a daily fever, for it causes these persons to be disturbed and anxious about many things from morning till evening and sometimes even during the night, whether they are asleep or lying awake. Although this condition may coexist with the state of grace and the absence of mortal sin, it is nevertheless an obstacle to the practice of fervent interior exercises and to the acquisition of a taste for God and for all the virtues, and this does lasting harm.

The second kind of fever occurs every other day and is known as fickleness. Although there are longer periods of respite than with the first kind, this second is often more dangerous. It is of two types, one arising from inordinate heat, the other from cold. That which arises from inordinate heat sometimes afflicts good persons, for when these have been touched by God or have become aware of this touch and are afterward abandoned by God, then they sometimes fall into fickleness. One day they choose one course of action, the next day another, and so on for a long time. At one time they wish to remain silent, at another to speak. First they want to enter one religious order, then a different one. First they want to give all their possessions to God, then they want to keep them. First they want to wander about the country, then they prefer to be enclosed in a hermitage. First they want to receive Communion often, and shortly afterward they think little of this. Sometimes they wish to recite many prayers aloud, and not much later they decide on long periods of silence. All of this is but a fickle search for novelty, which hinders and prevents a person from understanding interior truth and destroys the foundation and practice of all interior fervor.

Now the source of this fickleness in good persons is as follows: Whenever a person directs his intentions and the active impulses of his heart more toward virtue and exterior modes than toward God and unity with God, then even if he remains in God's grace—since he intends God in and through the virtues—his life is nevertheless inconstant, for he does not feel himself to be resting in God above all the virtues. He therefore possesses God without knowing him, for the one whom he is seeking in manifold ways and in the practice of the virtues he already possesses in himself, above his intentions, above the virtues, and above all particular modes. If a person is to overcome his fickleness and inconstancy, he must therefore learn to rest in God and in the sublime Unity of God above all the virtues.

The other type of fickleness, the one which arises from cold, characterizes all those persons who do seek God but who simultaneously seek and intend something else in an inordinate way. This fever comes from cold inasmuch as there is little of the heat of charity when things other than God also arouse and urge on the works of virtue. Such persons are fickle of heart, for in everything they do nature is secretly seeking its own; this often occurs without their knowledge, for such persons do not know themselves very well. They choose and abandon first one course of action, then another. First they go to one priest for confession and for counsel about their entire life, and the next day they choose a different priest. They like to seek advice about everything, but seldom do they follow anyone's advice. They are ready to excuse and justify everything for which others blame or reproach them. They are full of fine words, but there is little substance to these. They like to receive frequent praise for their virtues, but at the cost of little effort. They want their virtues to become manifest, and for this very reason their virtues are empty and have no savor either of God or of themselves. They want to instruct others but will scarcely let themselves be instructed or reproved. A natural inclination toward themselves and a hidden pride make these persons fickle. They are walking along the edge of hell; one false step and in they fall.

In some persons this fever of fickleness causes quartan fever, which recurs every fourth day and consists in an estrangement from God and from oneself, from truth and from every virtue. A person thereby falls into such confusion that he does not know what is wrong with him or what he should do. This illness is more dangerous than any of the previous ones.

From this estrangement a person sometimes contracts what is called double-quartan fever, that is, a state of indifference. Here the fourth day of the quartan fever is doubled, and from this a person can scarcely recover at all, for he is heedless and negligent of everything which is necessary for eternal life. He can fall into sin as easily as someone who never knew anything of God. If this can happen to someone who governs himself poorly in this state of abandonment, then this should instill a special fear in those who have never known anything of God, of the interior life, or of that interior savor which good persons enjoy in their exercises.

Christ as our model in these four modes

If we are not to go astray, we must walk in the light (cf. Jn 12:35) and keep our eyes fixed on Christ, who has taught us these four modes and has marked out the way before us. Christ, the resplendent sun, rose in the heavens of the most high Trinity and in the dawn of his glorious mother, the Virgin Mary, who was and is the dawn and daybreak of all the graces in which we are to rejoice eternally.

Now you should note that Christ possessed, and still possesses, the first mode, for he abode in oneness and unity. In him were and are gathered together and united all the virtues which have ever been practiced or will be practiced, as well as all the creatures who ever practiced or will practice these virtues. He was the only Son of the Father and was united with human nature. He was also interiorly fervent, for he brought to earth that fire which has enflamed all the saints and all good persons. He bore a felt affection for and fidelity to his Father and to everyone who is to enjoy him eternally. Throughout his life his devotion and his loving, uplifted heart burned with desire before his Father on behalf of the needs of all persons. All his works, both from without and from within, together with all his words, were thanksgiving and praise to the glory of his Father. Such was the first mode.

Christ, the lovable sun, shed his light still more brightly and with greater heat, for in him was and is the perfection of all graces and all gifts. For this reason, Christ's heart, his ways, his conduct, and his service flowed forth in kindness, meekness, humility, and generosity. He was so gracious and so lovable that his conduct and his being drew to himself all persons of goodwill. He was a spotless lily and a wildflower accessible to everyone; from him all good persons draw the honey of eternal sweetness and consolation. For all the gifts which his humanity ever received, Christ, according to that humanity, praised and thanked his eternal Father, who is the Father of all gifts and benefits. He also rested, according to the higher powers of his soul, above all gifts in the sublime Unity of God, from where all gifts flow forth. In this way he possessed the second mode.

Christ, the glorious sun, shed his light still more brightly, from a greater height and with greater heat, for throughout his life his corporeal powers and his power of feeling, his heart and his senses were called and invited by the Father to a higher glory and bliss, which he now savors with much feeling through these corporeal powers. He himself was inclined toward this through all his affections, both natural and supernatural, but he was nevertheless willing to remain in exile until the time which the Father had foreseen and ordained from all eternity. In this way he possessed the third mode.

When the fitting time arrived for Christ to gather together and bring into the eternal kingdom the fruits of all the virtues which had ever been practiced or ever would be practiced, then the eternal sun began to descend, for Christ lowered himself and delivered his earthly life into the hands of his enemies. In such need he was ignored and abandoned by his friends. His human nature was deprived of all exterior and interior consolation, and instead there was laid upon it misery, pain, scorn, and the oppressive burden of redeeming all our sins according to righteousness. He bore this with humble patience. In this state of abandonment he wrought the strong works of love and thereby bought back and regained our eternal inheritance. In this way he adorned the lower part of his noble humanity, for he suffered this pain for our sins. For this reason he is called the Savior of the world and has been raised in resplendent glory and placed at the right hand of the Father, from where he rules in power. At his sublime name every creature must forever bend the knee, whether in heaven, on earth, or in hell (cf. Phil 2:10).

If a person lives in genuine obedience to God's commandments in the practice of the moral virtues; if he practices the interior virtues according to the manner and urging of the Holy Spirit by following the attractions and inspirations of the Spirit as righteousness requires; if he is not self-seeking either in time or in eternity; and if in genuine patience he can evenly balance and endure darkness, oppressive burdens, and all kinds of misery, thanking God for them all and offering himself up to God in humble resignation: then he has received the first coming of Christ according to the way of interior exercises. He has gone out in the interior life and has had the vitality of his heart and the corporeal unity of his feelings interiorly adorned with rich virtues and gifts.

When a person has been thoroughly purified, set at rest, and drawn inward according to the lower part of his being, then he can be interiorly enlightened if God thinks the time has come and so commands. It can also happen that a person may be enlightened very early, at the beginning of his conversion, provided that he offers himself completely to the will of God and renounces all self-seeking, for it is on this that all depends. In this case a person must afterward follow in his exterior and interior life the ways and paths which have previously been described, but this should be easier for him than for another person who is ascending from below, for he will have received more light than the other.

B. The Second Coming, into the Higher Powers, Likened to a Spring with Three Streams

We now wish to go on and speak of the second manner of Christ's coming in interior exercises, one in which the three higher powers of the soul are adorned, enlightened, and enriched. We will liken this coming to a living spring with three streams. The spring from which these streams flow forth is the fullness of God's grace in the unity of our spirit. This grace subsists there in two ways: essentially, insofar as it abides there as a spring which is full to the brim; and actively, insofar as it flows forth in streams into each power of the soul according to the needs of each power. These streams are special influxes or workings of God in the higher powers, where God works by means of grace in many different ways.

The first stream, which unifies the memory

The first stream of God's grace which he makes flow forth in this coming is a pure simplicity which sheds its light upon the spirit to the exclusion of all distinctions. This stream takes its origin from the spring in the unity of the spirit and flows down from there, penetrating all the powers of the soul—the higher as well as the lower—and raising them above all restless multiplicity. It creates a state of simplicity in a person and both shows and bestows upon him an interior bond in the unity of his spirit. In this way a person is raised up in his memory and delivered from distracting impressions and from fickleness.

In this light Christ now calls a person to go out in accordance with the light and with this coming. He therefore goes out and finds that by means of this simple light which has been infused into him he has been firmly set in order and established in peace, penetrated by the light and confirmed in the unity of his spirit or mind. In this way he is raised up to and established in a new state of being. He turns inward and fixes his memory on total bareness, above the impressions of all sensible images and above multiplicity. He here possesses in an essential and supernatural way the unity of his spirit as his own dwelling place and as his eternal and personal inheritance. He constantly experiences a natural and supernatural inclination toward this same unity. By means of God's grace and purity of intention, this unity itself experiences an eternal, loving inclination toward its own higher Unity, where the Father and Son are united with all the saints in the bond of the Holy Spirit. A person hereby fulfills the requirements of the first stream, which calls him to unity.

The second stream, which enlightens the understanding

By means of fervent interior affection and a loving inclination, together with God's faithfulness, the second stream springs forth from the fullness of grace in the unity of the spirit. This stream is a spiritual resplendence which infuses its light into the understanding and reveals many kinds of distinctions, for this light truly makes manifest the distinctions among all the virtues. This, however, does not lie within our own power. Even if we constantly have this light in our souls, it is God who makes it be silent or speak, God who can reveal it or hide it, bestow it or take it away, at any time and in any place, for it is his light. He therefore works in this light when he wills, where he wills, upon whom he wills, and what he wills. The persons upon whom he works in this way have no need of revelations or of being caught up above their senses, for their life, their abode, their conduct, and their being are already in the spirit, above their senses and above their sensibility. It is there that God shows them what he wills as being necessary either for them or for other persons. Nevertheless God could, if he wished, deprive such persons of their external senses and interiorly reveal to them strange images and future occurrences in many different ways.

Now in accordance with this light Christ wills that these persons go out and walk in the light. The enlightened person will, then, go out and examine his state and his exterior and interior life to see whether he bears a perfect likeness to Christ according to both his humanity and his divinity, for we have been created in the image and likeness of God. He will also raise the illumined eyes of his enlightened understanding to the truth which is open to the understanding. There he will see and behold in a creaturely way the sublime nature of God and the fathomless attributes which are in God, for to a fathomless nature belong fathomless virtues and activities.

The sublime nature of the Godhead will be seen and beheld as simplicity and unicity, inaccessible height and unfathomable depth, incomprehensible breadth and eternal length, a dark stillness and a wild desert, a repose for all the saints in unity and a bliss common to itself and all the saints for eternity. A person could also behold many a wonder in the fathomless sea of the Godhead. Although we make use of sensible images because of the coarseness of the senses with which we give external expression to it, in truth it will be seen from within to be a fathomless good from which all particular forms or modes are excluded. But when we give external expression to it, then we attribute to it images and modes in many different ways, according to the degree of enlightenment of the particular human reason which brings it to expression.

This enlightened person will also see and behold the attributes of the Father within the Godhead: that he is almighty power and might; Creator,

Conserver, and Mover; and the beginning and end, cause and principle of all things. The stream of grace reveals this clearly to the enlightened reason.

The stream also reveals the attributes of the eternal Word: that he is unfathomable wisdom and truth, the exemplar and life of all creatures, the eternal rule which never changes, the one who beholds and sees through all things so that nothing remains hidden, and the one who shines through and enlightens all the saints in heaven and on earth according to the merits of each.

Since this resplendent stream reveals distinctions in many different ways, it also makes manifest to the enlightened reason the attributes of the Holy Spirit: that he is incomprehensible charity and generosity, mercy and graciousness, infinite fidelity and benevolence, an incomprehensibly great richness which flows forth to all things and an unfathomable goodness which flows through all heavenly spirits for their delight, a fiery flame which consumes everything in unity, an overflowing spring rich in savor according to each person's desire, one who prepares and introduces all the saints into their eternal bliss, and an embrace and interpenetration of the Father and the Son and all the saints in blissful unity.

In the simple nature of the Godhead all this is seen and beheld as undivided and devoid of distinctions, and yet, according to our manner of beholding them, these attributes exist individually and in manifold distinction one from another, for might and goodness, generosity and truth are, to our way of seeing things, very different from one another. Nevertheless, in the sublime nature of the Godhead all this subsists in unity and without division.

As regards the relations which constitute these personal attributes, however, these do subsist in eternal distinction, for the Father begets distinction. The Father ceaselessly begets the Son but is himself not begotten, just as the Son is begotten and cannot beget. Consequently, the Father has a Son for all eternity and the Son a Father: These are the relations of the Father to the Son and of the Son to the Father. Moreover, the Father and the Son breathe forth a Spirit, who is the will or love of them both. This Spirit neither begets nor is begotten, but must be eternally breathed forth as flowing out from them both. These three Persons are one God and one Spirit. All the attributes, together with the works which flow forth from them, are common to all three Persons, for they work in the power of a single nature.

The divine nature's incomprehensible richness, its sublimity, and its generosity which flows forth to all in common draw a person into a state of wonder. In particular, such a person wonders at the way God is common to all and flows forth upon all things, for he sees this incomprehensible essence as a bliss common to God and all the saints. He also sees the divine Persons flow forth in common, acting in grace and in glory, in nature and above nature, in all places and at all times, in the saints and in simple human beings, in heaven and on earth, in all rational, irrational, and material creatures, according to the merit, need, and capability of each. He sees that heaven and earth, the sun and the moon, the four elements, all creatures, and the course of the heavens were created for all in common. God, with all his gifts, is common to all. The angels are common to all. The soul is common to all its powers and to the entire body and all its members, and yet it subsists entirely in each member, for it may not be divided except by rational analysis. According to such analysis, the higher powers are distinct from the lower and the spirit is distinct from the soul, but in reality they are all one. In the same way, God belongs entirely and particularly to each of us and yet is common to all creatures, for all things exist through him, and it is within him and upon him that heaven and earth and all nature depend.

When a person thus beholds the marvelous richness and sublimity of the divine nature and all the manifold gifts which God offers and gives to his creatures, there grows within him an interior sense of wonder at such great and diverse richness and sublimity and at the infinite fidelity which God bears toward his creatures. This gives rise to a special interior joy in the spirit and a sense of great trust in God. This interior joy envelops and penetrates all the powers of the soul and the unity of the spirit.

The third stream, which enflames the will in love

By means of this joy and the fullness of grace, together with God's faithfulness, the third stream rises and flows forth in the same unity of the spirit. Like a fire, this stream enkindles the will and devours and consumes all things, reducing them to a unity. It flows over and through all the powers of the soul with rich gifts and with a special nobility, and it produces in the will an exceedingly fine and spiritual love which excludes all effort.

By means of this burning stream Christ speaks interiorly within the spirit: "Go out, through exercises which are in accordance with the manner of these gifts and this coming." Now through the first stream, which is a simple light, the memory is raised above sense impressions and is made firm and steadfast in the unity of the spirit. Through the second stream, which is an infused resplendence, the reason and understanding are enlightened so as to be able to know in a distinct way the various kinds of virtues and exercises and the mysteries of Scripture. Through the third stream, which is a burning heat breathed into the spirit, the exalted will is set aflame in a quiet love and is endowed with great riches. In this way a person becomes spiritually enlightened, for the grace of God abides like a spring in the unity of the spirit, its streams produce in the powers an outflux of all the virtues, and the spring of grace constantly calls for a reflux into the same source from which the outflux arose.

A person who has been established firmly in the bond of love will now make his abode in the unity of his spirit. He will also go out both in heaven and on earth with an enlightened reason and with overflowing charity, observing all things with clear discernment and giving all things in true generosity from the treasury of divine riches. A person who is enlightened in this way is called and invited to go out in four different ways: The first way is to go out to God and to all his holy ones; the second, to sinners and to all who are going astray; the third, to those who are in purgatory; and the fourth, to himself and to all good persons.

Now pay careful attention to the following: This person is first to go out and observe God in his glory with all his holy ones. He will see how God himself richly and generously flows forth with glory and incomprehensible delight to all his holy ones, in accordance with the desire of every spirit. He will also see how they themselves flow back, with all that they have received or could accomplish, into that same rich Unity from which all delight comes forth. This flowing forth of God constantly demands a flowing back again, for God is a flowing and ebbing sea which ceaselessly flows out into all his beloved according to their needs and merits and which flows back with all those upon whom he has bestowed his gifts in heaven and on earth, together with all that they possess or are capable of.

Of some God requires more than they can accomplish, for he reveals himself to be very rich, very generous, and infinitely good, and in so doing he calls for love and homage according to his merit. That is to say, God wishes to be loved by us according to his nobility, and in this all spirits fail. Love thereby becomes devoid of particular form or measure, for no spirit knows how to accomplish this or bring it about, since the love of all spirits is finite. For this reason their love is constantly begun anew, in the hope that God might be loved according to his demand and their desire. To this end, all spirits ceaselessly come together and produce a burning flame of love, so that they might bring to fulfillment the work of loving God according to his nobility. The power of reason shows clearly that this is impossible for creatures, but love constantly wishes to bring its love to fulfillment or else to be consumed and burnt to nothingness in its failure. Nevertheless, God is never loved as he deserves by any creature. For the enlightened reason it is a source of great delight and satisfaction that its God and its Beloved is so sublime and rich that he transcends all created powers and is loved as he deserves by no one except himself.

This rich, enlightened person bestows gifts on all the heavenly choirs and on all spirits—on each in particular in accordance with its merits—out of the riches of his God and out of the generous ground of his own being, which has been enlightened and which overflows with great wonders. Such a person passes among all choirs, orders, and beings, observing how God dwells in them in accordance with the merits of each. This enlightened person passes quickly in spirit among and through all the heavenly host; himself rich and overflowing in charity, he makes the entire celestial army rich and overflowing with new glory. All this has its source in the rich and overflowing Trinity and Unity of the divine nature and constitutes the first way of going out, namely, to God and to his holy ones.

This person will at times descend to sinners with great compassion and generous mercy, presenting them to God with fervent devotion and much prayer. He will also remind God of all the good which he himself is and which he can do, has done, and has promised to do, just as if he had forgotten this, for God wishes us to pray to him, while charity wishes to receive everything that it desires. This does not mean, however, that charity wants to be stubborn or self-willed; rather it leaves everything to God's own rich goodness and generosity, for God loves without limit and this puts a loving person most securely at peace. Since such a person bears a love common to all, he prays with great desire that God might let his love and mercy flow forth to pagans, Jews, and all unbelievers, so that God might be loved, known, and praised in heaven and that our own glory, joy, and peace might be spread to the ends of the earth. This is the second way of going out, namely, to sinners.

At times this person will behold his friends in purgatory, observing their misery, their yearning, and their grievous suffering. Seeing this, he will beseech and invoke God's gracious and generous mercy and will bring before him their good will, their great misery, and their yearning for God's rich goodness. He will also remind God that they died in love and that they are placing all their trust in his passion and mercy. You should also know that it can sometimes happen that an enlightened person will be inspired in a special way by the Spirit of God to pray for a particular thing, a particular sinner or soul in purgatory, or some spiritual good, in such a way that the person knows for certain that this is a work of the Holy Spirit and not the result of human stubbornness or self-will. This person may even be so fervently enflamed in his prayer that he receives spiritually the response that his prayer has been heard, and with this the Spirit stops urging him to pray.

This person will also come to himself and to all persons of good will, savoring and observing the unity and harmony which they have in love. He will then pray with great desire that God might let his customary gifts flow forth so that all these persons might remain steadfast in his love and in their eternal worship of him. This enlightened person will faithfully and discreetly instruct and teach, reprove and serve everyone, for he bears a love common to all. In this way he serves as a mediator between God and all human beings. He will also turn entirely inward, together with all the saints and all good persons, and will there peacefully possess the unity of his spirit and, in addition, the sublime Unity of God in which all spirits find their rest. This is a truly spiritual way of life, for all interior and exterior modes and virtues and all the higher powers of the soul are hereby supernaturally adorned in a genuinely fitting way.

Those who deviate from this path

There are some persons who are very subtle in their use of words and skillful in elucidating lofty matters and yet have not attained this enlightened state or this generous love toward all. In order that such persons might come to know themselves as they are and might also be recognized by others, I wish to make three points. Through the first they can come to know themselves and through the other two any intelligent person will be able to recognize them.

The first point is this: Whereas an enlightened person, by reason of a divine light, is simple, stable, and free of curious reflections, these persons are complex, unstable, and full of subtle reasonings. They have no taste for interior unity or for that rest which comes from being devoid of images. Through these signs they can come to know themselves.

The second point is this: Whereas an enlightened person has a wisdom infused into him by God, whereby he knows the truth distinctly and effortlessly, this other kind of person has subtle insights to which he cleverly turns his imagination and his powers of reflection and reason. But there is neither depth nor liberality in the way he presents his teaching, which instead is complicated, esoteric, and abstruse, so as to trouble, hinder, and lead astray those who are interiorly fervent. This teaching neither leads nor directs a person to unity but only shows him how to make clever observations in diversity. People who teach in this way hold stubbornly to their doctrine and opinions, as though no other opinion were as good as their own. They are unpracticed in all the virtues and careless of them, and they are spiritually proud in all they are and do. This is the second point.

The third point is this: Whereas an enlightened, loving person flows forth with a charity that is common to everyone whether in heaven or on earth, as you have already heard, this other kind of person sets himself apart in all things. He thinks he is the wisest and best person alive and wants others to think highly of himself and of his teaching. He thinks that all those whom he does not himself teach or counsel, as well as all who do not follow his way or look to him as their master, are certain to go astray. He is tolerant and even lax when it comes to fulfilling his own needs and thinks little of minor faults. He is neither righteous nor humble nor generous; he does not serve the poor and is not fervent or zealous; he does not feel any affection for the things of God and knows neither God nor himself in the way of true virtue. This is the third point.

You should note and reflect on these things and avoid them both in yourself and in all those persons in whom you recognize them. Do not, however, judge anyone as being guilty of these things unless you actually observe their effects. Otherwise your heart will not be pure enough to come to the knowledge of divine truth.

Christ as our model for giving ourselves to all in common

In order that we might desire and attain this state of having a love common to all more than any of the other states of which we have spoken—for it is the highest state of all—we wish to present Christ as our model, for he gave himself completely to all in common, does so still, and will do so for all eternity. He was sent to earth for the common benefit of all persons who wished to turn to him. To be sure, he says himself that he was sent only to the lost sheep of the house of Israel (cf. Mt 15:24), but this does not refer only to the Jews, since all those who are to contemplate God eternally—and only those—belong to the house of Israel. The Jews scorned the Good News and the Gentiles entered in and accepted it. In this way salvation has come to all Israel, that is, to all those who have been chosen from all eternity.

Now note how Christ with true faithfulness gave himself to all in common. His fervent and sublime prayer flowed forth to his Father on behalf of all those who wish to be saved. He went out to all in common in his love, his teaching, and his admonitions; in the way he tenderly consoled and generously gave; and in the way he kindly and mercifully forgave. His soul and body, his life and death, and his service to others were and are common to all. So, too, are his sacraments and gifts common to all. Christ never took any nourishment or anything else to satisfy the needs of his body without intending it to be for the common benefit of everyone who is to be saved, right up to the end of the world. Christ possessed nothing properly his own, but had it all in common: his body and soul, his mother and disciples, his cloak and tunic. He ate and drank for our sake, he lived and died for our sake. Although his pain, suffering, and misery were properly his own, the benefits and profit which resulted from them are common to all, and his glorious merits will be common to all throughout eternity.

Christ left on earth his treasure and his possessions, namely, the seven sacraments and the external goods of the holy Church. He acquired these goods through his death and intended them to be for all in common, even as his servants who live off these goods are meant to give themselves to all in common. All those who live on alms in the service of the Church, such as clerics and all who live in monasteries or hermitages, should give themselves to all in common, at least through their prayers. In the earliest days of the holy Church and of our faith, the popes, bishops, and priests were like this, for they converted the people, set the holy Church and our faith on a firm foundation, and sealed all this with their blood and their death. Such persons were simple and unified. They possessed a steadfast peace in the unity of their spirit, were enlightened with divine wisdom, and overflowed richly in faithfulness and charity toward God and all persons.

Today the situation is just the opposite, for those who hold the inheritance and possessions of the Church, which were given to them out of love and for the sake of their own salvation, are restless, agitated about many things, and unstable in the depths of their being. They have turned completely to worldly concerns and do not have thoroughly at heart the matters and concerns which have been placed in their hands. For this reason they pray with their lips, but their heart does not savor the meaning of their prayers, that is, they do not experience the heavenly wonders which lie hidden in Scripture, in the sacraments, and in their office. As a result, they are coarse and dull and are not enlightened with divine truth. Sometimes they seek to eat and drink well and to enjoy bodily comforts without moderation—and would to God that they were chaste of body. As long as they live in this way they will never attain enlightenment. Whereas those others were generous and outgoing in their charity, holding back nothing for themselves, nowadays they are sometimes greedy and rapacious, unwilling to do without anything. All this is completely contrary to the way the saints lived and to that service of all in common of which we have spoken. I am speaking here of the state of things in general. Everyone should examine himself in this regard and, if necessary, teach and correct himself. If this is not necessary, then a person should rest joyfully and peacefully in a clean conscience, serve and praise God, and be of service to himself and all human beings for the glory of God.

Since I wish to praise and glorify in a special way this state of giving oneself to all in common, I will also call to mind a special jewel which Christ left in the holy Church for the sake of all good persons. He did this at the supper which opened the great feast of the Passover during which Christ was to pass from this exile to his Father, after he had eaten the paschal lamb with his disciples and after the Old Law had been fulfilled. At the end of this festal meal he wished to give something he had long desired to give, namely, a special dessert with which he would bring the Old Covenant to an end and begin the New. He therefore took bread into his sacred and venerable hands, consecrated first his holy body and then his holy blood, gave them to all his disciples, and left them for all good persons in common for their eternal benefit. This gift, this dessert, is the joy and adornment of all great festivals and banquets both in heaven and on earth.

In this gift Christ gives himself to us in three ways: First he gives us his body, his blood, and his corporeal life, glorified in the fullness of joy and sweetness; he also gives us his spirit with its higher powers full of glory and gifts, of truth and righteousness; and he gives us his person, divinely resplendent, which raises his spirit and all enlightened spirits up to a state of sublime and blissful unity.

Now Christ wishes us to remember him as often as we consecrate, offer, and receive his body. Note carefully how we are to remember him. First, we should see and behold how Christ bends down to us with loving affection, great desire, and corporeal delight. With heartfelt warmth he pours himself into our corporeal nature, for he gives us what he received from our humanity, namely, flesh and blood and his corporeal nature. We should also see and behold his precious body, martyred, pierced, and wounded out of love and fidelity toward us. In this way we are adorned and nourished with Christ's glorious humanity in the lower part of our own humanity.

In the sublime gift of this Sacrament, Christ also gives us his spirit, which is full of glory and rich gifts, of virtues and ineffable marvels of charity and nobility. Through this indwelling of Christ with all of his richness, we are nourished, adorned, and enlightened in the unity of our own spirit and in our higher powers.

In addition, he gives us in the Sacrament of the Altar his sublime and incomprehensibly resplendent person, whereby we are led up to and united with the Father. The Father receives his adopted sons together with his natural Son, and in this way we enter into our inheritance of the Godhead in eternal bliss.

When a person has worthily recalled and considered all these things, then he should go out to meet Christ in accordance with every way in which Christ comes to him. He should raise himself up to receive Christ with his heart, with his desires, with heartfelt affection, with all his powers, and with fervent longing; it was in this way that Christ received himself. This longing could not be too great, for our nature is here receiving its own nature, that is, Christ's glorified humanity, full of joy and majesty. For this reason I wish that a person receiving Christ in this way might, as it were, be dissolved in an immersion of desire, joy, and delight, for he is receiving and being united with the most beautiful, most glorious, and most lovable of all the children of men. In this state of yearning and longing devotion, many a good has often been bestowed upon a person and many a hidden wonder from God's rich treasury has been revealed and disclosed.

When a person who is receiving Christ in this way reflects on the martyrdom and sufferings of Christ's precious body, he sometimes experiences such loving devotion and felt compassion that he desires to be nailed with Christ to the cross and to shed his heart's blood for the glory of Christ. He presses himself into the wounds and into the open heart of Christ his Savior. In this exercise many revelations and many good things have often been bestowed upon a person. This felt, compassionate affection, together with the strong power of the imagination applied to the fervent contemplation of the wounds of Christ, can at times be so intense that a person thinks he feels Christ's wounds and sufferings in his own heart and in all his members. If anyone were ever truly to receive the marks of Christ's wounds in any way, it would be such a person as this. In this way we respond properly to Christ as regards the lower part of his humanity.

We are also to dwell in the unity of our spirit and flow out with ample charity and clear discernment both in heaven and on earth. We hereby come to bear a likeness to Christ according to the spirit and so respond properly to him at this level.

In addition, through the person of Christ we will with a pure intention and in blissful love transcend ourselves and the created nature of Christ and come to rest in our inheritance, that is, in the divine Being in eternity.

Christ constantly wishes to give us this in a spiritual way, as often as we give ourselves to these exercises and make ready a place for him within ourselves. He also wishes us to receive him sacramentally and spiritually, as is fitting, proper, and reasonable. Even if a person does not have such feelings and desires, he may freely approach the Lord's table if he intends God's glory and praise and his own progress toward salvation, provided that his conscience is free of mortal sin.

C. THE THIRD COMING, INTO THE UNITY OF THE SPIRIT, LIKENED TO A VEIN OF WATER FEEDING A SPRING

The relationship of God to our spirit

The sublime, superessential Unity of the divine nature, where the Father and the Son possess their nature in the unity of the Holy Spirit, lies in the bare, essential being of our spirit, beyond the comprehension and understanding of all our powers.[11] In this sublime stillness God transcends every creature that is enlightened by a merely created light. This sublime Unity of the divine nature is both living and fruitful, for out of this same Unity the eternal Word is ceaselessly begotten of the Father. Through this birth the Father knows the Son and all things in the Son, and the Son knows the Father and all things in the Father, for they are one simple nature. From this mutual contemplation of the Father and the Son in eternal splendor there issues forth an eternal sense of well-being, a fathomless love, which is the Holy Spirit. By means of the Holy Spirit and of the eternal Wisdom, God inclines himself to every creature in distinct ways, bestowing gifts upon each one and enkindling each one in love according to his nobility and according to the state in which he has been placed and destined through his practice of virtue and through God's eternal providence. All good spirits in heaven and on earth are hereby moved to the practice of virtue and to righteousness.

---

11. Much careful attention has been given by Ruusbroec scholars in recent years to the terminology of "essential" (*weselijk*), "superessential" (*overweselijk*), and their corresponding noun forms, *wesen* and *overwesen* (which are here regularly translated as "essential being" and "superessential being"). The major conclusion of these studies is that such terminology is not to be understood as applying to a metaphysical order of "essences" but rather to the lived experience of loving union with God. See Albert Deblaere, "Essentiel (superessentiel, suressentiel)," *Dictionnaire de spiritualité* 4, pt. 2:1346–66, and the two articles by Joseph Alaerts in *Ons Geestelijk Erf* 49 (1975): 225–47, 337–65.

THE SPIRITUAL ESPOUSALS

cosmology

Now pay careful attention to a simile which I wish to use in this regard.[12] God created the empyrean or highest heaven as a pure and simple radiance encircling and enclosing all the heavens and every corporeal and material thing which he ever created. It is the exterior dwelling place and kingdom of God and of his saints and is filled with glory and eternal joy. Because this heaven is eternally resplendent and free of all admixture, there is within it neither time nor place, neither movement nor change, for it is securely established in a changeless state above all things. The sphere which is nearest to this fiery heaven is called the *primum mobile*, which is the source of all motion deriving from the highest heaven by means of God's power. From this motion the firmament and all the planets derive their courses, and this in turn is the principle of life and growth for all creatures, each according to its kind.

You should understand that in the same way the essential being of the soul is a spiritual kingdom of God, filled with divine radiance and transcending all our powers (unless one considers these powers as unified and undifferentiated in their ground, which is something about which I do not yet wish to speak). Now beneath this essential being of the soul, in which God reigns, there is found the unity of our spirit; this can be likened to the *primum mobile*, for in this unity the spirit is moved from above by the power of God, both naturally and supernaturally—it must be by his power, since of ourselves we possess nothing, neither in nature nor above nature. When this divine motion is supernatural, it is the first and principal cause of all virtue. In this divine motion some enlightened persons receive the seven gifts of the Holy Spirit, which are like seven planets enlightening a person's entire life and making it fruitful.

This is the way in which God possesses the essential unity of our spirit as his kingdom and in which he works and flows forth with gifts into that unity which is the source of all our powers and into all these powers themselves.

How a person is made ready for this third coming

You should now note very carefully how we can practice and possess the most fervent and interior exercises of our spirit when this is enlightened

---

12. In this paragraph Ruusbroec introduces several terms from ancient and medieval cosmology, which assumed that the earth was the immobile center of the universe and that the planets, sun, and stars revolved around it. In this system, the empyrean or highest heaven was conceived of as a sphere of fire or light surrounding all else. Next to it came the sphere known as the *primum mobile* ("the first moving thing"), which carried along the smaller spheres of the fixed stars and the planets in its daily revolution.

by created light. If a person is adorned with the moral virtues in his exterior way of life and if he has been raised to a noble state through interior exercises and has thus attained divine peace, then he possesses unity of spirit. His spirit is enlightened with supernatural wisdom, flows forth with generous charity in heaven and on earth, and raises itself up to flow back with honor and reverence into that same ground, the sublime Unity of God, from which all flowing forth arises. As creatures are more and more gifted by God, they experience a love which raises them up more and more and a devotion which draws them more and more fervently into their source, for God and all his gifts call us to himself, while we, through charity, virtue, and our likeness to God, wish to be in him. Through God's loving inclination of himself to us and his interior working in the inmost part of our spirit, as well as through our burning love and the total impulse of all our powers to enter the same Unity in which God dwells, there arises the third coming of Christ in interior exercises. This is an interior stirring or touch of Christ in his divine resplendence, and it takes place in the inmost part of our spirit.

The nature of this third coming

The second coming, of which we have already spoken, was likened to a spring giving rise to three streams. We wish to liken this third coming to the vein of water which feeds the spring, for just as there could be no streams without a spring, so too there could be no spring without a living vein. In the same way, God's grace flows into the higher powers like streams and thereby urges a person on and makes him ardent for the practice of all the virtues. God's grace also abides in the unity of our spirit like a spring, and in this same unity from which it arises it wells up just like a living, welling vein out of the living ground of God's richness, where neither faithfulness nor grace can ever fail. This is the touch that I mean.

A creature undergoes this touch passively, for here there is a union of the higher powers in the unity of the spirit, above the multiplicity of all the virtues, and at this level no one is active but God alone. God here acts out of the free initiative of his goodness, which is a cause of all our virtues and all our blessedness. In the unity of the spirit, where this vein wells up, a person is above works and above reason, though not without reason, for the enlightened reason, and especially the amorous power, feel this touch, but the power of reason cannot comprehend or understand the mode or manner of this touch, or how or what it is.[13] This is because this touch is a divine work, the source and irruption of all graces and gifts and the last intermediary between God and his creature. Above this touch, in the still being of the spirit, there hovers an incomprehensible resplendence; this is the sublime Trinity, from which this touch proceeds. There God lives and reigns in the spirit, and the spirit in God.

Our response to this coming and its effects

By means of this touch Christ says interiorly within the spirit, "Go out, in exercises that are in accordance with this touch." This profound touch draws and invites our spirit to the most interior exercises which a creature can practice in a creaturely way when enlightened by created light. At these words of Christ, the spirit raises itself, by means of the amorous power, above works to that unity in which the living vein of this touch wells up. This touch calls the understanding to know God in his resplendence and it draws the amorous power to enjoy God without intermediary. The loving spirit desires to do this more than anything else, in both a natural and a supernatural way.

By means of the enlightened reason the spirit raises itself up in interior observation, contemplating and observing its inmost depths where the touch abides. At this point, reason and all created light are unable to go further, for the divine resplendence which hovers there and which constitutes this touch blinds all created powers of vision by its presence, which is unfathomable. All powers of understanding which are enlightened by merely created light are here like the eyes of a bat when confronted with the sun's brightness. Nevertheless the spirit is constantly called and roused anew, by both God and itself, to fathom this deep stirring and to come to the knowledge of what God and this touch might be. The enlightened reason is constantly led to ask ever anew where the touch comes from and to make new soundings in order that it may follow this vein of honey to its source. But it knows as much about this on the first day of its attempt as it will ever know. Consequently the powers of reason and observation con-

---

13. "Above reason, though not without reason" (*boven redene, maer niet sonder redene*) may derive from the distinction made by Richard of St. Victor in *De gratia contemplationis* 1.6: We are "above reason when through divine revelation we know things which cannot be grasped by human reason," and we are "above reason and beyond reason when through divine illumination we know things which seem contrary to human reason." The expression "amorous power" (*minnende cracht*) in this same sentence of Ruusbroec is another term for the will.

fess, "We do not know what it is," for the divine resplendence which hovers there repulses and blinds all powers of understanding by its very presence. In this way God dwells in his resplendent glory above all spirits in heaven and on earth.

Those who, through the practice of virtue and interior exercises, have fathomed the depths of their being to its source, which is the door to eternal life, are able to experience the touch. God's resplendence shines there so brightly that all powers of reason and understanding are unable to go further and must passively give way before God's incomprehensible resplendence. But for a spirit which experiences this touch in its depths, even though reason and understanding fail when confronted with the divine resplendence and must remain outside the door, the amorous power desires to go further. Like the understanding, it has been called and invited, but it is blind and wishes only to enjoy. Now enjoying is more a matter of savoring and feeling than of understanding, and for this reason love goes in while understanding remains outside.

Here begins an eternal hunger which can nevermore be satisfied. This is an interior craving and striving on the part of the amorous power and of the created spirit to attain an uncreated good. Because the spirit desires to enjoy God and has been called and invited to this by him, it constantly wishes to fulfill this desire. Here begin an eternal craving and striving which can never be satisfied. Persons experiencing this are the most pitiable people alive, for they are afflicted with the disease of bulimia and so are filled with ravenous craving. Regardless of what they eat or drink, they are never satisfied, for their hunger is eternal. A created vessel cannot contain an uncreated good, and for this reason these persons suffer an eternally tormenting hunger, while God is like an overflowing stream which yet does not satisfy them. Here there are huge courses of food and drink of which no one knows except a person who is experiencing all this, but a thoroughly satisfying enjoyment of such fare is the one dish that is missing. As a result, the pangs of hunger return again and again. Even so, in the touch there flow streams of honey full of all delight, for the spirit savors these delights in every way that can be thought of or imagined. All this is, however, in a creaturely manner and beneath God, and for this reason there is a never-ending hunger and restlessness. Even if God gave such a person all the gifts which the saints possess and everything else which he is able to give, but without giving himself, the ravenous craving of the spirit would still remain voracious and unsatisfied. God's interior stirring and touch make us hunger and strive, for the Spirit of God is pursuing our spirit. The more there is of the touch, the more there is of the hunger and striving. This is a life of love at the highest level of its activity, above reason and understanding, for reason can here neither give love nor take it away, since our love has been touched by divine love. In my opinion, from this time on there can never again be any separation from God. God's touch within us, as far as we experience it, and our striving in love are both created and creaturely, and for this reason they can grow and increase as long as we live.

In this storm of love two spirits struggle—the Spirit of God and our spirit. God, by means of the Holy Spirit, inclines himself toward us, and we are thereby touched in love; our spirit, by means of God's activity and the amorous power, impels and inclines itself toward God, and thereby God is touched. From these two movements there arises the struggle of love, for in this most profound meeting, in this most intimate and ardent encounter, each spirit is wounded by love. These two spirits, that is, our spirit and God's Spirit, cast a radiant light upon one another and each reveals to the other its countenance. This makes the two spirits incessantly strive after one another in love. Each demands of the other what it is, and each offers to the other and invites it to accept what it is. This makes these loving spirits lose themselves in one another. God's touch and his giving of himself, together with our striving in love and our giving of ourselves in return—this is what sets love on a firm foundation. This flux and reflux make the spring of love overflow, so that God's touch and our striving in love become a single love. Here a person becomes so possessed by love that he must forget both himself and God and know nothing but love. In this way the spirit is consumed in the fire of love and enters so deeply into God's touch that it is overcome in all its striving and comes to nought in all its works. It transcends its activity and itself becomes love above and beyond all exercises of devotion. It possesses the inmost part of its creatureliness above all virtue, there where all creaturely activity begins and ends. This is love in itself, the foundation and ground of all the virtues.

Now our spirit and this love are both living and fruitful in virtues, and for this reason the powers cannot simply remain in the unity of the spirit. God's incomprehensible resplendence and his fathomless love hover above the spirit and from there touch the amorous power, and at this the spirit falls back into its activity, this time in a more sublime and fervent striving than ever before. The more fervent and noble the spirit, the faster will it transcend its activity and come to nought in love; then it falls back into new works. This is a heavenly way of life. In its craving, the spirit constantly intends to consume and devour God, but in fact it remains itself swallowed up in God's touch, becomes unable to proceed in all its activity, and itself becomes love above all works. In the unity of the spirit there is a union of the higher powers, and here grace and love abide essentially, above works, for this is the source of charity and all the virtues. Here there is an eternal flowing out in charity and in virtues, and an eternal movement inward marked by an interior hunger for savoring God, and an eternal abiding in simple, undifferentiated love.

All this is in a creaturely manner and beneath God. This is the most interior exercise a person can practice when enlightened by created light, whether in heaven or on earth; above this is only the contemplative life, which is lived in the divine light and after God's own manner. In this exercise a person cannot go astray or be deceived. It begins here in grace and will last eternally in glory.

PART FOUR: "TO MEET HIM."

I have now shown you how a free and uplifted person becomes able to see by the help of God's grace in interior exercises. This is the first thing that Christ requires and desires of us when he says, "See." As regards the second and third points (when he says, "The Bridegroom is coming. Go out."), I have described three manners in which Christ comes interiorly, of which the first manner has four different modes; I have also shown how we are to go out through exercises that are in accordance with all the ways in which God interiorly enkindles, teaches, and moves us by his coming. It remains for us to consider the fourth and last point, which is a meeting with Christ our Bridegroom. All of our interior, spiritual seeing, whether in grace or in glory, and all of our going out through the practice of virtue in various exercises are all for the purpose of meeting and being united with Christ our Bridegroom, for he is our eternal rest and the goal and reward of all our activity.

A. Introductory Remarks on the
Various Ways of Meeting God

As you know, every meeting is an encounter between two persons coming from different places which are separate from and set over against one another. Now Christ comes from above as an almighty Lord and generous Benefactor, while we come from below as poor servants who can do nothing of ourselves but have need of everything. Christ comes to us from within outward, while we come to him from without inward. It is this which gives rise to a spiritual meeting. This coming, this meeting between ourselves and Christ, occurs in two ways, namely, with intermediary and without intermediary.

Natural union with God, without intermediary

Now understand and note carefully that the unity of our spirit exists in two ways, namely, as it is in its essential being and as it is in its activity. According to its essential being, you should know that the spirit receives Christ's coming in its bare nature without intermediary and without interruption, for the being and life that we are in God, in our eternal image, is immediately and indivisibly united with the being and life that we possess in ourselves and that we are according to our essential being. For this reason the spirit, in the most intimate and highest part of its being, in its bare nature, ceaselessly receives the imprint of its eternal image and of the divine resplendence and becomes an eternal dwelling place of God. God possesses this dwelling place with his eternal presence and constantly comes to it afresh with new resplendence radiating anew from his eternal birth.[14] Where he comes, there he is present, and where he is present, there he comes. But he will never come where he has never been, for in him there is nothing fortuitous or changeable. Everything in which he is present is also present in him, for he never goes outside himself.

For this reason the spirit possesses God essentially in its bare nature, and God possesses the spirit, for it lives in God and God in it. In the highest part of its being it is also capable of receiving God's resplendence without intermediary, together with all that God can accomplish. By means of the resplendence of its eternal image, which shines within it both essentially and personally, the spirit immerses itself in the divine being as regards the highest part of its own vital being and there possesses in an enduring way its eternal blessedness. It then flows out again with all other creatures through the eternal birth of the Son and is established in its created being by the free will of the Holy Trinity. It here bears a likeness to the image of the sublime Trinity and Unity, according to which it was made. In its

---

14. This teaching about the birth of Christ in the soul, even more prominent in the writings of Eckhart, has its roots in the earliest Christian theology and is found in many of the Greek Fathers. The best modern study of the doctrine, from its beginnings up to Eckhart, is Hugo Rahner, "Die Gottesgeburt," in *Symbole der Kirche* (Salzburg: Otto Müller, 1964), pp. 13–87.

creatureliness it ceaselessly receives the imprint of its eternal image, just like a spotless mirror in which the image always remains and in which knowledge of it is ceaselessly renewed with fresh clarity each time you look at it. This essential unity of our spirit with God does not subsist in itself but remains in God, flows forth from God, depends upon God, and turns back to God as to its eternal cause. Accordingly it has never been separated from God and never will be, for this unity exists within us in our bare nature, and if a creature were to be separated from God in this respect it would fall into pure nothingness. This unity transcends time and place and is ceaselessly active according to God's own manner of acting, but it passively receives the imprint of its eternal image inasmuch as it is like God but is in itself a creature.

This is the nobility which we naturally possess in the essential unity of our spirit, which is at this level naturally united with God. This renders us neither holy nor blessed, for all persons, both good and bad, possess this unity within themselves; it is, however, the first principle of all holiness and blessedness. This, then, is the meeting and union between God and our spirit in our bare nature.

Meeting God with intermediary

Now pay careful attention to the meaning of my words, for if you understand well what I now wish to say as well as what I have already said, then you will have understood all the divine truth which any creature could teach you—and much more besides. In this same unity our spirit also exists in a second way, namely, as it is in its activity. In this respect it subsists in itself as in its created, personal mode of being. This is the originating source of the higher powers and the beginning and end of all creaturely activity which is performed in a creaturely manner, whether in the natural or the supernatural order. Nevertheless the unity is not active insofar as it is unity; it is the powers of the soul which act, but in whatever way they act they derive their power and potency from their originating source, that is, from the unity of the spirit, where the spirit subsists in its personal mode of being.

In this unity the spirit must always be either like God by means of grace and virtue or else unlike God because of mortal sin. This is because human beings have been created to the likeness of God, that is, in the grace of God, for grace is a deiform light which shines through us and makes us like God, so that without this light which makes us like God we cannot attain supernatural union with him. Even though we cannot lose God's image or our natural unity with God, if we lose our likeness to him, which is his grace, then we will suffer damnation.

For this reason, whenever God finds in us some capacity for receiving his grace, he wishes out of gratuitous goodness to give us life and make us like himself by means of his gifts. This happens whenever we turn to him with all our will, for in one and the same moment Christ comes to us and enters within us with intermediary and without intermediary (that is, with his gifts and above all gifts), and we come to him and enter within him with intermediary and without intermediary (that is, with our virtues and above all virtues). He imprints his image and likeness upon us, namely, himself and his gifts, delivers us from our sins, sets us free, and makes us like himself.

Meeting God without intermediary

In this same activity whereby God delivers us from sin, sets us free, and makes us like himself in charity, the spirit immerses itself in blissful love. Here there occurs a meeting and a union which are without intermediary and supernatural, and in this is found our highest blessedness. Although from God's side it is natural that he bestows gifts out of love and gratuitous goodness, from our side this is something accidental and supernatural, for previously we were strangers and unlike him, while afterward we attained a likeness to God and unity with him. This meeting and unity which the loving spirit attains in God and possesses without intermediary must take place in the essential ground of our being; it therefore remains a deep mystery to our understanding, unless the understanding apprehends it essentially in an utterly simple way.

In this blissful unity we will constantly rest in a state transcending ourselves and all things. All natural and supernatural gifts flow forth from this unity, and yet the loving spirit rests in this unity above all gifts. Here there is nothing but God and the spirit united with God without intermediary. In this unity we are received by the Holy Spirit, and we ourselves receive the Holy Spirit, the Father, the Son, and the divine nature in its entirety, for God cannot be divided. The spirit's inclination to blissful enjoyment seeks rest in God above all likeness. In the spirit's essential being, this inclination obtains and possesses in a supernatural way all that the spirit ever received there in a natural way.

All good persons possess this, but its nature remains hidden to them all their lives if they are not interiorly fervent and empty of all creatures. In the very moment in which a person turns from sin, he is received by

God in the essential unity of his being, the topmost part of his spirit, so that he might rest in God now and forevermore. He also receives grace and a likeness to God in the ground of his powers, so that he might constantly grow and increase in new virtues. As long as this likeness exists through charity and the practice of virtue, just so long does this unity in rest perdure, for it cannot be lost except through mortal sin.

The absolute necessity of God's grace and our response to it

Now all holiness and blessedness lie in the spirit's being led, by means of likeness and the mediation of grace or glory, to a state of rest in the essential unity. The grace of God is the path we must always follow if we are to arrive at that bare being in which God gives himself to us without intermediary in all his richness. Sinners and the damned spirits are in darkness precisely because they lack God's grace, which would have enlightened them, instructed them, and led them to this blissful unity. Nevertheless the essential being of the spirit is so noble that the damned cannot will their own annihilation, but sin causes such a state of darkness and unlikeness and raises so great a barrier between the spirit's powers and the essential being where God dwells that the spirit cannot attain union in its own being, which would be the spirit's proper place of eternal rest if it were not for sin. Whoever lives apart from sin lives in the likeness and grace of God and has God as his own possession. Grace is therefore necessary, for it drives away sin, prepares the way for us, and makes our entire life fruitful.

For this reason Christ is constantly coming to us through the mediation of grace and manifold gifts, while we in turn go to him through the mediation of our virtues and various exercises. The more interior the gifts he bestows and the more finely wrought his movements within us, the more interior and delightful will be the exercises of our spirit, as you have already heard concerning all the ways which have previously been described. There is in all this a constant renewal, for God is always giving new gifts and our spirit is always turning back to God in accordance with the ways in which it has been called and gifted by God, and in this encounter it constantly receives new and higher gifts. In this way a person is constantly advancing to a higher form of life.

This active meeting is always with intermediary, since God's gifts, together with our virtues and the activity of our spirit, constitute this intermediary. Such mediation is necessary for all persons and all spirits, for without the mediation of God's grace and of our freely willed and loving conversion no one can be saved.

God's meeting with us in unity and likeness

Now God beholds the abode and place of rest which he has made with us and in us, namely, our unity with him and our likeness to him. He wishes ceaselessly to visit the unity with new comings of his sublime birth and with a rich outflux of his fathomless love, for he desires to live in bliss within the loving spirit. He also wishes to visit the likeness of our spirit with rich gifts so that we might become even more like him and more fully enlightened in virtue. Christ wishes that we make our own dwelling in the essential unity of our spirit, abiding there with him above all creaturely activity and above all virtue. He also wishes us to continue actively in the same unity, rich and fulfilled with virtues and heavenly gifts. Moreover, he wishes us ceaselessly to visit both the unity and the likeness through every work we perform, for in each new moment God is born in us and from this sublime birth the Holy Spirit flows forth with all his gifts. Now we are to meet God's gifts by means of our likeness to him and are to meet his sublime birth by abiding in unity.

B. MEETING GOD WITH INTERMEDIARY

In every good work, through a pure intention

Now understand how in each of our activities we are to meet God, grow in likeness to him, and more nobly possess our blissful unity with him. Every good work, no matter how small, which is offered to God with love and an upright, pure intention merits an increase in our likeness to God and in our eternal life in him. A pure intention draws the scattered powers together in the unity of the spirit and directs the spirit toward God. A pure intention is the beginning, the end, and the adornment of all virtue. A pure intention offers praise, honor, and all virtue to God. It passes through itself, all the heavens, and everything else and finds God in the simple ground of its own being. An intention is pure when it intends only God and all other things in relation to God. A pure intention drives out hypocrisy and duplicity. A person should retain and practice such an intention above all else in all his works, for it keeps a person in God's presence and renders him clear of understanding, zealous in virtue, and free of needless fear both now and on the Day of Judgment. A pure intention is that "simple eye" which Christ says will keep a person's entire body (that is, all his works and his entire life) filled with light and free from sin (cf. Lk 11:34). A pure intention is the fervent, enlightened, loving inclination of the spirit and is the foundation of all spirituality. It contains within itself faith, hope, and love, for it trusts God and is faithful to him. It treads nature underfoot, establishes peace, drives out a spirit of murmuring, maintains all virtues in their full vitality, and bestows peace, hope, and confidence in God both now and at God's Judgment.

It is in this way that we ought to dwell in the unity of our spirit in both grace and likeness, constantly meeting God through the mediation of our virtue and offering him all our works and our entire life with a pure intention. If we do this, we will from hour to hour become more and more like him in each of our works. At the same time, and on the foundation of a pure intention, we will transcend ourselves and meet God without intermediary, resting with him in the ground of simplicity. There we will possess the heritage that has been prepared for us from all eternity.

The life and virtuous activity of all spirits consist in becoming like God through purity of intention, while the highest rest of these spirits consists in a simplicity which transcends all likeness. Nevertheless one spirit surpasses another as regards virtue and likeness to God and possesses its own essential being in itself according to the degree of its nobility. God suffices each spirit in particular, while each of the latter seeks God in the ground of its spirit according to the measure of its love, both here and in eternity.

Gradations in meeting God with intermediary, in accordance with the seven gifts of the Holy Spirit

Consider now the order and gradation of all virtues and all holiness, for I will show how we are to meet God through likeness to him so as to be able to rest with him in unity.[15]

Fear of the Lord

When a person lives in the fear of God through the practice of the moral virtues and of exterior exercises, through obedience and submis-

---

15. The seven gifts that Ruusbroec proceeds to discuss are based on Isaiah 11:1–3, a passage the Fathers of the Church regularly interpreted as referring to dispositions of soul resulting from the action of the Holy Spirit. They are commonly called "the gifts of the Holy Spirit," though Ruusbroec himself does not here use that particular term.

siveness to the holy Church and to God's commandments, and through a ready willingness to do all that is good with a pure intention, then he is like God by means of his faithfulness and by the concurrence of his will with God's regarding things to be done or left undone; in addition, he rests in God above and beyond his likeness to him. In other words, by means of faithfulness and a pure intention a person fulfills the will of God—in a greater or lesser measure depending on the degree of his likeness to God— and by means of love he rests in his Beloved over and above his likeness to him.

Kindness

If he responds well to what he has received from God, then God will give him the spirit of kindness and generosity. In this way he becomes generous of heart, merciful, and kind and so becomes more full of life and more like God. He feels that he is resting more deeply in God and acquiring more breadth and depth in the practice of virtue than was previously the case. As he becomes more like God, he also finds more savor in this likeness and in his rest.

Knowledge

If he responds well in this regard—by acting with great zeal and a pure intention and by striving against all that is opposed to virtue—then he will obtain the third gift, that of knowledge and discretion. He thereby becomes reasonable and discerning, knowing what to do and what to leave undone, when to give and when to take. Through a pure intention and divine love, such a person rests in God above himself in unity. He possesses himself through his likeness to God and performs all his works with greater delight, for he is obedient and submissive to the Father, reasonable and discreet through the Son, and kind and generous through the Holy Spirit. In this way he bears a likeness to the Holy Trinity and comes to rest in God by means of love and his pure intention. The entire active life consists in this.

If a person thus exerts himself with great zeal and discreetly follows his pure intention, refraining from all that is opposed to virtue and constantly prostrating himself in humility at the feet of Christ, then he will progress from hour to hour in virtue and in his likeness to God. If he behaves in this way, he cannot go astray. Nevertheless, if he keeps to the practice of manifold works in restlessness of heart instead of focusing on the purpose and reason for the works, then he will accordingly remain always in the active life. So too, if he remains more occupied with sacramental practices and with exterior signs and usages than with the purpose and the truth which are thereby signified, then he will always remain an exterior kind of person and will attain salvation through his works performed with a pure intention.

For this reason, if a person wishes to draw nearer to God and attain a higher kind of practice and life, then he must turn from the works to the reason for the works and from the signs to the truth which they signify. In this way he will become the master of his works and one who knows the truth, and so will enter upon the interior life.

Fortitude ———

God will then give him the fourth gift, which is the spirit of fortitude. He can thereby master pleasure and pain, gain and loss, hope and concern about earthly matters, and all kinds of obstacles and multiplicity. In this way a person becomes free and detached from all creatures. When a person is devoid of images, he is master of himself and becomes easily and effortlessly united in his being and interiorly fervent. Without obstacle, he turns freely to God with interior devotion, lofty desire, thanksgiving, praise, and a pure intention. He thereby finds savor in all his works and in his entire life, both interior and exterior, for he is standing before the throne of the Holy Trinity. He often receives interior consolation and sweetness from God, for whoever serves at such a table with thanksgiving, praise, and interior reverence often drinks of the wine and partakes of the food that is left over and of the scraps that fall from the Master's table (cf. Mt 15:27). Because of his pure intention, he constantly enjoys interior peace.

If he wishes to remain standing fast before God with thanksgiving, praise, and an upright intention, then the spirit of fortitude will be doubled within him. He will then descend neither toward bodily inclinations nor toward the desire for consolation, sweetness, rest, peace of heart, or any of God's gifts. Rather, he will forgo all gifts and all consolation for the sake of finding the one whom he loves.

Accordingly, whoever leaves behind and overcomes restlessness of heart and the things of this world is strong, while whoever forgoes and rises above all consolation and heavenly gifts is doubly strong. In this way such a person transcends all creatures and powerfully and freely gains possession of himself by means of the gift of spiritual fortitude.

THE SPIRITUAL ESPOUSALS

Counsel

When, then, no creature can overcome a person or stop him from standing firm in his pure, upright intention and in the praise of God, or from seeking and intending God above all God's gifts by means of this fortitude, then God will give him the fifth gift, that of counsel. Through this gift the Father draws a person from within, calling him to sit with all the chosen in union with him at his right hand; the Son says spiritually within him, "Follow me to my Father. One thing is necessary" (cf. Lk 10:42); and the Holy Spirit makes the heart expand and become enkindled with a burning love. This gives rise to a passionate way of life marked by interior restlessness, for whoever listens to this counsel is caught up in the storm of love so that nothing can satisfy him except God alone. For this reason such a person abandons himself and all things in order to find the one in whom he lives and in whom all things are one. A person will here direct his mind simply to God, mastering himself by means of his reason, renouncing all self-will, and freely awaiting the unity he desires until the day when God wills to bestow it.

The spirit of counsel thus works in him in two ways: Whoever follows the order and counsel of God, abandoning himself and all things and saying with insatiable, passionate, and burning love, "Thy kingdom come," is someone great; but whoever overcomes his own will, renouncing it in love and saying to God with reverent submissiveness, "Thy will be done in all things, not mine," is still greater and follows still more closely God's counsel.

When Christ our Lord was drawing near his passion, he spoke the same words to his Father in humble abnegation of himself. For him these were the most pleasurable and most honorable words he ever spoke, for us they were the most beneficial, for the Father the most lovable, and for the devil the most offensive, for in Christ's renunciation of his human will we have all been saved. For a loving, humble person, the will of God thereby becomes his highest joy and his greatest delight in the realm of spiritual feelings, even if he were to end up in hell, which is impossible. It is here that our human nature is reduced to its lowest point and God is raised to his highest, while the person himself becomes capable of receiving all God's gifts because he has denied himself, renounced his own will, and given all for all. He therefore requests and wills nothing except what God wishes to give, for God's will is his joy. Whoever surrenders himself in love is the freest person alive; he lives without care, for God cannot lose what is his.

JOHN RUUSBROEC

(margin handwritten: Tribulation)

Now note that although God knows all hearts, he nevertheless visits such a person and puts him to the test to see whether he can freely practice self-denial and so become enlightened, living a life that gives glory to God and is of benefit to himself. For this reason God sometimes moves him from his right hand to his left, from heaven to hell, and from a state full of delight to one of great misery. It then seems as if he has been scorned and abandoned by God and by all creatures. If he renounced himself and his will when he was formerly in a state of love and joy and accordingly sought not himself but the adorable will of God, then he will easily renounce himself in this condition of suffering and misery, again seeking not himself but always the glory of God. Whoever is willing to do great things is also willing to suffer great things, but suffering and enduring these things with resignation is nobler and of greater value in God's eyes and more satisfying to our own spirit than performing great deeds with the same resignation, for it is more contrary to our nature. Our spirit is thereby more exalted and our nature is brought lower through grievous suffering than through great deeds performed with equal love.

If a person remains in this state of resignation without preferring anything else, just like someone who neither wills nor knows any alternative, then he possesses the spirit of counsel in a twofold manner, for he satisfies God's will and counsel both in what he does and in what he suffers—all with self-abandonment and submissive obedience. His nature is thereby adorned to a higher degree and he is made capable of becoming enlightened in spirit.

Understanding

God will therefore give him the sixth gift, which is the spirit of understanding. This gift is what we previously likened to a spring with three streams, for this gift establishes our spirit firmly in unity, reveals the truth, and produces an ample love which embraces all in common. This gift can also be likened to the shining of the sun, for through its rays the sun fills the air with a simple resplendence; sheds light on the forms of all things, making clear the differences among all colors; and reveals its power and heat, which is conducive to the common good and the fruitfulness of the entire world.

The first effect of this gift: simplicity in the spirit. In the same way, the first ray of this gift produces simplicity in the spirit. This simplicity is penetrated by a special resplendence just as the air of the heavens is penetrated

126

by the light of the sun, for the grace of God, which is the foundation of all gifts, subsists essentially in our possible intellect like a simple light.[16] By means of this simple light our spirit is made firm, simple, and enlightened, full of grace and divine gifts. In this it is like God, by means of his grace and love.

Because it is like God and because it loves and intends God purely and simply above all his gifts, it cannot rest content in this likeness and in this created resplendence, for it has both naturally and supernaturally a fundamental inclination toward that unfathomable being from which it has issued forth; moreover, the Unity of the divine being eternally draws all likeness into union with itself. For this reason the spirit becomes immersed in a state of bliss and loses itself in God as in its eternal resting place. The grace of God is to God himself as sunlight is to the sun—a means and a way leading us to the latter. It therefore shines within us in a simple, onefold way and makes us deiform, that is, like God. This likeness constantly sinks away, dying in God and becoming and remaining one with him, for charity makes us become one with God and causes us to remain living in union with him. We nevertheless retain an eternal likeness to God whether in the light of grace or of glory, where we possess ourselves actively through charity and virtue, while we also retain unity with God above our works in the bareness of our spirit in the divine light, where we possess God in rest above all virtue. In other words, charity must remain eternally active as regards our likeness to God, while unity with God in blissful love is called to rest in him forevermore.

All this is what it means to give oneself to love, for in one and the same moment of time love is both active and at rest in its Beloved. The one element is strengthened by the other, for the higher the love, the greater the rest, and the greater the rest, the more fervent the love. The one lives in the other, so that whoever does not love does not rest, and whoever does not rest does not love. It does indeed seem to some good persons that they neither love nor rest in God, but this thought itself arises from love: Because a person desires to love more than he is able, he thinks that he is deficient, but in this very activity he savors both love and rest, for only a resigned, detached, and enlightened person can understand how one can actively love and blissfully rest.

Every lover, then, is one with God in rest and is like God in the works

---

16. The term "possible intellect" (*moghelijke verstane*) refers to the intellect (or understanding) considered in its receptivity to all being and, in particular, to the working of God's grace.

127

of love, for God, in his sublime nature of which we bear a likeness, subsists blissfully in eternal rest in accordance with the essential Unity of his being and also subsists actively in eternal activity in accordance with the Trinity. Each of these is the perfection of the other, for rest abides in the Unity and activity abides in the Trinity, and the two remain thus for all eternity. For this reason, if a person is to savor God, he must love, and if he wishes to love, he must have this savor. If he lets himself be satisfied with other things, then he can have no savor of what God is. We must therefore possess ourselves in a simple way in virtue and in our likeness to God and must also possess God above ourselves in rest and unity by means of love. This is the first point to be made concerning the gift of understanding: how a person who is common to all is made firm and stable.

The second effect of this gift: enlightenment in the understanding. When the air is filled with the sun's light, then the beauty and richness of the entire world are revealed, our eyes are enlightened, and we find joy in the great variety of colors. In the same way, when we have become simple and unified in ourselves and when our possible intellect has been enlightened and pervaded by the spirit of understanding, then we become able to recognize God's sublime attributes, which are the causes of all the works which flow forth from him. Although all persons can come to an understanding of these works—and of God, by means of his works—nevertheless no one can experience the attributes that give rise to these works or truly understand these attributes in their ground unless it is by means of this gift. It teaches us how to consider and come to know our own nobility; it also enables us, in the practice of the virtues and in all our exercises, to discern how we ought to live without straying from the eternal truth. Whoever is enlightened by this gift can live in the spirit and, with his enlightened reason, observe and understand correctly all things in heaven and on earth. Such a person therefore has his citizenship in heaven (cf. Phil 3:20) and sees and beholds with all the saints the nobility of his Lover: his incomprehensible height and unfathomable depth, his length and breadth, his wisdom and truth, his goodness and ineffable generosity, and all the other lovable attributes which are in God our Lover without number and without limit in his sublime nature, for he is all this himself.

This enlightened person then lowers his eyes upon himself and all other creatures, observing how God created them out of his gratuitous generosity and bestowed gifts upon their nature in many different ways and how God also wishes to endow them supernaturally and make them rich with himself if only they seek and desire this. All these observations of our reason about the manifold diversity of God's riches fill our spirit with joy, provided that by means of divine love we have died to ourselves in God and live and walk in the spirit, savoring the things that are eternal.

This gift of understanding reveals to us the unity which we have and possess in God through the blissful immersion of love and also reveals the likeness to God which we have in ourselves through charity and virtue. It provides us as well with a resplendent light in which we are able to live in the spirit with discernment, to contemplate and know God through spiritual likenesses, and to know ourselves and all things in accordance with the mode and measure of this light and in accordance with the will of God and the nobility of our understanding. This is the second point to be made concerning the gift of understanding: how a person who is common to all becomes enlightened.

The third effect of this gift: love in the will. According to the degree in which the air is made bright by the sun's resplendence, the heat produced will be more or less great and more or less conducive to the fruitfulness of everything. So too, if our power of reason and understanding is enlightened so as to know God's truth distinctly, then the will, that is, the amorous power, will be enkindled to the point of flowing forth richly in faithfulness and love toward all in common, for this gift establishes in us an ample love of all in common—a love which arises through the knowledge of the truth which we attain from the resplendence of this gift.

The simplest persons are those who are the most satisfied and most at peace with themselves. They are also the most deeply immersed in God, the most enlightened in their understanding, the most diversified in their good works, and the most wide-ranging in the way their love flows out to all in common. They also meet with the fewest obstacles, for they are the most like God, who is himself simplicity in his inmost being, resplendent clarity in his understanding, and love flowing out to all in common in his works. The more like God we are in these three respects, the closer is our union with him. For this reason we should abide simply in the ground of our being, observe all things with an enlightened power of reason, and flow through all things with a love common to all, just as the sun in the heavens remains simple and unchanged in itself while its resplendent light and heat are to be found universally in all parts of the world.

Now understand how we ought to live with an enlightened power of reason and a love common to all. The Father is the origin of the entire Godhead both essentially and personally. For this reason we should with humble reverence prostrate ourselves in the spirit before the Father's sublimity; we will thus possess humility, a foundation of all virtue. We should fervently worship, that is, honor and reverence the Father's might; we will thus be lifted up in spirit, for in his might he created all things from nothing and maintains them in being. We should offer praise, thanksgiving, and eternal service to God's love and faithfulness, which saved us from the enemy's bondage and from eternal death; we will thus become free. Before God's wisdom we should confess and lament the blindness and ignorance of human nature and should desire that all persons be enlightened and attain knowledge of the truth; God will thus be known and honored by them. We should beseech God's mercy on behalf of sinners, so that they might be converted and advance in virtue; God will thus be loved and desired by them. We should give generously out of God's rich goodness to all who are in need, so that they might be filled and flow back to God; God will thus be possessed by them all. In honor and reverence we should offer to the Father all the service and all the works which Christ in his humanity ever performed out of love; all our prayer will thus be heard. In Christ Jesus we should also offer the Father all the fervent interior devotion of the angels, saints, and all good persons; we will thus be united with them all in the glory of God. In addition, we should offer the Father the entire service of the holy Church and the sublime Sacrifice celebrated by all priests, together with all that we have been able to accomplish or understand in the name of Christ, so that through Christ we might meet God, become like him in a love common to all, transcend all likeness in simplicity, and be united with him in essential unity. We should constantly abide with God in unity, eternally flow forth with God and all the saints in a love common to all, constantly turn inward again with thanksgiving and praise, and in blissful love immerse ourselves in essential rest. This is the richest kind of life I know, and with it we possess the gift of understanding.

Wisdom

Now you should understand that in this inward movement of return the blissful Unity of God is just like an incomprehensible darkness devoid of particular form. By means of love and a pure intention the spirit turns within in two ways: actively, by offering all its virtues, and in blissful enjoyment, by offering itself above and beyond all its virtues. In this loving movement within there arises the seventh gift, which is the spirit of savorous wisdom. It pervades the simplicity of our spirit as well as our soul and body with wisdom and spiritual savor. This is a divine stirring or touch in the unity of our spirit, an influx and ground of all graces, gifts, and virtues. In this divine touch each person savors his exercises and his life in accordance with the power of the touch and the measure of his love. This divine stirring is the inmost intermediary between God and ourselves, between rest and activity, between particular forms and the absence of all form, and between time and eternity.

God produces this spiritual stirring within us at the very beginning, before bestowing any of his gifts, but it is actually recognized and savored by us last of all, for when we have lovingly sought God in all our exercises right into the inmost ground of our being, then we experience the influx of all God's graces and gifts. We experience this touch in the unity of our higher powers, above reason—though not without reason, for we do perceive that we are being touched. But if we try to determine what this touch is or where it comes from, then reason and all creaturely powers of observation fail. Even though the air is made bright with the sun's resplendence and even though a person's eyes are sharp and healthy, if he tries to follow the rays which bring this resplendence and to look directly at the orb of the sun, then his eyes will certainly fail in such an activity and will simply receive passively the shining of these rays. In the same way, the reflection of the incomprehensible light in the unity of our higher powers is so intense that all creaturely activity that proceeds by way of perceiving distinctions cannot but fail. Here, then, our active powers must submit passively to God's action, and this is the beginning of all gifts. If we were able to comprehend God, that would mean he was giving himself to us without intermediary; but this is impossible, for we are too narrow and small to comprehend him. For this reason he pours his gifts into us in accordance with the degree of our comprehension and the nobility of our exercises.

The fruitful Unity of God abides above the unity of our powers and constantly calls us to likeness to God in love and virtue. For this reason we are at all times touched anew, so that we might always be renewed more and more and become more like God in virtue. At each new touch our spirit falls into a state of hunger and thirst and wishes in this storm of love thoroughly to savor and penetrate this groundless abyss in order to find satisfaction. This gives rise to a never-ending, ravenous striving which never reaches its goal, for all loving spirits desire and strive after God—each according to its nobility and the degree in which it has been touched by God—but God nevertheless remains forever uncomprehended by us in our active desire of him. For this reason there remains in us an eternal hunger and an eternal desire to turn inward with all the saints. When we meet God, the heat and light are so infinitely intense that all spirits fail in their activity and vanish and melt away in the love which they experience in the unity of the spirit. As mere creatures they must here passively undergo

God's activity within them. Here too our spirit, God's grace, and all our virtues become a single, felt love which does not act, for our spirit has transcended its activity and has itself become love. Here the spirit is simple and unified, able to receive all gifts and capable of practicing every virtue. In this ground of felt love there lives that welling vein which is the illumination or interior activity of God which at all times moves and urges us on, draws us inward, and makes us flow forth with new works of virtue. With this I have shown you the ground and manner of all virtues.

C. Meeting God without Intermediary, in Three Different Modes

Now understand well what follows: The measureless illumination of God which, together with his incomprehensible resplendence, is a cause of all gifts and virtues is the same incomprehensible light which transforms and pervades our spirit's inclination toward blissful enjoyment. It does this in a way which is devoid of all particular form, since it occurs in incomprehensible light. In this light the spirit immerses itself in a rest of pure bliss, for this rest is modeless and fathomless. It cannot be known except through itself, for if we could know and comprehend it by ourselves it would lapse into some particular form or measure and would then not be able to satisfy us; instead, this rest would become an eternal state of restlessness. For this reason the simple, loving inclination of our spirit, immersed in rest, produces in us a blissful love, and such love is fathomless. Here, God's deep calls to deep (cf. Ps 42:8), that is, calls to all who are united with the Spirit of God in blissful love. This call is an overflow of essential resplendence, and this essential resplendence, enveloping us in fathomless love, makes us lose ourselves and flow forth into the wild darkness of the Godhead. Thus united—one with the Spirit of God, without intermediary—we are able to meet God with God and endlessly possess our eternal blessedness with him and in him. This most interior way of life is practiced in three manners or modes.

The first mode: emptiness

Sometimes a person living the interior life turns within himself in a simple way in accordance with his inclination toward blissful enjoyment. This occurs above and beyond all activity and all virtue, by means of a simple, inward act of gazing in blissful love. Here such a person meets God without intermediary, and an ample light, shining from out of God's Unity, reveals to him darkness, bareness, and nothingness. He is enveloped by the darkness and falls into a modeless state, as though he were completely lost; through the bareness he loses the power of observing all things in their distinctness and becomes transformed and pervaded by a simple resplendence; in the nothingness all his activity fails him, for he is overcome by the activity of God's fathomless love, while in the inclination of his spirit toward blissful enjoyment he overcomes God and becomes one spirit with him (cf. 1 Cor 6:17).

   Through this unity in the Spirit of God such a person enters a state of blissful savor and there possesses God's essential being. Being immersed in his own essential being, this person becomes filled with the fathomless delights and riches of God. From out of these riches there flow into the unity of the higher powers an embrace and a fullness of felt love, and from this fullness of felt love there flows into the heart and into the corporeal powers a felt and deeply penetrating savor. By means of this influx such a person becomes interiorly unable to move and powerless over himself and all his activity. In the inmost part of his being, in both soul and body, he neither knows nor feels anything except a unique resplendence accompanied by a felt sense of well-being and a penetrating savor.

   This is the first mode, which is characterized by emptiness, for it empties a person of all things, lifts him up above all virtues and activities, unites him with God, and provides a firm and stable basis for the most fervent interior exercises which a person can practice. When, therefore, any restlessness or any virtuous practice sets up an obstacle or interposes images between a good person and the bare introversion which he desires, then he will be hindered in this mode, since it consists in transcending all things to enter a state of emptiness. This is the first mode in the practice of the most interior exercises.

The second mode: active desire

   At times this interiorly fervent person turns to God in a way characterized by desire and activity, so that he might give God glory and honor and might offer him both himself and all his works, letting them be consumed in the love of God. At such times he meets God with intermediary, namely, the intermediary of the gift of savorous wisdom. This gift is the ground and source of all virtue, for it urges and moves every good person toward virtue in accordance with the degree of his love. It sometimes touches an interior person so deeply and enkindles his love so intensely that all God's gifts and all that God can bestow apart from himself are too small and unsatisfying and serve only to increase his restlessness. Such a person has an interior perception or feeling in the ground of his being, where all virtues have their beginning and end, where with ardent desire he offers God all these virtues, and where love has its abode. Here the hunger and thirst of love are so great that he surrenders himself at every moment and is unable to work any further, but rather transcends his activity and comes to nought in love. He hungers and thirsts for the taste of God and at each sudden illumination of God is seized by him and touched by him anew in love. Though living he dies; though dying he comes back to life. In this way the yearning hunger and thirst of love are constantly renewed within him.

This is the second mode, one which is characterized by desire. In it, love stands in a state of likeness and yearningly desires to be united with God. This mode is more honorable and more beneficial to us than the first since it is the cause of the first, for no one can enter a state of rest transcending activity unless he has previously loved in a way characterized by desire and activity. For this reason God's grace and our active love must both precede and follow, that is, must be practiced both before and after, for without works of love we cannot merit or attain God nor can we retain what we have gained by means of the works of love. Therefore no one should be empty of activity if he is master of himself and can give himself to the works of love. But whenever a good person lingers somewhat over any of God's gifts or over any creature, he will be hindered in this most interior exercise, for it is a hunger which cannot be satisfied by anything or anyone except God alone.

The third mode: both resting and working in accordance with righteousness

From these first two modes there arises the third, which is an interior life in accordance with righteousness. You should understand that God comes ceaselessly to us both with intermediary and without intermediary and calls us both to blissful enjoyment and to activity in such a way that the one will not be hindered by the other but rather constantly strengthened by it. An interior person therefore possesses his life in these two ways, that is, in rest and in activity, and in each he is whole and undivided, for he is completely in God when he blissfully rests and is completely in himself when he actively loves. He is exhorted and called by God at all times to renew both his rest and his activity, and his spirit's righteousness wishes to pay at each instant whatever God asks of it. For this reason the spirit turns inward both actively and with blissful enjoyment each time it experiences God's sudden illumination. In this way it is constantly renewed in all the virtues and becomes more deeply immersed in blissful rest, for each time God bestows something on us he gives himself as well as his gifts, while in each of its inward movements the spirit gives itself as well as all its works. By means of God's simple illumination and the spirit's inclination to be blissfully immersed in love, the spirit is united with God and is ceaselessly transported into a state of rest. In addition, by means of the gifts of understanding and of savorous wisdom, it is actively touched and at all times enlightened and enkindled in love.

To a person in this state there is spiritually revealed and held out before him all that one could desire. He is hungry and thirsty, for he sees angelic food and heavenly drink; he works intensely in love, for he sees his rest; he is a pilgrim and sees his fatherland; he strives for victory in love, for he sees his crown. Consolation, peace, joy, beauty, riches, and everything else that brings delight is revealed in God to the enlightened reason without measure in spiritual likenesses. Through this revelation and God's touch love remains active, for this righteous person has established for himself a truly spiritual life in both rest and activity; such a life will continue forever, though after this present life it will be transformed into a higher state.

It is in all this that a person's righteousness consists. He goes toward God with fervent interior love through his eternal activity, enters into God with his blissful inclination toward eternal rest, remains in God, and nevertheless goes out to creatures in virtue and righteousness through a love which is common to all. This is the highest point of the interior life. Anyone who does not possess both rest and activity in one and the same exercise has not attained this righteousness, while a person who has attained it cannot be hindered when he turns inward, for he does so both actively and in blissful enjoyment.

A person is, however, like a double mirror, receiving images on both sides, for in the higher part of his being he receives God with all his gifts and in the lower part he receives corporeal images through the senses. Now he can turn inward whenever he wishes and so practice righteousness without hindrance. But in this life a person is inconstant and accordingly often turns outward; without necessity or the direction of his enlightened reason he gets caught up in the activities of the senses and so falls into daily faults.

Still, in the loving inward movement of a righteous person these daily faults are just like a drop of water in a red-hot furnace. With this I conclude the description of the interior life.

Deviations from these three modes

Now there are some persons who appear to be good but who in fact live contrary to these three modes and to all the virtues. Let each person examine and test himself.

The first deviation: false emptiness

Anyone not drawn and enlightened by God is untouched by love and has within himself neither an active devotion full of desirous longing nor a simple, loving inclination toward blissful rest. Such a person cannot be united with God, for all who live without supernatural love are turned back upon themselves and seek their rest in things which are apart from God. All creatures are naturally inclined toward rest and therefore both the good and the bad seek rest in many different ways. Now notice that whenever a person is bare and imageless in his senses and devoid of activity in his higher powers, he enters a purely natural state of rest. All persons can find and possess this kind of rest in themselves by merely natural means, apart from God's grace, provided only that they can become empty of images and all activity. But a loving person cannot rest in such a state, for charity and the interior touch of God's grace do not lie inactive. For this reason an interior person cannot long remain in this state of natural rest.

Consider now the way in which a person practices this natural rest. It consists in sitting quietly in a state of idleness, without any interior or exterior exercises, in order to find rest and have it remain undisturbed. But it is not lawful to practice this kind of rest, for it produces blind ignorance in a person and makes him sink down into himself in inactivity. Such rest is nothing other than a state of empty idleness into which a person falls and in which he becomes forgetful of himself, of God, and of all things as regards any activity. This kind of rest is contrary to that supernatural rest in which a person possesses God, for the latter is a loving immersion of oneself characterized by a simple act of gazing in incomprehensible resplendence. This rest in God—which is always sought actively with fervent desire, found in blissful inclination, eternally possessed in a loving immersion of oneself, and still sought even when already possessed—this rest is raised as high above merely natural rest as God is raised above all creatures.

For this reason all those persons are deceived who have the intention of immersing themselves in a state of natural rest, neither seeking God through desire nor finding him in blissful love. The rest which they possess consists in an emptying of their inmost being, something to which they are inclined by both nature and custom. One cannot find God in this state of natural rest, but it does bring a person into that state of emptiness which can be attained by pagans, Jews, and all persons, no matter how evil, provided only that they can live in their sins without suffering the reproaches of conscience and can empty themselves of images and all activity.

The rest which one attains in this state of emptiness is both satisfying and deep. In itself it is not sinful, for it arises naturally in everyone whenever he empties himself of activity. But if a person seeks to practice and possess it without performing works of virtue, then he falls into spiritual pride and a state of self-complacency from which hardly anyone ever recovers. Such a person sometimes thinks that he has obtained and become what he will in fact never attain. When a person thus possesses this state of empty rest and considers all loving devotion to be an obstacle, he remains resting upon himself and is living contrary to the first mode which unites a person with God; this is the beginning of all spiritual error.

I will now offer a simile to clarify this. The angels which lovingly and blissfully turned to God with all that they had received from him found salvation and eternal rest, but those who turned toward themselves and complacently sought rest in themselves in natural light attained a rest which was both short and unlawful. They were blinded and cut off from the eternal light and fell instead into darkness and eternal restlessness. This is the first deviation, one in which a person attains rest through false emptiness.

The second deviation: active self-seeking

Now understand that when a person wants to rest in a state of emptiness without interior yearning for God and devotion to him, he is liable to all kinds of error, for he has turned away from God and toward himself with a natural love, seeking and desiring consolation, sweetness, and whatever else pleases him. In this he is like a merchant, for in all that he does he is turned back upon himself and seeks and intends his own rest and profit more than God's glory. A person who lives like this in a state of natural love is constantly closed in upon himself through his self-seeking and lack of detachment.

Some of these persons lead an arduous life marked by great works of penance in order to become known and renowned for their great holiness and also in order to merit a great reward, for all natural love thinks much of itself and likes to receive honor in this life and a great reward in eternity. There are others who have many special preferences and who pray fervently for many particular favors from God. Such persons are often deceived, for at times they receive from the devil the things that they desire, but they then attribute this to their own holiness and conclude that they were worthy of these things. Because these persons are proud and are neither touched by God nor enlightened by him, they remain closed in upon themselves. Even a small consolation may bring them much joy, for they are unaware of all that they lack. In their desire they are inclined with their whole being toward interior savor and toward spiritual pleasure of a purely natural kind. This is called spiritual impurity, for it is a disordered inclination directed by natural love and constantly turning back upon itself to seek its pleasure in all things. In addition, such persons are always spiritually proud and obstinate, so that their desire and appetite are sometimes so intensely focused on the things which they want and which they stubbornly seek to obtain from God that they are often led astray; some even become possessed by the devil.

These persons live in a way which is completely contrary to charity and to that loving movement within oneself whereby a person offers up himself and all that he can do for the honor and love of God, so that nothing can bring him rest or satisfaction except that incomprehensible good which is God alone. Charity is a bond of love which raises us up above ourselves; through it we renounce ourselves and become united with God and God with us, whereas natural love turns back upon itself and upon its own pleasure and so remains ever alone. It is true that in exterior activity natural love resembles charity as closely as two hairs on the same head, but the intentions in the two cases are different: With his heart uplifted, a good person constantly seeks, intends, and desires the glory of God, whereas in the case of natural love a person is always intent on himself and his own profit.

Consequently, whenever natural love opposes and overcomes charity, a person falls into four sins, namely, spiritual pride, avarice, gluttony, and lust. It was in this way that Adam fell in Paradise, and all human nature with him, for he loved himself with a disordered natural love and therefore turned away from God and in his pride scorned God's commandment. He also avariciously desired knowledge and wisdom, gluttonously sought the pleasures of taste and appetite, and was finally moved to lust. Mary, however, was a living paradise. She found the grace which Adam had lost, and much more besides, for she is the mother of love. She actively turned to God in charity, conceived Christ in humility, and generously offered him with all his sufferings to the Father. She never tasted consolation or any other gift in a gluttonous way, and her entire life was lived chastely. Whoever follows her overcomes all that is contrary to virtue and enters the kingdom where she reigns with her Son for all eternity.

The third deviation: living contrary to righteousness

When, therefore, a person possesses natural rest in a state of empty idleness, intends himself in all his works, and remains obstinately turned away from God through self-seeking, he cannot be united with God, for he lives without charity in a state of unlikeness to God. Here begins the third and most harmful deviation of all, namely, an unrighteous life, which is full of spiritual errors and all kinds of perversity. You should now pay careful attention so as to understand it well.

Those guilty of this deviation are, in their own estimation, contemplatives. They think they are the holiest persons alive, but in fact they live in a way that is contrary to and unlike God, all the saints, and all who are good. Note well my meaning and you will be able to recognize them in both their words and their deeds. Because of the natural rest which they feel and possess within themselves in a state of emptiness, they conclude that they are free and are united with God without intermediary. They also believe that they are above all the practices of the holy Church, above God's commandments, above the law, and above all virtuous works which might be practiced in any manner, for they consider this state of emptiness to be so great a thing that it must not be disturbed by any works, however good they might be, since the emptiness is nobler than all virtue. They therefore live in a state of pure passivity without performing any activity directed either to God or neighbor, just as if they were a tool which is itself idle and awaits the time when its master wishes to work, for if they did anything themselves, then God would be hindered in his own work. For this reason they are empty of every virtue, so empty that they have no wish either to praise or thank God. They do not know, love, will, pray, or desire, for in their opinion they already possess everything that they could pray for or desire. They are accordingly poor in spirit, for they have no will of their own and have abandoned all things, living without any personal preference. They think that they are empty, that they have overcome all things, and that they already possess everything to which the practices of the holy Church are ordered and directed. They therefore claim that no one, not even God himself, can give them anything or take anything from them, for in their opinion they have transcended all exercises and all virtues by entering a state of pure emptiness and being freed of every virtue. They also say that it is harder work to become free of virtue in this state of emptiness than it is to acquire virtue.

They accordingly wish to be free and to obey no one, neither pope nor bishop nor parish priest. Although they may appear otherwise in their outward behavior, interiorly they are submissive to no one, whether in their will or in their works, for they are in every respect empty of all that concerns the holy Church. For this reason they say that as long as a person strives after virtue and desires to do the adorable will of God he is imperfect, for he is still amassing virtues and knows nothing of this spiritual poverty and emptiness. In their estimation they are even raised above all the choirs of saints and angels and above every reward which could be merited in any way. They therefore say that they can never increase in virtue or merit any more reward or even sin ever again, for they claim to live without will, to have handed their spirit over to God in rest and emptiness, to be one with God, and to have become nought in themselves. Consequently they hold that they may freely do whatever their corporeal nature desires, for they have arrived at a state of innocence and are bound by no law. If their nature is drawn toward something which it desires and if this proves a hindrance or obstacle to their spirit's state of emptiness, then they satisfy the desire of their nature so that the emptiness of their spirit might remain undisturbed. They accordingly do not observe fastdays or feastdays or any of the commandments except insofar as they do so to be seen by others, for they live without conscience in all things.

I hope that there are not many such persons to be found, for they are the most wicked and harmful persons alive and can hardly ever be converted. They are sometimes possessed by the devil and are then so cunning that they cannot easily be bested with arguments from reason, though we can clearly show from Scripture, the teaching of Christ, and our faith that they are deceived.

There is another group of wicked persons who are in certain respects different from those just described. They too consider themselves to be empty of all activity and to be no more than an instrument with which God produces whatever he wishes in the way he wishes. They therefore claim to be in a state of pure passivity, without works, and say that the works which God performs through them are nobler and more meritorious than those of any person who performs his own works in the grace of God. They say that they are persons who passively allow God to act in and through themselves, so that it is not they who act but rather God who performs all their works. They also say that they cannot sin since it is God who performs the works while they themselves are completely empty; only what God wills is wrought in them, nothing else. Such persons have abandoned themselves interiorly, renouncing all activity in their state of emptiness and living without preference for a single thing. Their mode of life is one of humble abandonment, and they are very well able to suffer and endure with equanimity whatever befalls them, for they consider themselves to be an instrument with which God works as he wills. In many respects and in many of their works they behave in the same way as good persons, but in some respects they are different, for they believe that everything to which they feel interiorly driven—whether it is something lawful or unlawful—comes from the Holy Spirit. In this and in similar points they are deceived, for the Spirit of God neither wills, counsels, nor produces in any person things which are contrary to the teachings of Christ and of holy Christianity.

Such persons are hard to recognize except by someone who is enlightened and who possesses the gift of the discernment of spirits and of divine truth, for some of them are subtle and so are able to disguise and gloss over their errors. They are also so self-willed and hold so fast to their own ideas that they would rather die than abandon a single point to which they are attached, for they consider themselves to be the holiest and most enlightened persons alive. These differ from the previously described group inasmuch as they say they can make progress and gain merit, whereas the others hold that they cannot merit anything more because they possess themselves in a state of unity and emptiness beyond which they can rise no higher since there is here no more activity.

A synthesis and refutation of these errors

These are all wicked persons, the worst alive, and are to be avoided as much as the enemy from hell. If you have understood well the teaching which I have previously set before you in many different ways, then you clearly perceive that they are in error, for they live in a way that is contrary to God, to righteousness, and to all the saints. They are all precursors of the antichrist, preparing for him the way that leads to all unbelief, for they all wish to be free without following God's commandments or practicing virtue and to be empty and united with God without love and charity. They also wish to be contemplatives without focusing their gaze in love and to be the holiest persons alive without performing the works of holiness. They claim to be resting in him whom they do not love and to be raised up to him to whom they direct neither their will nor their desire. They say that they are empty of all virtue and all devotion in order not to be a hindrance to God in his work. They admit that God is the Creator and Lord of all creatures, but they do not wish to praise or thank him. They also admit that he is infinitely powerful and rich and yet claim that he is unable to give them anything or take anything from them and that they themselves cannot make further progress or gain merit. Some hold the contrary opinion and say that they gain more merit than other persons since it is God who performs their works while they in their emptiness passively undergo God's activity and are themselves worked by him; in this, they say, lies the highest merit.

This is altogether deceitful and impossible. The work which God performs within himself is eternal and unchangeable, for it is himself whom he works and nothing besides. In this activity there can be no question of progress or merit on the part of any creature, for here there is nothing but God, who can neither increase nor decrease. Creatures, however, have their own proper activity through God's power, both in the order of nature and grace and in that of glory, and if their works come to an end here in the order of grace, they will continue for all eternity in glory. Now if it were possible, which it is not, for a creature to come to nought as regards his activity and to become as empty as he was when he did not yet exist—that is, for him to become one with God in every respect, as was then the case—then he could not gain merit any more than he did then; he would be no more holy or blessed than a rock or a piece of wood, for we cannot attain salvation without our own works, without loving and knowing God.[17] God would indeed be blessed, as he is from all eternity, but that would be of no avail to us.

All that they say about this state of emptiness is therefore nothing but deceit. They seek to disguise all their wickedness and error by proposing them as nobler and higher than any virtue and try cunningly to gloss over what is most wicked so as to make it seem best of all. Such persons are contrary to God and all his saints but are very much like the damned spirits in hell, for the damned spirits are without love and knowledge and are

---

17. In this sentence Ruusbroec illustrates the erroneous practical conclusion that some were drawing from the doctrine of exemplarism. In fact, he says, once we have been created it is no longer possible "to become one with God in every respect," as was the case when we were only "living ideas" in the mind of God.

empty of praise and thanksgiving and all loving devotion—this is the very reason they are damned for all eternity. For these persons, the only thing lacking is for their time to fall into eternity, and then justice will be revealed in their works.[18]

D. Christ and the Saints as Our Models in the Interior Life

Christ, the Son of God, who in his humanity is the head of all good persons and the model for how they ought to live, was and is and will evermore remain—together with all his members, that is, all the saints—full of love and desire, of thanksgiving and praise of his heavenly Father. It is true that his soul was and is blessedly united with the divine essence, but he could not and never will arrive at a state of empty idleness, for his glorious soul and all who are blessed have a never-ending loving devotion—just like those who hunger and thirst and, having savored God, can never again be satisfied. Yet this same soul of Christ enjoys God—as do all the saints—above and beyond all desire, there where there is nothing but oneness, namely, the eternal blessedness of God and of all his chosen ones.

This is why the blessedness of Christ and of all his saints consists in both blissful enjoyment and activity; this is likewise the life of all good persons, in accordance with the degree of each one's love. This is a righteousness which will never pass away. For this reason we should adorn ourselves both from without and from within with virtues and upright behavior, just as the saints did. We should also lovingly and humbly offer up ourselves in God's sight together with all our works. We will thereby meet God through the mediation of all his gifts, be touched with a love that is felt, and be filled with faithfulness toward everyone. In this way we will flow forth and flow back again in true charity and will be firmly established so as to abide in simple peace and likeness to God. Through this likeness, as well as through blissful love and God's resplendence, we will become

---

18. As an aid to understanding this vehement opposition to heretics—which Ruusbroec shared with the medieval Church in general and which led him in other treatises to advocate burning such persons at the stake—see Karl Rahner, "What Is Heresy?" in *Theological Investigations*, vol. 5, trans. Karl-H. Kruger (Baltimore: Helicon Press, 1966), pp. 468–81 (= sec. 1, "The Christian Attitude towards Heresy").

immersed in a state of unity and will meet God with God without intermediary in blissful rest. Thus we will eternally abide in God and constantly flow forth and ceaselessly turn back within. With this we will
possess a truly interior life in all its perfection. May God help us that this
might come about. Amen.

BOOK THREE: THE
CONTEMPLATIVE LIFE

A fervent lover of God who possesses God in blissful rest, who possesses himself in dedicated and active love, and who possesses his entire life in virtues and righteousness will—by means of these three points and the hidden revelation of God—enter the contemplative life. Indeed, God freely desires to choose this fervent and righteous lover and raise him to a state of superessential contemplation in the divine light in accordance with the divine mode of being. This contemplation establishes us in a state of purity which transcends all our understanding, for it is a special adornment and heavenly crown and is, in addition, an eternal reward for all our virtues and for our entire life. No one can attain this through knowledge or subtle reasoning or through any exercises; the only persons who can attain divine contemplation are those whom God wishes to unite with himself in his Spirit and to enlighten through himself—no one else can attain this.

The hidden divine nature is eternally active in contemplation and love as regards the Persons and is constantly in a state of blissful enjoyment insofar as the Persons are embraced in the Unity of the divine being.[19] All interior spirits are one with God through their loving immersion in this embrace, which takes place within God's essential Unity; they are that same oneness which the divine being is in itself according to the mode of

---

19. For a proper understanding of book three of the *Espousals*, it is important to note the constant allusions to the dialectical relationship between work and rest, a relationship so very evident in the two clauses of this particular sentence of Ruusbroec. As regards God's own life, the active pole of the dialectic is characterized by such notes as the distinctions among the three Persons, the begetting of the Son, the creation of all things in the Son, the breathing forth of the Holy Spirit, and the Father and the Son's love of all things in the Spirit. On the other hand, the pole of blissful rest is characterized by the Persons' being embraced in the divine Unity, "beyond the distinction of Persons," in a state of "essential bareness" where all names and distinctions "pass away into simple ineffability, without mode and without reason." As noted in the Introduction to this volume, much of the strength of Ruusbroec's mystical theology lies in his insistence that both poles are always present, both in God's life and in the life of contemplatives.

blessedness. In this sublime Unity of the divine nature, the heavenly Father is the origin and beginning of every work which is wrought in heaven and on earth. In the hidden depths in which our spirit is immersed, he speaks the words: "See, the bridegroom is coming. Go out to meet him." We wish to explain and clarify these words as they relate to the state of superessential contemplation, which is the ground of all holiness and of all the life which can ever be lived.

Few persons can attain this divine contemplation because of their own incapacity and because of the hidden, mysterious nature of the light in which one contemplates. For this reason no one can properly or thoroughly understand its meaning through any learning or subtle reflections of his own, for all words and all that can be learned or understood in a creaturely manner are alien to and far beneath the truth which I mean. However, a person who is united with God and enlightened in this truth can understand the truth through itself. To comprehend and understand God as he is in himself, above and beyond all likenesses, is to be God with God, without intermediary or any element of otherness which could constitute an obstacle or impediment. I therefore beseech everyone who does not understand this or feel it in the blissful unity of his spirit not to take offense at it but simply to let it be as it is. What I want to say is true; Christ, the eternal truth, said it himself at many places in his teaching, if only we are able to manifest and express it well. Whoever, then, wishes to understand it must have died to himself and be living in God and must turn his gaze to that eternal light which is shining in the ground of his spirit, where the hidden truth is revealing itself without intermediary.

PART ONE: "SEE."

Our heavenly Father wishes us to see, for he is the Father of light (cf. Jas 1:17). Accordingly, in the hidden depths of our spirit he eternally, ceaselessly, and without intermediary utters a single, fathomless word, and only that word. In this word he gives utterance to himself and all things. This word, which is none other than "See," is the generation and birth of the Son, the eternal light, in whom all blessedness is seen and known.

If our spirit is to contemplate God with God without intermediary in this divine light, three things are necessary. The first is that a person must be exteriorly well ordered, interiorly unhindered, and as empty of all his exterior works as if he were not even performing them, for if he is interiorly disturbed through any virtuous work he will be troubled by images, and as long as this lasts he will not be able to contemplate. Secondly, he must interiorly cleave to God with devoted intention and love, just as if he were a burning, glowing fire which can never be extinguished. As long as he feels himself to be in this state, he will be able to contemplate. Thirdly, he must lose himself in a state devoid of particular form or measure, a state of darkness in which all contemplatives blissfully lose their way and are never again able to find themselves in a creaturely way.

In the abyss of this darkness in which the loving spirit has died to itself, God's revelation and eternal life have their origin, for in this darkness an incomprehensible light is born and shines forth; this is the Son of God, in whom a person becomes able to see and to contemplate eternal life. This divine light is shed upon a person in the simple being of his spirit, where the spirit receives the resplendence which is God himself above and beyond all gifts and creaturely activity in the empty idleness of the spirit, where the spirit has lost itself in blissful love and receives God's resplendence without intermediary. The spirit ceaselessly becomes the very resplendence which it receives. See, this hidden resplendence, in which a person contemplates all that he desires in accordance with his spirit's mode of emptiness, is so great a resplendence that the loving contemplative neither sees nor feels in the ground of his being, in which he is at rest, anything other than an incomprehensible light. In the simple bareness which envelops all things, he feels and finds himself to be nothing other than the same light with which he sees.

This is the first point, describing how a person is made capable of seeing in the divine light. Blessed are the eyes that see in this way, for they possess eternal life.

PART TWO: "THE BRIDEGROOM IS COMING."

When we have thus become able to see, we can joyfully contemplate the eternal coming of our Bridegroom, which is the second point of which we wish to speak. What is this eternal coming of our Bridegroom? It is a new birth and a new illumination which knows no interruption, for the ground out of which the resplendence shines forth and which is the resplendence itself is both living and fruitful. The revelation of the eternal light is therefore ceaselessly renewed in the hidden depths of the spirit. See, all creaturely activity and all exercises of virtue must here cease, for here God works himself alone in the most sublime nobility of the spirit, where there is only an eternal contemplating of and gazing at the light with the light and in the light. The coming of the Bridegroom is so fast that he has always come and is always abiding with fathomless richness and yet is personally and ceaselessly coming anew with such new resplendence that it seems as if he had never previously come. This is because his coming occurs beyond time in an eternal now, which is ever received with new pleasure and new joy.

See, the delight and joy which the Bridegroom brings at his coming is fathomless and without measure, for it is his very self. For this reason the spirit's eyes, with which it contemplates and gazes at its Bridegroom, are opened so wide that they will never again be closed, for the spirit's gaze and contemplation remain eternally caught up in God's hidden revelation, and the spirit's capacity for comprehending is opened so wide for the coming of the Bridegroom that the spirit itself becomes the very breadth which it comprehends. In this way God is comprehended and seen with God; in this lies all our blessedness.

This is the second point, describing how we ceaselessly receive the eternal coming of our Bridegroom into our spirit.

PART THREE: "GO OUT."

A. OUR ETERNAL BEING IN GOD
BEFORE OUR CREATION IN TIME

The Spirit of God now speaks within our own spirit in its hidden immersion: "Go out, into a state of eternal contemplation and blissful enjoyment after God's own manner." All the richness which is in God by nature is something which we lovingly possess in God—and God in us—through the infinite love which is the Holy Spirit. In this love a person savors all that he can desire. By means of this love we have died to ourselves and through a loving immersion of ourselves have gone out into a state of darkness devoid of particular form. There the spirit is caught up in the embrace of the Holy Trinity and eternally abides within the superessential Unity in a state of rest and blissful enjoyment. In this same Unity, considered now as regards its fruitfulness, the Father is in the Son and the Son in the Father, while all creatures are in them both. This is beyond the distinction

148

of Persons, for here we can only make distinctions of reason between fatherhood and sonship in the living fecundity of the divine nature.

This is the origin and beginning of an eternal going forth and an eternal activity which is without beginning, for it is a beginning without beginning. Since the almighty Father has perfectly comprehended himself in the ground of his fruitfulness, the Son, who is the Father's eternal Word, goes forth as another Person within the Godhead. Through this eternal birth all creatures have gone forth eternally before their creation in time. God has thus seen and known them in himself—as distinct in his living ideas and as different from himself, though not different in every respect, for all that is in God is God.

This eternal going forth and this eternal life which we eternally have and are in God apart from ourselves is a cause of our created being in time. Our created being depends upon this eternal being and is one with it in its essential subsistence. This eternal being and life which we have and are in God's eternal wisdom is like God, for it both abides eternally and without distinction in the divine essence and, through the birth of the Son, flows forth eternally as a distinct entity, its distinctness being in accordance with God's eternal idea of it. In these two ways it is so like God that he ceaselessly knows and expresses himself in this likeness as regards both the divine essence and the Persons. Although there are here distinctions and differences of a rational kind, this likeness is nevertheless one with the very image of the Holy Trinity which is the wisdom of God, in which God contemplates himself and all things in an eternal now that has no before or after. He sees himself and all things in a single act of seeing; this is God's image and likeness as well as our image and likeness, for in this act God expresses both himself and all things. In this divine image all creatures have an eternal life apart from themselves, as in their eternal Exemplar.

B. ATTAINING OUR ETERNAL IMAGE
IN THE CONTEMPLATIVE LIFE

It is to this eternal image and likeness that the Holy Trinity has created us. God therefore wills that we go out from ourselves into this divine light, supernaturally pursuing this image which is our own life and possessing it with him both actively and blissfully in a state of eternal blessedness. We will find that the bosom of the Father is our own ground and origin, in which our life and being have their beginning. From out of this ground, that is, from out of the Father and all that lives in him, there shines an eternal resplendence, which is the birth of the Son. In this resplendence, that is, in the Son, the Father is himself revealed together with all that lives in him, for he gives to the Son all that he is and all that he has, with the single exception of the property of fatherhood, which he retains himself. For this reason all that in the Father lives still concealed in unity lives also in the Son as having flowed forth in open manifestation; so too, the simple ground of our eternal image constantly abides in a state of darkness devoid of particular form, while the infinite resplendence which shines forth from there reveals and manifests the hidden mystery of God in particular forms.

All persons who have been raised above their creaturely state into the contemplative life are one with this divine resplendence and are this re-splendence itself. Through this divine light—and as regards their un-created being—they see, feel, and find themselves to be the same simple ground from out of which the resplendence shines without measure in a divine way and in which it eternally abides devoid of particular form according to the simplicity of the divine essence. For this reason interior, con-templative persons will go out in accordance with the mode of their contemplation, above and beyond reason and distinction and their own cre-ated being. Through an eternal act of gazing accomplished by means of the inborn light, they are transformed and become one with that same light with which they see and which they see. It is in this way that contempla-tives pursue the eternal image to which they have been created; they con-template God and all things without distinction in a simple act of seeing in the divine resplendence.

This is the noblest and most beneficial contemplation which a person can attain in this life, for in such contemplation a person remains free and master of himself in the best possible way. With each loving movement within, he is able to grow in nobility of life beyond anything that is hu-manly understandable: He remains free and master of himself in the prac-tice of the interior life and of virtue; in addition, his gazing into the divine light raises him above all interiority, all virtue, and all acquisition of merit, for it is the crown and reward to which we aspire and which we now have and possess in a certain way, for the contemplative life is a heavenly life. If, however, we were set free from this present exile, we would have a still greater capacity in our creatureliness to receive this resplendence, and then God's glory would in every respect shine through us in a better and nobler way.

All this is the way above all ways in which a person goes out into a state of divine contemplation and an eternal act of gazing and in which he is transformed and formed over in the divine resplendence.

PART FOUR: "TO MEET HIM."

This going forth of a contemplative also takes place in love, for by means of blissful love he transcends his creaturely state and finds and savors the riches and delight which God is himself and which he causes ceaselessly to flow forth into the hidden depths of the spirit, where the spirit bears a likeness to God's own nobility.[20]

When an interior, contemplative person has thus attained his eternal image and, in this purity and by means of the Son, has possessed the Father's bosom, then he is enlightened with divine truth. He continually receives the eternal birth and goes out into a state of divine contemplation in accordance with the mode of the light. Here arises the fourth and last point, which is a meeting in love; it is in this more than anything else that our highest blessedness resides.

You should know that the heavenly Father, as a living ground and with all that lives in him, has turned actively toward his Son as toward his own eternal wisdom, and that this same wisdom, together with all that lives in it, has actively turned back toward the Father, that is, toward that same ground from which it comes forth. In this meeting between the Father and the Son there arises the third Person, the Holy Spirit, who is the love of them both and who is one with them in the same nature. In a way characterized by both activity and blissful enjoyment, the Spirit embraces and penetrates the Father and Son and all that lives in both of them with such great riches and joy that all creatures must remain silent before this, for the incomprehensible wonder which resides in this love eternally transcends the understanding of all creatures. But when a person understands this wonder and savors it without amazement, then has his spirit been raised above itself and been made one with the Spirit of God; it savors and sees—

---

20. The close parallelism between this fourth part of book three and the preceding third part should be noted. In part three, Ruusbroec writes that contemplatives "are transformed and become one with that same light with which they see and which they see," that light being the Son of God. In part four, there is a similar transformation—only this time through the Holy Spirit—whereby a person's spirit is "raised above itself and. . . made one with the Spirit of God," who is the love of the Father and Son. These two transformations are clearly on the level of what the mystic calls an "active meeting," characterized by distinction of Persons. In the same two parts of the book there is also a meeting or union that is not active, but "blissful," occurring "beyond distinction." In part three, contemplatives are said to feel themselves to be the same simple ground from out of which the divine resplendence shines forth but which itself is in a state of darkness, devoid of particular form, while in part four contemplatives are described as encompassed in "that dark stillness in which all lovers lose their way."

without measure, like God himself—the riches which it has itself become in the Unity of the living ground where it possesses itself in accordance with the mode of its uncreated being.

Now this blessed meeting is actively renewed in us without ceasing in accordance with God's own mode of being, for the Father gives himself to the Son and the Son to the Father in an eternal sense of well-being and a loving embrace. This is constantly renewed in the bond of love, for just as the Father ceaselessly sees all things anew in the birth of the Son, so too are all things loved anew by the Father and the Son in the flowing forth of the Holy Spirit. This is the active meeting of the Father and the Son, in which we are lovingly embraced by means of the Holy Spirit in eternal love.

Now this active meeting and this loving embrace are in their ground blissful and devoid of particular form, for the fathomless, modeless being of God is so dark and so devoid of particular form that it encompasses within itself all the divine modes and the activity and properties of the Persons in the rich embrace of the essential Unity; it thereby produces a divine state of blissful enjoyment in this abyss of the ineffable. Here there is a blissful crossing over and a self-transcending immersion into a state of essential bareness, where all the divine names and modes and all the living ideas which are reflected in the mirror of divine truth all pass away into simple ineffability, without mode and without reason. In this fathomless abyss of simplicity all things are encompassed in a state of blissful blessedness, while the ground itself remains completely uncomprehended, unless it be through the essential Unity. Before this the Persons must give way, together with all that lives in God, for here there is nothing other than an eternal state of rest in a blissful embrace of loving immersion.

This is that modeless being which all fervent interior spirits have chosen above all things, that dark stillness in which all lovers lose their way. But if we could prepare ourselves through virtue in the ways I have shown, we would at once strip ourselves of our bodies and flow into the wild waves of the Sea, from which no creature could ever draw us back.

That we might blissfully possess the essential Unity and clearly contemplate the Unity in the Trinity—may the divine love grant us this, for it turns no beggar away. Amen. Amen.

THE SPARKLING STONE

INTRODUCTION: THE FOUR THINGS NECESSARY FOR A PERFECT LIFE

A person who wishes to live in the most perfect state within the holy Church must be someone who is zealous and good, who is interiorly fervent and spiritual, who is lifted up to the contemplation of God, and who goes forth to all in common. When these four things are found together in a person, then his state is perfect; he will constantly grow and increase in grace, in all the virtues, and in knowledge of the truth before God and all upright persons.

PART ONE: A SYNOPSIS OF THE FIRST THREE OF THESE POINTS

A. A GOOD PERSON

Now you should note three things which make a person good. The first thing which a person must have in order to be good is a purified conscience, free from any reproach of mortal sin. For this reason, whoever wishes to be good must examine himself with great care, starting from the time when he was first able to sin. He must be cleansed of sins committed from that time onward in accordance with the precepts and customs of the holy Church. The second thing which makes a person good is the need to obey God, the holy Church, and his own conscience in all things. He must be equally obedient to all three. If he is, he will live without doubt or anxiety and will remain constantly free of interior reproach in all his works. The third thing which is proper to every good person is that he primarily intends God's glory in all his works. But if because of restlessness in the multiplicity of his activities he does not keep God constantly before his eyes, then at least he must intend and desire to live according to God's holy will.

These three things, when possessed in this way, make a person good. Whoever lacks a single one of them is not a good person and does not abide in God's grace. But whenever a person resolves in his heart to bring about these three things in his own life, then in that very moment—regardless of how evil he was previously—he becomes a good person, open to God and full of God's grace.

B. A SPIRITUAL PERSON

If this good person is to go on and become an interiorly fervent and spiritual person, then three further things are necessary: The first is a heart unencumbered by images; the second is spiritual freedom in his desires; and the third is an experience of interior union with God. Now everyone who considers himself spiritual should examine himself.

Whoever wishes to have his heart unencumbered by images must not possess anything with affection, and in associating with others he must not cleave to anyone with voluntary attachment, for all association and affection which are not purely for the sake of God's glory encumber a person's heart with images, since such association and affection are born not of God but of flesh (cf. Jn 1:13). For this reason, if a person is to become spiritual he must renounce all fleshly affection and cleave to God alone with longing and affection, possessing God in this way. All encumbrance from images and all inordinate affection for creatures are thereby driven away. By possessing God with affection a person is interiorly set free from images, for God is a spirit whom no one can properly represent through images. In his exercises a person should make use of good images, such as our Lord's passion and anything else which can stir a person to greater devotion; in possessing God, however, a person must descend to that imageless bareness which is God himself. This is the first thing necessary for a spiritual life and is its very foundation.

The second thing is interior freedom, which means that a person can be raised to God in all his interior exercises without hindrance and without the encumbrance of images. Such exercises are thanksgiving, praise, worship, devout prayers, fervent affection, and all the other things which longing and affection can bring about with the help of God's grace and fervent zeal for all spiritual exercises.

By means of these interior exercises a person attains the third thing necessary for a spiritual life, which is that he experiences spiritual union with God. Whoever, then, in his interior exercises ascends freely and without images to his God and intends nothing but God's glory will savor God's goodness and will experience true interior union with God. It is in this union that an interior, spiritual life reaches its perfection, for from this union a person's desire is touched ever anew and awakened to new interior works, while in this very activity the spirit ascends to new states of union. In this way, activity and union are constantly renewed, and this renewal in work and in union constitutes a spiritual life.

You can thus see how a person becomes good through moral virtues and an upright intention and how he becomes spiritual through interior virtues and union with God. Without these things a person can be neither good nor spiritual.

C. A CONTEMPLATIVE

You should also know that if this spiritual person is to become a contemplative three more things are necessary: The first is that he must experience the depth of his being as having no ground and must possess it in this way; the second is that his exercises must be devoid of particular form or measure; and the third is that his turning within himself must be characterized by the enjoyment of God. Now take care to understand, you who wish to live in the spirit, for it is to you alone that I am speaking.

The union with God which a spiritual person experiences whenever this union becomes manifest to his spirit is one which is without ground, that is, it is infinitely deep, infinitely high, and infinitely long and wide. In this very manifestation a person's spirit realizes that, by means of love, it has itself been immersed in this depth, raised to this height, and sent forth into this length. It feels itself to be wandering in this breadth, living in this unknown knowledge, and—through this intimate experience of union—immersed in unity, even as, through all its dying, it feels itself to be immersed in the life of God and to be one single life with God. This is the first thing necessary for a contemplative life and is its very foundation.

This gives rise to the second thing, which is that a person's exercises are above reason and without particular form, for God's Unity, which every contemplative spirit possesses in love, eternally calls and draws the divine Persons and all loving spirits into its own self. Everyone who loves experiences this attraction—in a greater or lesser degree according to the measure of his love and the nature of his exercises. Whoever perceives this attraction and abides in it cannot fall into mortal sin. But a contemplative, who has renounced himself and all things and who experiences no contrary pull inasmuch as he possesses nothing as his own but remains empty of all things, can constantly enter the inmost part of his spirit in a state of bareness and freedom from images. There an eternal light is revealed to him, and in this light he experiences the eternal call of God's Unity. He also feels himself to be an eternal fire of love, which desires above all else to be one with God. The more he perceives this attraction and call, the more he feels it, and the more he feels it, the more he desires to be one with God, for he desires to pay the debt which God demands of him.

The eternal call of God's Unity creates in the spirit an eternal fire of love. But when the spirit ceaselessly pays its debt, an eternally consuming fire is enkindled within it, for in the transformation brought about by God's Unity all spirits come to nought in their works and feel only that they are being consumed by the fire of God's simple Unity. No one can experience or possess this simple Unity of God unless he stands before God in measureless resplendence and in a love that is above reason and devoid of particular form. By standing before God in this way the spirit feels within itself an eternal fire of love. In this fire it finds neither beginning nor end and feels itself to be one with this fire of love. The spirit remains constantly on fire within itself, for its love is eternal; it also feels that it is constantly being consumed in the fire of love, for it has been drawn into and transformed by the Unity of God. If the spirit observes itself when it is on fire in love, it will be aware of distinction and difference between itself and God; but when it is consumed in this fire, then it is onefold and without distinction and accordingly feels nothing but unity, for the measureless flame of God's love consumes and devours all that it can enfold in its own self.

You can thus see that this Unity of God which draws all things to itself is nothing other than a love which has no ground and which lovingly draws the Father and the Son and all that lives in them into a state of eternal enjoyment. In this love we will ceaselessly burn and be consumed by fire for all eternity, for in this lies the blessedness of all spirits. For this reason we must place our entire life on the foundation of a groundless abyss. Then we will be able to plunge eternally in love and immerse ourselves in a depth which has no ground. Through the same love we will ascend and transcend ourselves as we rise to an incomprehensible height. In this formless love we will wander about, and it will lead us to the measureless breadth of God's love. In it we will flow forth and flow out of ourselves into the uncomprehended abundance of God's riches and goodness. In it we will also melt and be dissolved, revolve and be eternally whirled around in the maelstrom of God's glory.

Through each of these images I have shown a contemplative what his being and his exercises are like. No one else can understand this, for a contemplative life cannot be taught to others. But whenever the eternal truth is revealed in the spirit, then all things necessary are taught.

PART TWO: PARTICULAR POINTS ABOUT THE CONTEMPLATIVE LIFE

A. INTRODUCTORY REMARKS ON THE SYMBOLISM OF THE SPARKLING STONE

The Spirit of God therefore says in St. John's Book of Revelation: "To the one who overcomes"—that is, to the one who overcomes and transcends himself and all things—"I will give the hidden bread of heaven"—that is, an interior, hidden savor and heavenly joy—"and I will give him a sparkling stone. On this stone a new name will be written, unknown to everyone except him who receives it" (Rv 2:17). This stone is called a pebble because it is so small, for even if a person steps upon it, it does not hurt. This stone is shining bright and is as red as a fiery flame; it is small, round, smooth all over, and very light.

By this sparkling stone we mean our Lord Jesus Christ, for according to his divinity he is a beam of the eternal light, a ray of God's glory, and a spotless mirror in which all things have their life. Whoever overcomes and transcends all things is given this sparkling stone, through which he receives light, truth, and life. The stone is also like a fiery flame, for the fiery love of the eternal Word has filled the whole world with love and wishes all loving spirits to be consumed in the fire of love. This stone is also so small that a person scarcely feels it when he treads it underfoot. For this reason it is called a *calculus*, that is, a pebble. This is what St. Paul means when he says that the Son of God emptied himself and made himself lowly, taking the form of a slave and becoming obedient even to death on the cross (Phil 2:7–8). The Lord himself says through the mouth of the Prophet: "I am a worm and not a man, the scorn of men and an outcast of the people"

(Ps 22:7). He made himself so small in this temporal order that the Jews trod him underfoot and did not even feel it, for if they had recognized God's Son they would not have dared crucify him. He is still small and unrecognized in the hearts of all who do not love him. This noble stone of which I am speaking is also completely round and equally smooth all over. Its roundness teaches us that the divine truth has neither beginning nor end, while the fact that it is smooth and even all over teaches us that he will weigh all things evenly and give to each according to his deserts; whatever each is given will be his eternally. The last characteristic of this stone which I will consider is the fact that it is especially light, for the eternal Word of the Father has no weight, even though it bears up heaven and earth by its power. It is equally near all things, even though no one can overtake it, for it transcends and precedes all creatures and reveals itself where it wills and to whom it wills. In and through its lightness our heavy human nature has risen above all the heavens and sits crowned at the right hand of the Father.

This, then, is the sparkling stone which is given to a contemplative; on it is written a new name, unknown to everyone except him who receives it. You should know that all spirits receive a name when they return to God—each a special name in accordance with the nobility of its service and the depth of its love. This name is different from that first name of innocence which we received at baptism and which is adorned with the merits of our Lord. Having lost that name of innocence through sin, if we still wish to follow God—especially through three works which he desires to work in us—then we will be baptized a second time in the Holy Spirit. It is then that we will receive a new name, which will remain with us for eternity.

B. GOD'S UNIVERSAL CALL TO UNION WITH HIM

Now understand the free works of our Lord which he works in everyone who is open to them. The first of these, which God works in all persons in common, is that he calls and invites them all to union with him. As long as a sinner ignores this call, he must do without all the other gifts of God which would follow it.

JOHN RUUSBROEC

THE FIVE KINDS OF SINNERS
WHO IGNORE THIS CALL

I have observed that all sinners are divided into five groups. The first consists of those who are careless of good works. They wish to live in bodily comfort according to the desires of their senses and so are caught up in the world's busyness and in the manifold concerns of the heart. None of these are capable of receiving God's grace, and even if they were they would not be able to retain it.

The second group is made up of those who have knowingly and deliberately fallen into mortal sin. At the same time they also perform good works, constantly stand in fear and awe of God, love those who are good, and in a spirit of trust request their prayers. Nevertheless, they will remain unworthy of God's grace as long as their turning from God and their attachment to sin overcome and outweigh their love and their turning to God.

The third group of sinners consists of all unbelievers and of those who err in their faith. Whatever good works they perform and whatever way of life they lead, without faith they cannot be pleasing to God, for true faith is the foundation of all holiness and virtue.

The fourth group is comprised of those who fearlessly and shamelessly live in the state of mortal sin and who pay no attention to God or his gifts or any virtue. They regard the entire spiritual life as hypocrisy and deceit. They do not wish to have anything said to them about God or virtue, for they have firmly adopted the position that there is no God and no heaven or hell. They accordingly wish to know about nothing except what they actually feel or have present before them. Such persons are all rejected and scorned by God, for they are sinning against the Holy Spirit. They can nevertheless be converted, but this comes about only rarely and with difficulty.

The fifth group of sinners is made up of hypocrites, those who perform exterior good works not for God's glory or for their own salvation but rather to acquire a reputation for holiness or some fleeting thing. Although they seem good and holy exteriorly, interiorly they are false and turned away from God, lacking in God's grace and every virtue.

OVERCOMING SIN WITH
THE HELP OF GOD'S GRACE

I have thus described for you five groups of sinners who have all been called to union with God. But as long as a sinner wishes to remain in the service of sin, he remains deaf and blind and is incapable of tasting or feeling all the good things which God desires to work in him. If, however, the sinner enters into himself, and if upon doing so he becomes displeased with his sinful life, then he begins to draw near to God. If he wishes to respond to God's call and invitation, he must freely resolve to forsake sin and do penance. In this way he will come to be of one mind and one will with God and will receive God's grace.

Accordingly, we will first of all look upon God and see that out of his gratuitous goodness he ceaselessly calls and invites all persons—both good and bad, without exception—to union with himself. Secondly, we will experience God's grace as flowing forth to everyone who responds to God's call. Thirdly, we will clearly realize and understand in our own being that we can become one life and one spirit with God, provided that we deny ourselves in all things and follow God's grace to the highest point to which it leads us, for God's grace works in an orderly way within every person, in accordance with the measure and manner in which he is able to receive it. This means that through the universal working of God's grace every sinner receives the wisdom and strength to forsake sin and turn to virtue, provided that he wishes to do so. By means of the hidden cooperation of God's grace, every good person is able to overcome every sin, resist every temptation, fulfill every virtue, and persevere in the highest state of perfection, if only he is submissive to the grace of God in all things. All that we are and all that we have received both from without and from within are the free gifts of God. For these we ought to thank him and with these we ought to serve him if we are to be pleasing to him. But there are some gifts of God which are an aid to and an occasion of virtue for the good, whereas for the wicked they are an aid to and an occasion of sin; such gifts are health, beauty, wisdom, riches, and worldly honor. These are the lowest and least valuable of God's gifts, ones which he gives for the benefit of all—both his friends and enemies, both the good and the wicked. With these gifts the good serve God and his friends, while the wicked serve the world, their flesh, and the devil.

DIFFERENCES AMONG THOSE WHO RECEIVE GOD'S GIFTS AND RESPOND TO HIS CALL

Hired servants and faithful servants

You should also observe that some persons receive God's gifts as his hired servants, while others do so as his faithful servants.[1] These differ from one another in all their interior activities, that is, in love, in intention, in feeling, and in all the works and exercises of the interior life.

Now note well what follows: All who love themselves so inordinately that they do not wish to serve God except for the sake of their own profit and reward cut themselves off from God and live bound up in self-love, since they seek and intend themselves in all they do. In all their prayers and good works they seek temporal things or else strive after eternal things for the sake of their own advantage and benefit. Such persons have an inordinate devotion to themselves and accordingly remain always alone, for they lack that authentic love which would unite them with God and all his beloved. Although such persons appear to keep the law and commandments of God and of the holy Church, they do not keep the law of love, for everything they do is done of necessity and not out of love; that is, they act only to avoid damnation. Because they are interiorly unfaithful, they dare not trust God, so their entire interior life is one of doubt and fear, toil and misery. On the right side they see eternal life, which they are afraid of losing, and on the left they see the eternal pains of hell, which they are afraid of receiving. All the prayer and labor and good works which they can perform in order to dispel this fear are of no avail, for the more inordinately they love themselves, the more they fear hell. It is in this that you can see how their fear of hell arises from their self-love.

Now the Prophet and also the Book of Wisdom say: "The fear of God is the beginning of wisdom" (Ps 111:10; Prv 1:7). By this is meant the fear which is exercised on the right side, the fear of losing one's eternal blessedness, for such fear arises from everyone's natural inclination to be blessed, that is, to see God. Therefore, even if a person is unfaithful toward God, if he observes himself from within he will feel this inclination drawing him out of himself to that blessedness which is God. He will fear losing this blessedness, for he loves himself more than God and loves blessedness in a misguided way, namely, for his own sake. It is for this reason that he does not dare trust God. Nevertheless it is written that the fear of the Lord is the beginning of wisdom as well as a law for the unfaithful servants of God, for it compels a person to forsake sin, to strive after virtue, and to perform good works, and these things prepare a person exteriorly to receive God's grace and become a faithful servant.

---

1. The kinds of distinctions Ruusbroec will draw among hired servants, faithful servants, secret friends, and hidden sons are rather common in earlier Christian texts. For example, both John Cassian (*Collationes* 11.7) and St. Bernard (*De diligendo Deo*, ch. 12–14) discuss the differences among slaves (*servi*), hirelings (*mercenarii*), and sons (*filii*).

In that very hour when, with God's help, a person is able to overcome his self-love—that is, when he becomes so empty of himself that he dares trust in God for all that he needs—he pleases God so much by doing this that God gives him his grace. Through this grace he experiences genuine love, and this love drives away doubt and fear and makes the person trust and hope. In this way he becomes a faithful servant and comes to love God and direct his mind to him in all he does. This is the difference between a faithful servant and an unfaithful one.

Faithful servants and secret friends

We can also observe what a great difference there is between the faithful servants and the secret friends of God. By means of God's help and grace, the faithful servants resolve to keep God's commandments, that is, to be obedient to God and to the holy Church in all kinds of virtue and good behavior. This is called an exterior life or an active life. But the secret friends of God resolve to keep not only God's commandments but also his lifegiving counsel, that is, to maintain a loving and fervent adherence to God for the sake of his eternal glory, together with a voluntary renunciation of everything apart from God on which a person could set his desire and affection. God calls and invites such friends to turn within, giving them powers of discernment in interior exercises and revealing to them the many hidden ways of leading a spiritual life. On the other hand, God sends his servants outward, so that they might faithfully serve him and his people in all manner of exterior good works. In this way God bestows his grace and his aid according to each person's ability to receive them, that is, according to each person's degree of conformity with God, whether in exterior good works or in the interior exercises of love.

Now no one can accomplish or experience these interior exercises unless he is wholly and entirely turned inward toward God, for as long as a person has a divided heart he is always looking outward and is unstable of mind, easily swayed by the pleasures and pains of temporal matters, since these are still alive in him. Although he keeps God's commandments, he constantly remains interiorly unenlightened, ignorant of what interior exercises are and how they are to be practiced. Since he knows and feels that he has his mind directed to God and desires to do his holy will in all his works, he allows himself to be satisfied with this, for he finds himself to be free of hypocrisy in his intentions and faithful in his service. He is pleased with himself because of these two points and thinks that exterior good works performed with an upright intention are holier and more beneficial than interior exercises, since with God's help he has chosen an active way of life. He accordingly devotes himself more to performing exterior works with clear discernment than to showing interior affection toward him for whose sake he performs such works. This is why his mind is filled more with images of the works he performs than with God, for whose sake he does them. Because he is so filled with images in his works, he remains an exterior kind of person and is incapable of responding to God's counsel. His exercises are more exterior than interior, more sensual than spiritual. Even though in matters of exterior service he is our Lord's faithful servant, what God's secret friends experience is hidden from and unknown to him.

This is why some insensitive and outwardly turned persons are always criticizing and reproving those who are turned inward, for they think that the latter are guilty of idleness. This was why Martha complained to our Lord about her sister Mary because she was not helping her serve (Lk 10:38–42). It seemed to Martha that she was herself performing a great and useful service while her sister just sat idly by. But our Lord judged between the two of them. He did not blame Martha for her service, for that was good and useful, but rather for her anxiety and for being troubled and oppressed by the multiplicity of her exterior works. But Mary he praised because of her interior exercises, for he said that one thing was necessary and that she had chosen the better part, which would not be taken from her.

This one thing which is necessary for everyone is divine love, and the better part is an interior life marked by a loving adherence to God. This is what Mary Magdalen chose and it is also what God's secret friends choose. Martha, however, chose an exterior, active life that was free of hypocrisy, and this is the other part or way by which a person may serve God—but it is less good and less perfect. This is the part that the faithful servants choose for love of our Lord.

Now there are some foolish persons who want to be so idle that they do not wish to act or be of service when their neighbor is in need. These persons are neither secret friends nor faithful servants of our Lord but are completely false and deceived, for no one can follow God's counsel if he is not willing to keep God's commandments. For this reason, our Lord's secret friends are always his faithful servants in cases of need, though not all the faithful servants are secret friends, for the exercises which characterize the latter may be unknown to them. I have thus shown you the difference between the secret friends and the faithful servants of our Lord.

THE SPARKLING STONE

Secret friends and hidden sons

There is another difference that can be observed, one which is deeper and more subtle, namely, that which exists between the secret friends and the hidden sons of God. Through their interior exercises these two groups do indeed stand equally upright in God's presence. There is, however, a certain self-centered quality to the interiority of the friends. They choose their loving adherence to God as the best and highest state which they can or wish to attain; for this reason they cannot transcend themselves or their works so as to reach a state of imageless bareness, for their works and their very selves constitute an image and intermediary. Even though they feel a union with God in their loving adherence to him, still they constantly find distinction and otherness in this union between themselves and God, for that simple passing over into a state of bareness devoid of images is neither known nor loved by them. The highest level of their interior life is accordingly always marked by reasonings and particular forms. Even though they have a clear understanding of all genuine virtues and possess the power of distinguishing among them, that simple gaze with open mind into the divine resplendence remains hidden from them. Even though they feel themselves to be raised up to God in the strong fire of love, they retain something of their own self and so are not consumed and burnt to nought in the unity of love. Even though they wish to live constantly in God's service and please him forever, they do not wish to die in God to all the self-centeredness of their spirit and to lead a life completely conformable with God. Even though they attach little weight and importance to all the consolations and rest which might come to them from without, they attach great importance to God's gifts and their own interior works—the consolations and sweetness which they experience from within. They thus rest along the way and do not fully die so as to attain the highest victory in a love which is bare and devoid of particular form. Even if they could practice and know with clear discernment all the fullness of lovingly cleaving to God and all the interior paths of ascent which one could practice in God's presence, nevertheless they could not discover or come to know that formless passing over and that rich wandering in superessential love whose beginning and end, whose way and manner can never be found.

There is, therefore, a great difference between the secret friends and the hidden sons of God, for the friends experience within themselves nothing more than a loving, life-giving ascent which is marked by particular forms, while over and above this the sons experience a simple, deathlike passing over into a state devoid of form. The interior life of our Lord's friends is an upward-tending exercise of love in which they wish to remain forever, along with something of themselves, but they experience nothing of how a person possesses God through bare love in emptiness of self, above and beyond all exercises. Still, they are constantly ascending to God in true faith, awaiting God and their eternal blessedness with genuine hope, and cleaving to God and staying anchored in him through perfect charity. Accordingly, things go well for them, for they are pleasing to God and God is in turn pleasing to them.

Such persons are nevertheless not assured of eternal life, for they have not yet entirely died in God to themselves and to their self-centeredness. To be sure, all who remain steadfast in their exercises and in that turning to God upon which they have resolved have been chosen by God from all eternity and have had their names and works eternally inscribed in the living book of God's providence. But those who choose other things, who turn their inward gaze from God to sin and to whatever is opposed to God, and who remain in this state suffer a different outcome: Even though their names were known and inscribed by God because of the righteousness which they had practiced in an earlier period of time, since they did not persevere in this until death their names are stricken from the Book of Life and they will never again be able to savor God or any of the fruits of virtue.

It is for this reason incumbent upon all of us to examine ourselves carefully and to have our turning to God adorned with fervent interior affection and with exterior good works. We will then be able to look forward with hope and joy to God's judgment and to the coming of our Lord Jesus Christ. If, however, we could renounce ourselves and all self-centeredness in our works, then with our bare and imageless spirit we would transcend all things and in this bareness be led directly by the working of God's Spirit. We would then experience with certainty that we were perfect sons of God, for God's Apostle St. Paul says that all who are led by the Spirit of God are sons of God (Rom 8:14).

Nevertheless you should know that all faithful and good persons are the sons of God, for they have all been born of God's Spirit, who lives in them and moves and impels each one in a particular way—according to his capability—to the virtues and good works through which a person becomes pleasing to God. Because of the inequality in the ways they turn to God and in their exercises, I call some of them faithful servants, others secret friends, and still others hidden sons; yet they are all servants, all friends, and all sons, for they all serve, love, and direct their minds to the one God and they all live and act out of God's free Spirit. God permits and allows his friends to do or to refrain from doing anything which is not against his commandments, for those who are bound by God's counsel have this bond itself as a commandment. Accordingly, no one is disobedient or contrary to God except a person who does not keep his commandments, for we must do or refrain from doing all the things which God commands or forbids in Scripture or in the holy Church or in our conscience; otherwise we are disobedient and lose God's grace. But as for the faults which we commit daily, both God and our reason bear with these, for we cannot avoid them. Such faults do not make us disobedient, for they do not drive away God's grace or our interior peace. Still, we should constantly be sorry for such faults, however small they are, and guard against them as best we can.

With this I have explained for you what I said at the beginning, namely, that everyone must in all things be obedient to God, to the holy Church, and to his own conscience, for I do not want anyone to be wrongly offended by my words. I hereby let stand all that I have said.

C. THE NATURE OF THE CONTEMPLATIVE LIFE AND HOW WE ENTER IT

"But," you say, "I would very much like to know how we become hidden sons of God and attain the contemplative life." Well, I have reflected on this in the following way.

DYING IN GOD THROUGH FAITH AND LOVE

As I have said already, we must always live and be attentive in the practice of all the virtues, while above and beyond all virtues we must pass away and die in God. In other words, we must die to sin and be born of God into a life of virtue, and we must deny ourselves and die in God into an eternal life. All this occurs in the following order:

If we have been born of God's Spirit, then we are sons of grace. Our entire life is accordingly adorned with virtues, so that we overcome all that is contrary to God; as St. John says, "Everyone born of God overcomes the world" (1 Jn 5:4). In and through this birth all good persons become the sons of God. The Spirit of God enkindles and moves each such person

169

in a special way toward those virtues and those good works for which he is ready and capable. Thus these persons are all pleasing to God, each in a special way according to the greatness of his love and the nobility of his exercises. Nevertheless they do not feel that they have securely attained God or been assured of eternal life, for they can still turn away and fall into sin. I therefore call such persons servants or friends rather than sons.

But when we rise above ourselves and in our ascent to God become so unified that bare love can envelop us at that high level where love itself acts, above and beyond all virtuous exercises—that is, in our source, out of which we have been spiritually born—we will then come to nought, dying in God to ourselves and to all that is our own. In this death we become hidden sons of God and discover in ourselves a new life, which is eternal. It is of these sons that St. Paul speaks: "You are dead, and your life is hidden with Christ in God" (Col 3:3).

Now the order in which all this takes place is as follows: In our approach to God we must carry before us all our works and our very selves as an eternal offering to God, while when we enter God's presence we will leave behind ourselves and all our works. Dying in love, we will transcend all our creatureliness and attain to God's superessential richness. There we will possess God in an eternal dying to ourselves. The Spirit of God speaks of this in the Book of Revelation: "Blessed are the dead who die in the Lord" (Rv 14:13). Rightly does he call the dead blessed, for in remaining eternally dead they have immersed themselves in the blissful Unity of God and are constantly dying anew in love through the transforming power of that same Unity as it draws them to itself. Moreover, the Spirit of God also says: "They will rest from their labors, and their works will follow them" (Rv 14:13). In that condition marked by particular forms in which we find ourselves when we have been born of God into a spiritual and virtuous way of life, we carry our works before us as an offering to God. But in that formless state in which we die in God into an eternal and blessed life, our good works follow us, for they are one life with us. In our approach to God through the virtues God lives in us, but when we have transcended ourselves and all things it is we who live in God. If we have faith, hope, and love, then we have received God and he is living in us together with his grace. He sends us forth as his faithful servants to keep his commandments and calls us back to himself as his secret friends, provided that we follow his counsel. And if we live contrary to the ways of the world, he openly reveals us as being his sons. But above all else, if we are to savor God or experience eternal life within ourselves, we must enter God through our faith, above reason.

THE SPARKLING STONE

Being Transformed through the Eternal Word

There we will abide—unified, empty, and imageless—raised up through love to the open bareness of our mind, for when we transcend all things in love and die to all rational observations in a dark state of unknowing, we become transformed through the working of the eternal Word, who is an image of the Father. In the empty being of our spirit we receive an incomprehensible resplendence which envelops and pervades us in the same way that the air is pervaded by the light of the sun. This resplendence is nothing other than an act of gazing and seeing which has no ground: What we are is what we see, and what we see is what we are, for our mind, our life, and our very being are raised up in a state of oneness and united with the truth which is God himself. In this simple act of seeing we are therefore one life and one spirit with God. This is what I call a contemplative life. When we cleave to God in love we are practicing what is called the better part, but when we gaze at our superessential being in the way just described we possess God whole and entire.

Characteristics of This Life

Modelessness

This contemplation is always accompanied by an exercise which is devoid of particular form or mode. This is a life in which we ourselves come to nought, for when we go out of ourselves into a dark, modeless state which has no ground, the simple ray of God's resplendence is always shining there. It is in this ray that we have our ground, and it draws us out of ourselves into our superessential being and into a state in which we are immersed in love. This immersion in love is always accompanied and followed by a modeless exercise of love, for love cannot stand idly by but wishes to know and savor thoroughly the fathomless riches which abide in the ground of its being. This is a hunger which is never satisfied. Constantly to strive after something and always fall short is to swim against the stream. One can neither leave it nor grasp it, neither do without it nor attain it, neither speak about it nor remain silent about it, for it is above reason and understanding and transcends all creatures. We can therefore not reach it or overtake it. We will, however, see into our inmost being, where we will experience God's Spirit driving and enkindling us in the restless-

171

ness of love. We will also see above ourselves, where we will experience God's Spirit drawing us out of ourselves and devouring us in his own self, that is, in that superessential love with which we are one and which we possess in a fuller and deeper way than anything else.

This possession is a simple, fathomless savoring of all that is good and of eternal life. In this savoring we are swallowed up above reason and apart from reason in the deep stillness of the Godhead, which is never moved. That this is so is something that can be known in no other way than by experience, for neither reason nor any exercise can come to know how or who or where or what this is. It is for this reason that our ensuing exercise always remains modeless, that is, without manner or particular form, for we can neither grasp nor understand the fathomless good which we savor and possess, nor can we ever enter into it of ourselves through our exercises. We are, therefore, poor in ourselves but rich in God, hungry and thirsty in ourselves but drunken and satisfied in God, active in ourselves but idle and empty of everything in God. We will remain thus for all eternity, for without the exercise of love we can never attain God; anyone who feels or believes differently is deceived.

One single life in God

We accordingly live wholly in God insofar as we are in possession of our blessedness, and we live wholly in ourselves insofar as we exercise ourselves in love of God. Even though we live wholly in God and wholly in ourselves, this is still only one life, though as regards our experience of it there are two opposite aspects, since poverty and riches, hunger and satisfaction, activity and idle emptiness, are complete opposites. Nevertheless our highest nobility lies precisely here, both now and for eternity. We cannot wholly become God and lose our creaturely state—that is impossible. But if we remained entirely in ourselves, separated from God, we would be miserable and deprived of salvation. We will therefore feel ourselves as being entirely in God and entirely in ourselves. Between these two feelings there is nothing but God's grace and the exercise of our love, for at the highest level of our experience God's resplendence shines upon us, teaching us the truth and moving us to every virtue and to an eternal love of God. We ceaselessly pursue this resplendence right into the ground from which it arises, where we experience nothing but the expiration of our spirit and the immersion of ourselves in a simple, groundless love from which we will never emerge.

THE SPARKLING STONE

Continuing reality of our immersion in God

If we could always remain there with our simple gaze, we would constantly experience this, for our immersion and transformation in God continues forever, without interruption, provided that we have gone out of ourselves and possess God in the immersion of love. If we do possess God in the immersion of love—that is, if we become lost to ourselves—then God is our own possession and we are his, eternally and irretrievably immersing ourselves in our own proper source, which is God himself. This immersion is essential and is characterized by habitual love.[2] It therefore continues whether we are asleep or awake and whether we are aware of it or not. This immersion accordingly does not earn for us any new degree of reward, but it maintains us in the possession of God and of all the good that we have already acquired.

This immersion is like a river, which constantly and without turning back flows into the sea, which is its proper resting place. In the same way, if we have come into the possession of God alone, then our essential immersion through habitual love is always and irreversibly flowing into an experience which is without ground. We possess this experience as our own resting place. If we were always simple and unified and if we always saw with the same wholeness of vision, we would always have the same experience.

Transformation through God's resplendence

Now this immersion takes place over and above all virtues and all exercises of love, for it consists in nothing other than an eternal going out of ourselves as we see clearly before us an otherness toward which we are inclined as toward a state of blessedness that lies outside ourselves. In other words, we feel an eternal inclination toward something which is different from what we are ourselves. This is the most intimate and hidden distinction which we can feel between ourselves and God, for beyond this there is no further difference.

Nevertheless our power of reason remains standing with its eyes open in darkness, that is, in a groundless state of unknowing. In this darkness the fathomless resplendence remains covered and hidden from us, for its

---

2. "Essential" is to be understood in its special Ruusbroeckian sense of referring to what is taking place at the inmost level of our being, the locus of immediate, loving union with God.

overwhelming groundlessness blinds our reason. It does, however, envelop us in simplicity and transform us through its own inmost self, so that our own activity is brought to nought by God and we are introduced into a state of loving immersion in which we possess our blessedness and are one with God.

Knowledge of this union with God

When we are thus united with God, there remains in us a life-giving knowledge and an active love, for without our own knowledge we cannot possess God and without the exercise of love we can neither be united nor remain united with God. If we could be blessed without our knowledge, then a rock, which possesses no knowledge, could likewise be blessed. If I were lord of all the earth but did not know it, what good would that be? We will accordingly always know and feel that we are savoring and possessing. Christ himself bears witness to this when he speaks of us to his Father in the following words: "This is eternal life, that they know you, the only true God, and him whom you have sent, Jesus Christ" (Jn 17:3). You can thus see that our eternal life lies in clear knowledge.[3]

D. OUR UNION WITH GOD IS NOT AN IDENTIFICATION: FOUR WAYS OF EXPERIENCING THIS UNION

I just said that we are one with God, something to which Scripture bears witness. I now wish to say that we must forever remain different from God, which is also taught us by Scripture. We must understand and experience both these points if we are to be on the right path. I therefore say that from the face of God and from our own most profound experience there shines upon our inner eye a resplendence which teaches us the truth about love and all the virtues. In this resplendence we are especially taught to experience God and ourselves in four ways.

---

3. These lines are a particularly clear instance of Ruusbroec's distance from those mystics who rigorously follow the *via negativa*, a point emphasized in the Introduction to this volume.

THE SPARKLING STONE

The First Way: Experiencing God within Us through His Grace

In the first way we experience God within us through his grace. When we become aware of this, we cannot remain idle, for just as the sun brightens and gladdens the world and makes it fruitful through its radiance and heat, so too does God act through his grace: He enlightens, gladdens, and makes fruitful everyone who wishes to obey him. If we would experience God within us and have the fire of his love burn within us forever, we must of our own free will help him enkindle it in four manners: We must remain united with the fire within us through interior fervor; we must go out of ourselves to all persons with fidelity and fraternal love; we must descend beneath ourselves through penitence, the performance of every kind of good work, and resistance to our inordinate desires; and in the flame of this fire we must rise above ourselves through works of devotion, thanksgiving, praise, and fervent prayer, even as we constantly cleave to God through an upright intention and felt affection.

God hereby remains dwelling in us through his grace, for in these four manners are contained all the exercises which we can practice with the help of reason in particular forms. No one can be pleasing to God without these exercises, and whoever is most perfect in practicing them is nearest to God. They are therefore necessary for everyone, and no one can rise above this level except a contemplative. In this first way we therefore experience God within us through his grace, provided we wish to belong to him.

The Second Way: Experiencing Ourselves as Embraced by God

Secondly, if we are living a contemplative life we will experience ourselves as living in God. From out of this life in which we experience ourselves as living in God, there shines upon our inner eye a resplendence which enlightens our reason and serves as an intermediary between ourselves and God. If with our enlightened reason we remain standing within ourselves in this resplendence, we will feel our created life in its essential being constantly being immersed in its eternal life. But when we follow this resplendence above and beyond reason with a simple gaze and a willing inclination of our very self right into our highest life, then we experience the transformation of our being in its entirety in God. We thus experience ourselves as being completely embraced by God.

JOHN RUUSBROEC

THE THIRD WAY: EXPERIENCING
OURSELVES AS ONE WITH GOD

There follows a third kind of experience, namely, that we feel ourselves to be one with God, for by means of our transformation in God we feel ourselves to be swallowed up in the groundless abyss of our eternal blessedness, in which we can never discover any difference between ourselves and God. This is the highest of all our experiences and can be experienced in no other way than by our being immersed in love. Accordingly, when we are raised up to and drawn into this highest of all our experiences, all our powers stand empty and idle in a state of essential enjoyment. They are not, however, annihilated, for in that case we would lose our creaturely status. As long as with open eyes and a spirit that is so inclined—but without rational reflection—we stand empty and idle, we can contemplate and enjoy.

THE FOURTH WAY: EXPERIENCING
AN EAGER CRAVING FOR GOD

At the very moment when we try to examine and observe what it is that we are experiencing, we slip back into the activity of reasoning, at which we become aware of distinction and difference between ourselves and God. We then find God to be outside us in all his incomprehensibility, and this constitutes the fourth way of experiencing God and ourselves. We here find ourselves standing in God's presence. The truth which we receive from his face bears witness to the fact that God wishes to be wholly ours and that he wishes us to be entirely his. At the very moment when we feel that God wishes to be wholly ours, there arises in us an amazed and eager craving which is so ravenous, so deep, and so empty that even if God gave us everything he could give—but without giving us himself—that could not satisfy us. In feeling that he has given and delivered himself to our unfettered desire, to enjoy him in every way we could possibly wish, and in learning—through the truth that comes to us from his face—that everything we savor is but a drop in the ocean compared with all that we still lack, our spirit is buffeted as in a storm by the heat and restlessness of love. The more we savor, the greater becomes our hunger and desire, for the one is the cause of the other. This makes us strive without attaining satisfaction, for we feed on God's immensity without being able to consume it, and we strive after his infinity without being able to reach it. We can therefore not enter God, nor he us, for in this restlessness of love we are unable to deny ourselves. For this reason the heat is so extreme that the exercise of love between ourselves and God flashes back and forth like lightning in the sky, and yet we cannot be consumed by it.

In this storm of love our works are above and beyond reason and devoid of particular form, for love is craving what is impossible. Reason bears witness that love is in the right, but it can neither advise love nor hold it back, for as long as we interiorly see that God wishes to be ours, God's mercy touches our eager craving. This gives rise to the restlessness of love, for God's outward-flowing touch enkindles restlessness and demands our own activity, namely, that we love the love which is eternal. But his inward-drawing touch draws us out of ourselves and calls us to dissolve into nothingness in unity with God. In this inward-drawing touch we feel that God wishes us to be his, for in this touch we must renounce ourselves and allow him to bring about our blessedness. When, however, he touches us with his outward-flowing touch, he leaves us to ourselves, making us free, placing us in his presence, teaching us to pray in spirit and make requests in freedom, and revealing to us his incomprehensible riches in as many forms as we can envision. Whatever we can imagine as containing consolation and joy is found in him in an incomparable degree.

Accordingly, when we experience that he with all his riches wants to be ours and to dwell with us always, then all the powers of our soul open wide—above all, our eager craving. All the streams of God's grace flow forth. The more we savor this grace, the more do we desire to savor it; the more we desire to savor it, the more deeply do we open ourselves to God's touch; the more deeply we open ourselves to his touch, the more does the flood of his sweetness flow through and around us; and the more this flood flows through and around us, the more do we feel and know that God's sweetness is incomprehensible and without ground. It is for this reason that the Prophet says, "Taste and see, for God is sweet" (Ps 34:9). He does not say, "Taste and see how sweet," for God's sweetness is beyond measure, so we can neither grasp it nor take it wholly into ourselves. God's bride in the Song of Songs also bears witness to this when she says, "I have sat in the shadow of him whom I desired, and his fruit is sweet to my taste" (2:3).

JOHN RUUSBROEC

E. THE DIFFERENCE BETWEEN
THE STATE OF CONTEMPLATIVES ON EARTH
AND THAT OF
THE SAINTS IN HEAVEN

THE OPAQUENESS OF OUR MORTAL STATE

There is a great difference between the enlightenment of the saints and the highest enlightenment which we can attain in this life. It is God's shadow which enlightens our interior desert on earth, but on the high mountains of the Promised Land there is no shadow. Still, it is one and the same sun and one and the same resplendence which enlighten both our earthly desert and also those high mountains. But the state of the saints is gloriously transparent, so that they receive this resplendence directly, without intermediary, while our state is still mortal and opaque. This constitutes the intermediary which causes our understanding to be so darkened by a shadow that we cannot know God and heavenly realities as clearly as do the saints. As long as we live in this shadow, we cannot see the sun itself; rather, as St. Paul says, our knowledge is through likenesses and through things which are hidden (cf. 1 Cor 13:12). Nevertheless, the shadow cast by the shining of the sun is light enough that we can apprehend the distinctions among all the virtues as well as every truth which is beneficial to our mortal state. If, however, we are to become one with the sun's resplendence, we must follow the way of love and go out of ourselves into a state devoid of form. With blinded eyes we will then be drawn by the sun into its own resplendence, where we will attain unity with God. If we understand and experience this, we have attained the contemplative life proper to our state.

THREE DIFFERENT STATES

The state of the Jews in the Old Testament was one of coldness and of the night. They lived in darkness and sat in the shadow of death, as the prophet Isaiah says (9:1). This shadow of death was the result of original sin, which is the reason they had to be without God. Our own state in the Christian faith is still in the coolness of dawn, for the day has dawned for

178

us. We therefore walk in the light and sit in God's shadow, for God's grace is an intermediary between him and ourselves. Through this grace we will overcome all things, die to all things, and pass without hindrance into a state of unity with God. The state of the saints, however, is hot and bright, for they live and walk in the middle of the day. With open and enlightened eyes they see the sun in its brilliance, for they are pervaded and suffused by God's glory. According to the degree of each one's enlightenment, they taste and know the fruit of all the virtues which have been gathered by all the blessed spirits. But the most sublime food of all, surpassing every other, is that they taste and know the Trinity in the Unity and the Unity in the Trinity and that they find themselves united with these. This inebriates them and gives them rest in God's very self.

OUR FORETASTE OF HEAVENLY GLORY

This is what the bride desired in the Book of Love when she said to Christ: "Show me, you whom my soul loves, where you feed your flock and where you rest in the middle of the day" (Sg 1:7), that is, in the light of glory, as St. Bernard says.[4] All the food which is given us in the shadow of the morning is but a foretaste of the food that is to come in the midday of God's glory. Still, God's bride glories in having sat in God's shadow and in the fact that his fruit was sweet to her taste. Whenever we feel that God is touching us from within, we are tasting his fruit and his food, for his touch is his food. This touch both draws in and flows out, as I said earlier. When it draws us in, we become wholly God's, learning how to die and how to see. But when it flows out, he wishes to be wholly ours, teaching us how to live in the richness of the virtues. When his touch draws us in, all our powers fail; we are then sitting under his shadow, and his fruit is then sweet to our taste, for God's fruit is the Son of God, whom the Father begets in our spirit. This fruit is so infinitely sweet to our taste that we can neither swallow nor assimilate it; on the contrary, it consumes us and absorbs us into itself.

---

4. Not only this specific reference to the middle of the day as the time of God's resplendent glory, but also everything that Ruusbroec writes in the preceding section about the periods of darkness, dawn, and midday is based on St. Bernard's *Sermones super Cantica canticorum* 33.4–6. On Ruusbroec's dependence on Bernard, both here and elsewhere in his writings, see Albert Ampe, "Bernardus en Ruusbroec," *Ons Geestelijk Erf* 27 (1953): 143–79.

Our New Name

Whenever the touch of this fruit draws us into itself, we abandon and overcome all things. In overcoming them, we taste that hidden bread of heaven which gives us eternal life, for we are thereby receiving the sparkling stone which I discussed earlier, on which our new name was written before the world began. This is that new name which no one knows except him who receives it. Whoever feels himself to be united with God savors this name in accordance with the degree of his virtue, of his ascent to God, and of his unity with him. In order that everyone might receive his name and possess it forever, the Lamb of God—that is, our Lord's humanity—delivered himself up to death and opened for us the Book of Life, in which the names of all the elect stand written. No one of these names can be blotted out, for they are one with that living book which is the Son of God. That same death broke open for us the seals of this book, so that all virtues might come to fulfillment in accordance with God's eternal providence.

Therefore, to the extent that each person can overcome himself and die to all things, to that same extent he will feel the Father's touch drawing him inward and will savor the sweetness of the Son's inborn fruit; by means of this savor the Holy Spirit will reveal to him that he is an heir of God. No one is exactly like anyone else as regards these three points, which is why everyone receives a special name, one which is continually being renewed through new grace and new works of virtue. For this reason all knees bend at the name of Jesus, for he struggled on our behalf and was victorious. He enlightens our darkness and brings all virtues to their highest degree of perfection. His name is therefore exalted above every other name (Phil 2:9), for he is the sovereign prince of all the elect. In his name we have been called and chosen and have been adorned with grace and virtues as we await God's glory.

F. FOLLOWING CHRIST UP THE MOUNT TABOR OF OUR BARE MIND

In order that Jesus' name might be extolled and glorified in us, let us follow him up the mountain of our bare mind, just as Peter, James, and John followed him up Mount Tabor. In our Dutch tongue the term Tabor means an increase of light. If we are like Peter in knowing the truth, like James in overcoming the world, and like John in being full of grace and possessing the virtues in righteousness, then Jesus is leading us up the mountain of our bare mind to a barren, secret place and is manifesting himself to us in the glory of the divine resplendence. In Jesus' name, his heavenly Father opens for us the living book of his eternal wisdom. God's wisdom envelops our bare mind and the simplicity of our spirit in a simple, formless savoring of all that is good. This takes place in an undifferentiated way, for here there is both seeing and knowing, tasting and feeling, subsisting and living, having and being, and all this is entirely one when we are thus raised above ourselves in God. But before we are thus raised up, each of us remains standing in some particular form or mode, and our heavenly Father, in his wisdom and goodness, bestows gifts upon each of us in particular, in accordance with the nobility of each person's being and exercises.

For this reason, if we were to remain always with Jesus on Tabor, that is, on the mountain of our bare mind, we would experience a constant increase of new light and new truth, for we would continually hear the Father's voice taking hold of us as it flowed forth with grace and drew us in toward unity. All who follow our Lord Jesus Christ hear the Father's voice, for he is speaking of them all when he says: "These are my chosen sons, in all of whom I am well pleased" (cf. Mt 3:17). Through the Father's good pleasure each person receives grace, in accordance with the measure and way in which God is pleased with him. In and through the mutuality of our pleasure in God and God's pleasure in us, genuine love is practiced, so that everyone savors his name, his service, and the fruit of his works. In this, all who are good remain hidden from those who live according to the world's ways, for the latter are dead before God and are nameless; they can therefore neither experience nor savor what is proper to the living.

God's outward-flowing touch makes us alive in our spirit, fills us with grace, enlightens our reason, teaches us to know the truth and to distinguish among the virtues, and keeps us standing in God's presence with such great strength that we can bear all savor, all experience, and all God's outward-flowing gifts without having our spirit fail us. But God's inward-drawing touch calls us to be one with him and to expire and die in a state of blessedness, that is, in that one love which enfolds the Father and the Son in a single state of blissful enjoyment. When, therefore, we have climbed with Jesus up that mountain where we are free of images—provided we have followed him there with a single, simple gaze, with interior delight, and with blissful yearning—we then experience the fierce heat of the Holy Spirit as it burns and melts us into God's own Unity. There, where we are one with the Son and have been lovingly brought back to our source, we hear the Father's voice as it draws us inward through its touch, for he addresses all his chosen ones in his eternal Word: "These are my beloved sons, in whom I am well pleased."

You should know that the Father with the Son, and the Son with the Father, have taken eternal delight in the Son's assuming our human nature, dying for us, and bringing all the elect back to their source. Accordingly, if we have been raised up by the Son to our origin, we hear the Father's voice as it draws us inward and enlightens us with eternal truth. This truth reveals to us the expansive good pleasure of God, in which all good pleasure has its beginning and end. All our powers then fail us and we fall down in open contemplation. All become one and one becomes all in the loving embrace of the threefold Unity. When we experience this Unity, we become one being, one life, and one blessedness with God. All things are then fulfilled and renewed, for when we are baptized in the powerful embrace of God's love each person's joy is so great and so special that he can neither think about nor observe the joy of anyone else. He becomes blissful love, which is itself everything, so that a person neither needs nor is able to seek anything else.

G. SIX THINGS LEADING TO THE ENJOYMENT OF GOD

THE THREE LOWER THINGS

If a person is to enjoy God, three things are necessary, namely, true peace, interior silence, and loving adherence. Whoever would find true peace between himself and God must love God in such a way that he can freely and for God's glory renounce everything that he does or loves in an inordinate way, as well as everything that he possesses or could possess in a way contrary to God's glory. This is the first thing and is necessary for everyone. The second thing is interior silence, which means that a person must be empty and free of the images of everything he ever saw or heard. The third thing is a loving adherence to God, an adherence which is itself blissful enjoyment, for if a person cleaves to God out of pure love and not for the sake of his own advantage then he enjoys God in truth and feels that he loves God and is loved by him.

182

THE SPARKLING STONE

The Three Higher Things

There are three other things which are higher and which give a person a firm foundation and render him capable of enjoying and experiencing God whenever he wishes. The first of these is to rest in him whom one enjoys. This takes place when the lover is overcome and possessed by his Beloved in bare, essential love. Here the lover is lovingly immersed in his Beloved, so that each is entirely the other's, both in possession and in rest. There follows the second thing, which is called falling asleep in God. This occurs when the spirit sinks away from itself without knowing how or where this takes place. There then follows the third and last thing which can be expressed in words. It takes place when the spirit sees a darkness which it cannot enter by means of the power of reason. In this state a person feels that he has died and lost his way and that he has become one with God, without difference. When he feels himself to be one with God, then God himself is his peace, his enjoyment, and his rest. This is an entirely fathomless abyss, in which a person must die to himself in a state of blessedness and come back to life through the virtues in whatever way love and its touch require.

If you experience these six things within yourself, then you have experienced everything which I told you previously or could tell you. In turning within yourself you will find it as easy to contemplate and to enjoy as to lead your normal, natural life. From out of this richness there arises that common life of which I promised to speak at the beginning of this treatise.

CONCLUSION: THE COMMON LIFE

A person who has been sent down by God from these heights into the world is full of truth and rich in all the virtues. He seeks nothing of his own but only the glory of the one who sent him. He is accordingly righteous and truthful in all things and has a rich and generous foundation which rests on God's own richness. He will therefore always flow forth to all who need him, for the living spring of the Holy Spirit is so rich that it can never be drained dry. Such a person is a living and willing instrument of God with which God accomplishes what he wishes in the way he wishes. Such a person does not attribute these accomplishments to himself but gives God the glory. He stands ready and willing to do all that God commands and is strong and courageous in suffering and enduring all that God sends him. He therefore leads a common life, for he is equally ready for contemplation or for action and is perfect in both.

No one can possess this common life unless he is a contemplative, and no one can contemplate or enjoy God unless he has within himself these six things, ordered in the way I have previously described. For this reason, all those persons are deceived who consider themselves contemplatives and yet love, practice, or possess any created thing in an inordinate way, or who think they are enjoying God before they have become free of images, or who rest before they have come to enjoy God. Such persons are all deceived, for we must devote ourselves to God with an open heart, a peaceful conscience, and an unveiled countenance and must live without hypocrisy in sincerity and truth. We will then rise from virtue to virtue, contemplating God, enjoying him, and becoming one with him, just as I have said. May God grant that we all attain this. Amen.

A MIRROR OF ETERNAL BLESSEDNESS

INTRODUCTION*

My dearly beloved in our Lord, I have a firm hope and confidence that the Lord has foreseen, called, chosen, and loved you from all eternity—and not you alone, but all who have truly made their religious profession before his glorious face in his convent, freely and sincerely choosing to serve, praise, and love him forever. For them this is a true witness and a sure sign that God has of his free goodness foreseen, chosen, and called them to live with his beloved friends in his convent. But if you are still a beginner, then embrace the religious life by making your profession in love and genuine holiness. Choose this sincerely and with a free heart and then you will feel that you have been eternally chosen by God. For the sake of his beloved elect, he sent his only Son, who is one with him in substance and one with us in our nature. The Son lived for us, taught us, and loved us unto death, delivering and freeing us from all our enemies and from all our sins. He did this for all of us in common and left all his sacraments for us as his common gift. For this reason, if you have decided to make your choice in love, that is a sign that you have been chosen from all eternity.

In order that you might believe and firmly trust him in this, he left you as his gift his body and blood to be your food and drink. Its savor will pervade your entire nature and will nourish you all the way to eternal life. He wishes to live and dwell in you and, as both God and a human being, to be himself your life and to be entirely yours, provided that you wish to be entirely his and to live and dwell in him as a heavenly and godlike person.

This is precisely the order and way of eternal life: that you are his and

---

*The text of *A Mirror of Eternal Blessedness* is in many manuscripts accompanied by a total of seventy lines of verse, some preceding, some following the treatise itself. These lines of verse were almost certainly not composed by Ruusbroec himself and have accordingly not been translated here. On this point, see Albert Ampe, "De bestemmelinge van *Spieghel* en *Trappen,*" *Ons Geestelijk Erf* 45 (1971): 263–77. In addition, within the text itself there are four short passages, totaling forty-six lines, in rhymed couplets. There is no reason to doubt that these passages are from Ruusbroec; in the present translation they are rendered as prose.

not your own and that you live for him and not for yourself, just as he became yours and lives for you and remains yours for all eternity. You must therefore live for, praise, love, serve, and intend his eternal glory rather than any reward, comfort, savor, consolation, or anything else which could accrue to you from such behavior, for genuine love does not seek its own advantage; it thereby possesses both God and everything else, since it overcomes nature through grace. Therefore give to Christ your Bridegroom all that you are and all that you have and are capable of, and do so with a free and generous heart. He will then give you in return all that he is and all that lies in his power. Never will you have seen a more joyful day than that. He will open for you his glorious and loving heart and the inmost part of his soul, all full of glory, grace, joy, and faithfulness. There you will find your joy and will grow and increase in heartfelt affection. The open wound in his side will be your door to eternal life and your entranceway into that living paradise which he is himself. There you will taste the fruit of eternal life which grew for us on the wood of the cross, that fruit which we had formerly lost through Adam's pride and have now regained through the lowly death of our Lord Jesus Christ. He is our living paradise, for within him and from out of him flows the spring of eternal health, while from his wounds flows balm, a medicine which cures every sickness, for its aroma is so strong that it drives away all the devil's serpents and awakens those who have died in their sins, bestowing upon them grace and eternal life.

In the inmost depths of our Lord Jesus Christ flow streams of honey surpassing every conceivable taste and sweetness. If you can enter there and experience and savor him, you will easily overcome the world, yourself, and everything else, for he will show you the way of love which leads to his Father, the way which he walked himself and which he himself is. He will there reveal to you how his humanity is a worthy offering to his Father. He has given you this humanity together with everything he suffered, so that with it you might boldly appear at the court of his heavenly Father, for he has brought about peace and set us free. You should therefore present and offer Christ, your sacrifice, with a humble and generous heart as the treasure through which you have been delivered and redeemed. He in turn will offer you, with himself, to his heavenly Father as the beloved fruit for whose sake he underwent death, and the Father will receive you, with his Son, in a loving embrace. See, here all sins are forgiven, every debt is repaid, every virtue is brought to perfection, and the beloved is possessed by the lover in love. In this possession you will find and feel yourself to be living in love and love in you. This is the source of all true holiness, for no one comes to the Father except through the Son (cf. Jn 14:6) and through his passion and death, which he endured in love. Those who wish to ascend and enter in any other way are deceived; such persons are thieves and murderers (cf. Jn 10:1) and belong in the fires of hell.

But if the Son has offered you to the Father together with himself and his death, then you are embraced in love. This love has been given you as a pledge with which you have been purchased for the service of God and as a security with which you have been made an heir in God's kingdom. God cannot go back on his pledge, for it is all that God himself is and is capable of. See, this pledge and security is the Holy Spirit, who is the dowry or treasure with which Jesus your Bridegroom has made you an heir in his Father's kingdom.

Take great care, then, to hold fast to your pledge and your dowry in a unity of love with Jesus, your beloved Bridegroom, for in the unity of love are constantly born anew all who live honorably for God and serve him. There are three groups in which the entire family of those who serve God is included.[1] The first group consists of virtuous persons of good will who are always overcoming sin and dying to it. The second group is made up of interior persons, rich and full of life, who practice all the virtues to a high degree of perfection. The third group consists of exalted, enlightened persons who are always dying in love and coming to nought in unity with God. These are the three states or orders in which all the ways of holiness are practiced. When all three coalesce in one and the same person, then he is living according to God's most holy will. Now note well these states or lives together with what distinguishes them one from another. I will show and explain them to you, so that you might know yourself better and not think you are better or holier than you are.

---

1. Under partially different terminology (the life of virtue, the interior life, and the living life), Ruusbroec follows in this treatise the same threefold division used in *The Spiritual Espousals*.

PART ONE: THE LIFE OF VIRTUE

The first group of persons will now be discussed. The first and lowest of the lives which are born of God and which the Holy Spirit bestows and urges on is called the life of virtue. It consists in dying to sin and increasing in virtue and begins in the following way.

A. RESPONSIVENESS TO GOD'S GRACE

The Holy Spirit reveals his grace in a person's heart. If, then, a person wishes to accept God's grace, he opens his heart and will to God and receives God's grace and interior working with a joyful spirit. At once his affection toward God outweighs and overcomes his inordinate affection toward all creatures, though it does not overcome every inordinate inclination or desire of his nature, for a holy life is a knightly service in which one must hold fast in the battle. For this reason, if you wish to begin a good life and remain in it forever, you must sincerely intend and love God above all things. This intention will always lead you toward what you love, and in love you will practice, embrace, and possess what you love. You will base your entire life on this and always be occupied with your Beloved with great desire. You will thus savor and experience God's goodness each time you turn within, and so you will love God purely for his eternal glory, so that you might love him for all eternity. This is the root of a holy life and of that genuine love which is imperishable and which you will always practice through forgetting and renouncing yourself. Therefore hold yourself above all things so as not to seek your own advantage in love—seek neither savor nor consolation nor anything else which God can give you for your own comfort in time or in eternity, for that is contrary to charity and is a tendency of our nature which makes genuine love wither away. It is also very hard for this tendency to be overcome by fearful and foolish persons who fancy themselves wise and are always seeking their own advantage.

B. FOUR WAYS OF LOVING

Moreover, you should know that everything you can desire—and much more besides—will be given you by love without your having to do anything, for if you truly have divine love, you have all that you can desire. Having such love is nothing other than always and eternally loving God without ceasing. In this way you will die to all self-centeredness, and love will be your life.

There is a love which is above and beyond your comprehension. This love is the Spirit of our Lord. In this love you will be raised up to dwell and rest in unity with God, above your power of rational understanding.

There is also a love which is within you. This is God's grace and your own good will. In this love you possess the richness and fullness of all your virtues. God thereby lives and dwells within you with his grace and his gifts, while you can become ever more pleasing to him.

There is in addition a love which is between you and God. This love is a holy desire which rises up to God's glory, accompanied by thanksgiving, praise, and all the exercises of love. This love between you and God, together with these exercises, will always be renewed through the touch of the Holy Spirit and the good will and affection of your heart.

There is finally a love which is beneath you. This love is an outflow of charity toward your neighbor through works of mercy, in every way that your neighbor stands in need and you are aware of these needs. In this love you will hold to your good practices and your rule, to good customs and good works, and to an orderly way of performing exterior works in accordance with God's commandments and the ordinances of the holy Church.

If you know what love is and if you respond properly to its demands in these four ways, then you have mastered yourself and are able to overcome the world, dying more and more to sin and practicing a life of virtue. For this reason you should be free of images and be master of yourself. Take your soul in hand, for then you will be able, as often as you wish, to raise your eyes and heart to heaven, where your treasure and your Beloved are. In this way you will lead one life with him. Do not let God's grace be idle within you, but direct yourself in genuine affection both upward in the praise of God and downward in the practice of all kinds of virtue and good works. In the practice of all exterior works let your heart be empty and undisturbed, so that through and above all things you might see him whom you love as often as you wish. For those who love this is easy to do, for where your Beloved is, there your eyes are directed, and where a person's treasure is, there is his heart, as our Lord himself says (Mt 6:21). You should therefore practice love with great diligence and heartfelt affection before the face of the Lord, for that is God's counsel and is also that "better part" of your life which you are to choose and practice above all else (cf. Lk 10:42). Although this is the higher and better part, you must nevertheless hold to good order and to your rule, to your good practices and customs, and to every good work and exterior exercise.

This is the lowest and least part of that holy way of life which God desires of you and of everyone else and which you owe him by right as well as in virtue of his commandments. You should practice it without worry or anxiety of heart and always do so in God's sight, for the Scriptures praise exterior works very much but condemn anxiety.

C. ATTENTIVENESS AT PRAYER

In addition, whenever you are reading, singing, or praying, if you are able to understand the words, then pay attention to their sense and meaning, for you are serving in God's presence. But if you do not understand the words, or if you are raised to a higher state, then remain in it and keep your gaze fixed simply on God as long as you can, always intending and loving God's glory. And if during a period of choral prayer or during your other exercises distracting thoughts or images come into your mind—no matter from where they come—do not get upset over this, for we are all unstable; when you come back to yourself and become aware of all this, quickly direct your attention and your love back to God. Even though the enemy shows you his booths and his wares, if you do not buy anything with affection, nothing of all that remains with you.

D. RECOLLECTION AND A DESIRE FOR WISDOM

If, then, you wish easily to win the victory, choose to raise your mind to a state of interior recollection, preferring to give yourself more to the interior exercises of love than to the exterior practice of good works. If you know how to turn inward to God in interior exercises, and if on the other hand your nature is inclined to follow its desires outward in speaking and hearing about things which are in accord with the comfort and satisfaction of the senses, then if you follow the inclinations of nature you will go backward and become cooler in love and in every virtue. You will fall from God's grace and God will scorn and reject you, so that your situation will become worse than that of a worldly person who has never experienced God. But if you are willing to struggle against the inclinations and desires of nature, you will certainly win the victory, so that grace, love, and the praise of God will grow and increase more and more from day to day.

Moreover, a simple, unlettered person who would like to live in accordance with God's holy will should with a humble heart pray and beseech God to give him the spirit of wisdom, so that he might live in a way which is pleasing to God and in accordance with his holy will. If he is able to receive the gifts of knowledge and wisdom without becoming proud and conceited, God will certainly give them to him. If this does not occur, then he should remain in his simplicity and serve God in all innocence as best he knows how, for this will be best for him.

E. RESTRAINING THE SENSES

Furthermore, when you are called upon to speak with any other person, whether a religious or a layperson, be prudent, careful, and well ordered in your words and bearing, so that no one may take offense at you. You should also prefer always to remain silent and to listen rather than to speak. Be upright, truthful, and sincere in your words and in your deeds, in what you do and in what you leave undone, and always keep your interior conduct fixed in God's sight. When in the give-and-take of conversation you recognize and feel images and obstacles coming between you and God, you should feel shame over this and should with a simple gaze turn quickly inward before the face of your God. As long as you remain so much the master of yourself that you can always turn inward when you wish to do so, you will live in peace and without fear of mortal sin. I therefore advise you to avoid and flee from worry and anxiety of heart as well as from the instability and manifold concerns of others, especially if they are worldly persons unschooled in the spiritual life. Seek and desire a unified, interior, recollected life and practice it as long as your state of recollection and your act of gazing inward with the eyes of your understanding are as easy and simple as turning outward and seeing things with your bodily eyes.

When you must use your five senses in cases when you or your neighbor is in need, then guard your ears and eyes so that nothing draws them to itself with desire, affection, or satisfaction so as to flood your heart with images and set up a barrier between yourself and God. Otherwise, inordinate desire and affection will hold you captive and you will lose your mastery over yourself and be deprived of your ability to turn freely inward to God, in whom all your beatitude resides. Be careful too in matters of food and drink and in tending to the needs of your body, so that you do not live according to the demands of your flesh and the desires of nature, for if you seek the satisfaction of your desires either in yourself or in any creature, you will have turned aside from the true way and become unable to live for God and to die to sin.

F. RESISTING TEMPTATION AND CONFESSING ONE'S SINS

Moreover, if impure images enter your mind in dreams when you are asleep or, when you are awake, through something you see, hear, or imagine, or through the influence of the enemy, in such a way that you are moved to satisfy impure inclinations and the desires of nature, then make the sign of the cross upon your heart and pray a Hail Mary, asking God to have pity on you. Ask also for the help and prayers of all the saints and all good persons. Place before your eyes the loss of God's glory, condemnation to the pains of hell, the offense given to God, and separation from him and from all his beloved. At this you will feel a justified fear and will struggle bravely, relying on the death of our Lord and on his help and his grace. He will not abandon you, but you will surely gain the victory and constantly grow in grace and in the increase of virtue.

When you come to your confessor to go to confession, you need not mention what you have dreamed about or imagined, for talking about or listening to such things is sometimes unseemly and confusing. Besides, there is no sin in what we dream or in what simply enters our mind, for no one can avoid such things, since we do not cause them ourselves. But the pleasure and satisfaction that arise from all this constitute venial sin, and when a person feels and recognizes this pleasure and willingly remains with it without a struggle, then the sin is greater. But if a person desires and seeks this pleasure by reflecting on impure images, the sin is greater still. Furthermore, if a person is careless in his relations with any other person, whether in words or deeds, in signs or any other way, and if he wishes to carry this out in practice, then he becomes filled with images and loses mastery of himself. Impure desires and longings grow in him more and more, so that his power of reason becomes blinded, his love of God disappears, and he falls into a life like that of beasts, even if he does not go so far as sinning in exterior acts. If a person finds himself in such a state and wishes to be reconciled with God, he should confess his sins to God and to a priest with a contrite and humble heart and he will certainly obtain pardon.

G. SPIRITUAL ABANDONMENT AND CONSOLATION

Moreover, if you feel slothful, oppressed, and sad in nature, without any savor, desire, or attraction for spiritual things; if you feel poor, miserable, abandoned, and deprived of all God's consolation; and if everything seems unpleasant and you have no taste or desire for any exercises, whether exterior or interior, but feel so heavy that you could sink through the ground: then do not become anxious, but place yourself in the hands of God and desire that his glory and his will be fulfilled. This dark, oppressive cloud will soon pass over and the bright light of the sun, our Lord Jesus Christ, will shine upon you with more grace and consolation than you ever felt before. This is something which will come to you through your self-renunciation and humble abandonment in all your suffering and heavy oppression. God's grace will fill and enlighten all your inmost being, and you will then feel that God loves you and that you are pleasing to him. Your heart and senses will become filled with joy and your entire nature will be awakened with divine consolation and a sense of well-being experienced in both body and soul, while all the blood in your veins will grow warm and flow through all your members. Your heart will open wide to receive new gifts from God with deep desire for newness of life, and your desires will mount up to God like a fiery flame of devotion in thanksgiving and praise. Your mind will meanwhile descend in a sense of unworthiness and of humble self-disdain, and your reason will reveal to you your sins, your shortcomings, and your many failings. At this you will feel displeasure and sorrow and will reflect on the fact that you are unworthy of all consolation and honor from God but that he has bestowed these on you out of his everlasting faithfulness and the free and generous goodness and mercy which he has toward you. Such reflections will stir your desires to even more ardent thanksgiving and praise.

For this reason, if you have self-knowledge you should always descend in a sense of unworthiness and self-disdain and then rise again with great veneration and reverence toward God, who spared you in your sins and now, graciously and without merit on your part, has filled you with his consolation and divine gifts. Therefore strive to rise toward God through desire and to descend into yourself through humility, and then you will grow and increase in both and God's grace will flow within you. Out of the sense of well-being which you will feel in your nature, you will sometimes laugh and sometimes cry, just like a person who is drunk. You will also have many unusual experiences, known only to those who have such love. Desire and affection will make your heart expand, so that you will love, thank, and praise God and yet fall short in all this, for all that you are able to do will seem as little or nothing compared to what you will wish to do and what love will rightly demand of you. Through such desire your heart will suffer a painful wound. The pain will constantly increase and be renewed through the practice of desirous affection for God, so that you will grow weak from love. Sometimes it will seem that your heart and senses will be broken to pieces, that your nature will die and come to naught through the impatience of its desires, and that this impatience will have to last as long as you live. But then, when you least expect it, God will hide himself and withdraw his hand, placing between himself and you a darkness which you will not be able to see through. You will then lament, moan, and groan like a poor, abandoned exile. "Now are the poor abandoned to God," says the Prophet (Ps 10:14). Then let God have what is his own, and prefer to live outcast and scorned in his house rather than to dwell in the tents of the proud (cf. Ps 84:11).

H. CHRIST'S EXAMPLE IN SUFFERING

If God has hidden himself from your sight, you are nevertheless not hidden from him, for he lives within you and has left you the gift of his mirror and image, namely, his Son Jesus Christ, your Bridegroom. You are to bear him in your hands, before your eyes, and in your heart. St. Paul says that the Son of God humbled himself, coming down from heaven and taking the form of a slave so that he might serve us (cf. Phil 2:7). In deep humility, he himself says through the Prophet: "I am a worm and no man" (Ps 22:7). When he had lovingly and reverently served his heavenly Father and us for thirty-three years, the time came when he would bring his service to completion by dying in genuine love for our sake and for his Father's glory. In his time of greatest need he was abandoned and deprived of consolation in the lower part of his being by God, by his chosen friends, and by all the world, while from his deadly foes he received ridicule, scorn, insults, opprobrium, and many wounds. He was obedient to his Father unto death and freely and lovingly suffered all the evil which his foes could invent and devise under the influence of the devil. He prayed for us and for them, pardoning their sins as he said, "Father, forgive them their sin, for they do not know what they are doing" (Lk 23:34). He was heard because of his reverence (Heb 5:7), for the sake of all who would ever acknowledge and repent of their sins. He well knew, from the moment of his soul's creation, that he would have to suffer and die for the sins of the world. Nevertheless, when the time came for him to die, his tender nature was oppressed by fear of suffering and he asked his heavenly Father if it were possible to take away the cup of his suffering so that he would not have to drink of it (cf. Mt 26:39). But his prayer was not answered, for his Father did not wish to spare him but rather to have him scourged and handed over to death. In the higher part of his being Christ was always of one will with his Father. Although his human nature was oppressed by fear, he was nevertheless obedient and overcame his lower will by saying: "Let not my will but yours be done" (Mt 26:39).

There is a lesson for us in this: When we pray to obtain pardon for our sins or those of others, we ought not to stop or hold back until we are heard; but when we pray for or desire the cessation of the pains or sufferings which we are undergoing because of our sins or the sins of others, we ought to practice self-abandonment and undergo such suffering obediently, even if it leads to death. Therefore, if we live in suffering without personal preference, we will always be victorious and never lose. Note this in what follows, for the second group of persons will now be discussed.

PART TWO: THE INTERIOR LIFE

A. RIGHTEOUSNESS AND THE BEATITUDES

God's Claim on Us

When Christ handed himself over to the will of his Father, the love in his spirit was so strong and ardent and the fear in his human nature so great that a bloody sweat flowed from his body onto the ground (cf. Lk 22:44). In his willing surrender of himself he redeemed us through his love so that we might serve him and his Father, and through his passion and death he paid and remitted our debt. We are therefore necessarily his, whether we are saved in heaven or damned in hell. The heavenly Father created us from nothing, so we will rightly belong to him. The Son of God redeemed us through his death, so we will rightly die to sin and serve and live for him. The Father and Son, with the Holy Spirit, have loved us from all eternity and have taken possession of us through their love, so it is altogether right that we love them in return. The three Persons are one God, one substance, and one nature, which is why we serve them in common: Whoever serves one of them serves the other two as well.

Our Following of Christ

Now Christ says in St. Matthew's Gospel: "Blessed are those who hunger and thirst for righteousness" (Mt 5:6). It is right to give God what we owe him. When Christ abandoned his own will to the will of his Father he thereby purchased us and through his death paid our debt. If, then, we wish to follow him, we must renounce our own will and live according to his. In that way his purchase of us will be confirmed. We must also restrain our senses, overcome our nature, take up our cross, and follow Christ. In this way we will repay the debt which he paid on our behalf. Through his death and our own willing penitence we are united with him and become his faithful servants, belonging to his kingdom. But when we die to our own will in favor of his, so that his will becomes ours, then we become his disciples and his chosen friends. Moreover, when we are raised up through love and when our mind stands bare and imageless, just as it was created by God, then we are led by the Spirit of God and become God's sons. Mark these words and their meaning and live accordingly.

When Christ, the Son of God, resolved to die out of love for us, he handed over his life into the hands of the enemy, even unto death. In this way he was a faithful servant of his Father and of all the world. He also gave over his own will to that of his Father. In this way he practiced the highest degree of righteousness and taught us all truth. He raised his spirit to a state of eternally blessed enjoyment and said: "It is consummated. Father, into your hands I commend my spirit" (Jn 19:30; Lk 23:46). To these words, and on behalf of all good persons who follow Christ, the Prophet David replied when he said: "You have redeemed me, Lord, God of truth" (Ps 31:6). We cannot redeem ourselves, but when we follow Christ to the best of our ability in the way I have shown, then our works are joined with his and are ennobled through his grace. He therefore redeemed us not through our works but through his, and through his own merits he saved us and set us free.

If we are to experience and possess this freedom, then his spirit must enflame ours with love and immerse it in the abyss of his grace and his free goodness. It is there that our spirit is baptized, set free, and united with his spirit. It is there that our self-will dies in God's will, so that we cannot possibly will anything other than what God wills, for his will has become ours. This is the root of genuine charity. When we are born again of God's Spirit, our will becomes free, for it is then one with the free will of God. Through love our spirit is there raised and taken up into unity of spirit, of will, and of freedom with God. In this divine freedom a person's spirit is raised up in love above its own nature, that is, above suffering, labor, and reluctance, above anxiety and care, above fear of death, hell, and purgatory, and above all the oppressive burdens which can overcome body and soul in time and in eternity, for consolation and desolation, giving and taking, death and life, and everything that can occur for weal or woe all remain beneath that loving freedom in which a person's spirit is united with God's Spirit.

JOHN RUUSBROEC

The Life of the Beatitudes

These persons who have not held onto anything of their own are poor in spirit and are therefore blessed, for God's love is their life.[2] They are still more blessed through being meek and humble. For this reason, however much their nature is weighed down with burdens, they always enjoy peace of heart and of spirit. Thirdly, they are blessed because they mourn and lament their daily transgressions and the sins of all, as well as the fact that God is not known, loved, and honored as he so richly deserves. This gives rise to the fourth beatitude, which is a hunger and thirst and an eternally ardent desire that God be loved and praised by all creatures in heaven and on earth. From this comes the fifth beatitude, namely, a heartfelt, humble, generous desire that God let his grace and mercy flow forth in heaven and on earth so that all might be filled with his gifts and might thank and praise him for all eternity. This gives rise to the sixth way of being blessed, which is proper to those who receive God's grace and gifts with hearts that are pure and free of images. Such persons stand upright in thankful praise and are the ones who see God. From this vision of God arises the seventh beatitude, which consists in a person's turning lovingly inward to God and to God's peace. This movement within involves a person's heart and senses, body and soul, and all his powers, and takes place in the company of all who are blessed or who are able to become so, that is, all who are participating in or pursuing this loving introversion into God and into the vision of divine peace. All who experience this within themselves are blessed and are peacemakers, for they are at peace with God, with themselves, and with all creatures. For this reason they are called sons of God; it is of them that the Prophet says: "You are gods and sons of the Most High" (Ps 82:6). But immediately afterward he adds: "You will die like men and fall like any of the princes" (82:7). This refers to the final way in which our beatitude comes to perfection, for just as through the power of our Lord Jesus Christ we rise up to the vision of God's peace when we are sons of God, so too we must descend with him into poverty, misery, temptation, and struggle against the world and the devil. In this struggle we must live and die as poor persons, just as Christ, the Son of the living God and a prince above all creatures, did before us. He came down, indeed fell down, under the feet of all sinners in poverty, misery, hunger, thirst, temptation, scorn, struggle, need, ridicule, disgrace, and every oppressive burden which he could bear, whether exteriorly or interiorly. In all this he

---

2. This section of the treatise is based on the beatitudes in Matthew 5:3–12.

remained as obedient and meek as a lamb, and in order to save us for his kingdom he died as a poor and wretched person.

Nevertheless, if we wish to be saved and to remain with him for all eternity, we must keep ourselves in his grace—that is, we must chasten and crucify our flesh and our nature by resisting sin, temptation, and that evil will and desire which can rise up within us against God's glory. Then we will always be able to ascend with our Lord Jesus Christ to his heavenly Father as free sons and will also be able to descend with him in suffering, temptation, and every kind of oppression as his faithful servants. Even if we were so experienced and practiced in virtue that we could turn inward with Christ as often as we wanted, we would still have to suffer persecution, for we will be unstable and prone to having a multitude of thoughts and images fall into our mind as long as we live here in this temporal order. That is why Christ says, "Blessed are they who suffer persecution for righteousness' sake, for the kingdom of heaven is theirs" (Mt 5:10). The kingdom of heaven is Christ living within us with his grace. Now the kingdom of God suffers violence, and in the power of Christ, who lives within us and fights with us, we will win and seize the kingdom (cf. Mt 11:12). When people curse, execrate, and persecute us, and when in speaking falsely they utter all manner of evil against us because we are serving God, Christ says that on that day we will rejoice, for our reward in heaven will be full and overflowing (cf. Mt 5:11–12). Moreover, no one will receive a crown without having struggled lawfully (cf. 2 Tm 2:5).

THE LAST BEATITUDE AND THE EUCHARIST

It is therefore better to be with Christ in tribulation and suffering than to be without him in a state of joy and delight, for he says through the Prophet: "I will deliver the person who is suffering, for he placed his hope in me, and I will protect him because he acknowledged my name. He has called upon me and I will hear him. I am with him in his suffering. I will free him and glorify him" (cf. Ps 91:14–15). And in another place the same Prophet David says: "Lord, you have prepared a table for us in the sight of all who brought tribulation and suffering upon us" (Ps 23:5).

This table is the altar of God, where we receive the living food which gives us life and strengthens us in all our suffering, allowing us to win the victory over all our foes and over everything which stands in our way. It is for this reason that Christ himself says to all human beings: "Unless you eat my flesh and drink my blood, you have no life in you" (Jn 6:53). He goes on to say: "Whoever eats my flesh and drinks my blood has eternal life, for he lives in me and I in him" (Jn 6:54, 56). This mutual indwelling is eternal life. Since here on earth we have to live in a condition of spiritual struggle, we need the food which has the power to strengthen us, so that we might win the victory in our struggle and might keep struggling even as we are winning the victory. This food is the hidden bread of heaven which is given only to those who are victorious in the struggle and which is known only by those who receive and savor it. Listen now to my words and note their sense and meaning.

B. THE EUCHARIST AND
ITS ROLE IN THE SPIRITUAL LIFE

MARY'S FOURFOLD EXAMPLE

If you wish to receive the body of our Lord in the blessed Sacrament in such a way that it will be for God's glory and your own salvation, then you should have within you the same four things which Mary, the mother of God, had within herself and was practicing when she conceived our Lord. For this reason you should be her disciple and maid, sitting at her feet so that she might teach you by her example how you are to live, for she is the sovereign mistress of all virtue and all holiness. The first thing which Mary possessed and which you yourself must possess is purity, the second is a true knowledge of God, the third is humility, and the fourth is a desire arising from your free will.

Purity

Note now the first thing, purity, in Mary, who is your mirror. From the moment of her conception she was pure of all transgressions and of all inclination toward transgressions, whether venial or mortal. God's messenger, the angel Gabriel, therefore spoke to her in the following way: "Hail, full of grace, the Lord is with you" (Lk 1:28). Everything which is full of grace is pure, and everything which is pure is full of grace. Therefore, if you wish to be full of grace and receive our Lord, you must be pure with Mary. Observe and examine the state of your conscience and repent of everything you find there which is displeasing to God. Confess these things to God and to your confessor with a humble heart. Above all do not let yourself forget or remain silent about those things which weigh most heavily on your conscience and of which you are most afraid and ashamed, but accuse yourself as if you were your own mortal enemy. In that way you will become pure and spotless. As regards other faults—the common kind which occur daily and which no one can avoid—speak but briefly about them and do not let them upset you. But you should have deep sorrow and heartfelt contrition for all your sins and have the good intention of always doing what is right and avoiding every sin, both venial and mortal. Above everything else, have great faith and loving trust in God, for these are the things which forgive sins, just as our Lord says at many places in the Gospels: "Your faith has saved you" (Mt 9:22 par.; Mk 10:52 par.; Lk 7:50, 17:19). This is the first point, showing how to be pure with Mary so as to receive our Lord.

But above all else you should avoid long confessions with many words, for they would rob you of peace and lead you into error and scrupulosity. If you speak much in the confessional when there is no need of that—as in the case of venial sins—and if you try to set your mind at rest through your own doing rather than through trust in God, then you will always remain unenlightened and uninstructed by God and will not be able to discern the difference between what is great and small, weighty and light in your transgressions. Moreover, if it should happen that you omit something which you are accustomed to confess but which it was not necessary to confess, you will then become troubled, oppressed, and grieved as though you had not been to confession or perhaps even worse, because instead of the faith, hope, and love of God which should rightly fill your conscience there is found there instead anxiety, fear, and a natural self-love. You must avoid all that if you wish to be pure and to remain with Mary in her chamber.

True knowledge of God

There follows the second thing, which no one can have unless he is pure of conscience, and that is a true knowledge of God. Mary possessed this in a higher degree than anyone who ever lived, with the exception of her Son, who is himself the wisdom of God. Nevertheless, when the angel brought the message to Mary, she was afraid and wondered what sort of greeting this could be. Then the angel said: "Do not be afraid, Mary, for you have found favor with the Lord. You will conceive and bear a Son, whom you will name Jesus. He will be great and will be called the Son of the Most High, and the Lord (that is, the heavenly Father) will give him

the throne of David his father (that is, the power of David), and he will
reign in Jacob's house forever, and of his kingdom there will be no end."
Then Mary said to the angel: "How will this come about, for I do not know
man?"—that is, "I intend to remain a virgin." Then the angel replied: "The
Holy Spirit will descend upon you from above and the power of the Most
High will overshadow you. Therefore the Holy One who will be born of
you will be called the Son of God. And know that your cousin Elizabeth
has conceived a son in her old age; this is the sixth month for her who was
considered barren, for nothing is impossible with God" (Lk 1:26–37).
When Mary heard these words and understood them well, she was instructed by the angel and even much more by the Holy Spirit.

Humility

Then she said: "Behold the handmaid of the Lord" (Lk 1:38). At the
very moment when God raised her to the highest place, she set herself in
the lowest place. The wisdom of God taught her this, for whatever has
been raised to the heights can remain standing only in and through humility; the fall of the angels from heaven shows this clearly. What is higher
than the Son of God, yet what is lower than the servant of God and of all
the world, Christ himself? Again, what is higher than the mother of God,
yet what is lower than the handmaid of God and of all the world, Mary
herself?

Desire

She also handed over her will to God's freedom with great desire and
said further to the angel: "Let it be done to me according to your word"
(Lk 1:38). When the Holy Spirit heard this, it was so pleasing to him, the
very love of God, that he sent Christ into Mary's womb—Christ, who has
delivered us from every evil. We have thus learned from Mary and from
the angel how we have received the Son of God in our human nature.

FIVE POINTS OF EUCHARISTIC DOCTRINE

You should also know how we are to receive the same Son of God in
body and soul in the blessed Sacrament. The Jewish Law teaches us this
through types and figures and the Christian Law teaches us through Holy
Scripture. Moreover, our Christian faith raises us above both natural un-

derstanding and the Scriptures, and above all doubt, and sets us firmly in *doubt*
God's grace. In addition, we are instructed by the writings and practices
of the holy Church, which has existed from the beginnings of holy Christianity and which cannot err, as well as by many things which the saints
have written for us. I therefore want to tell you five points concerning this
holy Sacrament which are useful for all Christians to know. The first point
concerns the time when our Lord gave himself to his disciples in the Sacrament. The second point deals with the matter and form of the Sacrament
and the third with the way or manner in which he gave himself. The fourth
point explains the reason why he gave himself in a concealed and hidden
way in the Sacrament, rather than openly in the form he then was and is
now in heaven. The fifth point will consider the different kinds of persons
who approach the blessed Sacrament, some for their eternal salvation and
others for their damnation.

The first point: the time of the Sacrament's institution

I will first consider the time and the prefiguring of our Sacrament.
When God through Moses led the children of Israel out of Egypt (which
he did on the fourteenth day of the April moon, which always begins in
March—this was the first Jewish Passover), Moses ordered on God's behalf
that the people in every house should eat a roast lamb and cover the door-
posts and lintel of the house with the lamb's blood. In this way they were
protected against sudden death and every evil, for in that same night our
Lord killed the firstborn in all of Egypt, both humans and animals. Moses
then led the Lord's people out of Egypt through the Red Sea into the desert, where our Lord fed them for forty years with heavenly bread. This
was a prefiguring of our Sacrament. All the signs and figures of the Jews
have been fulfilled, while our Sacrament will remain until the end of the
world, when it too will pass away. But the truth which is concealed within
it is eternal life, and this will remain for all eternity.

Now understand the following comparison: Whenever a great king or
a wise lord of a manor wishes to make a pilgrimage to a distant country, he
calls together his most trusted associates and commends to them his land,
his people, his children, and his household, so that they might govern and
preserve all things in peace until the time of his return. In the same way,
when Christ—the eternal wisdom of the Father, the King of Kings and
Lord of Lords—had completed his pilgrimage in this land of his exile, he
wished to return to his fatherland and on the Last Day come back to earth
for the Judgment. Therefore, on the day before he was to die he held a

great feast, an evening meal. To it he invited the greatest princes in all the world, the Apostles, for he wanted to hand over to their care his sacraments, his people, and his kingdom. At this feast the paschal lamb was prepared, which they all ate in accordance with the Jewish Law. This paschal lamb was a prefiguration of our Sacrament, and at this time that prefiguration came to an end, 1,486 years after Moses had led the Jewish people out of Egypt. At this feast Christ brought the Jewish Law to an end, for this was its last Passover, and at the same time he began our law and our own paschal feast. He was immeasurably powerful, wise, rich, and generous, and even though in his human nature he was experiencing a heavy burden, in his spirit he was nevertheless a joyful and bountiful host. He had particularly dear guests, namely, his Apostles, and because he was going to die the next day and so take his leave of them, he wished to make his last testament, which he would leave to his Apostles and, through them, to all believers until the Last Day. He sealed this testament with his death, as did all the Apostles after him.

This testament which Christ left us is himself in the Sacrament, together with everything he is able to accomplish as both God and a human being. This feast is therefore a great one, for it is both blessed and eternal. Jesus Christ, the Son of Mary and the King of heaven and earth, instituted this feast and was also chosen by his heavenly Father as the first Christian bishop. He accordingly celebrated the first Mass of all time, at which he ordained his priests and consecrated them bishops, just as Moses had offered the first sacrifice under the Jewish Law when he ordained and consecrated Aaron and his sons priests and bishops and gave them the power and authority of governing God's people until the coming of Christ. And so when Christ had come and had served us for thirty-three years as both God and a human being, he brought the Jewish Law to an end, for it was a prefiguration, and then he himself instituted the first sacrifice under the Christian dispensation, for he was the first bishop. He consecrated his priests and bishops and gave them and their successors his power so that they might rule and govern his people in spiritual matters until the Last Day, when he will come again for the Judgment. It was in the evening that he instituted our celebration of the Mass.

The second point: the matter and form of the Sacrament

In the same way that Melchisedek, the high priest of Abraham's time, offered bread and wine as a genuine prefiguration of our Sacrament and also as its matter, so too Christ, our high priest, in his sacrifice took bread into his holy and venerable hands, raised his eyes to his almighty Father in heaven, thanked him, blessed the bread, broke it into pieces, and said: "Take and eat, this is my body." Afterward, in the same way, he took the cup of wine into his holy and venerable hands, once more thanked his Father, blessed the wine, and gave it to his disciples, saying: "Drink, all of you, from this, for this is the cup of my blood, of a new and eternal covenant, a mysterious sign of faith, which will be poured out for you and for many for the forgiveness of sin."[3]

You here find the matter and the form of our Sacrament: The matter is the bread and wine, the form is the words which our Lord spoke: "This is my body; this is my blood." When he said, "This is my body," he transformed the substance of the bread into the substance of his body, not in such a way that the bread was annihilated but rather that in ceasing to be bread it became the body of our Lord. This was not a new body but the same one which was sitting there at the table eating and drinking with his disciples; the body they had before them in the Sacrament was the same one they were seeing with their bodily eyes as it sat before them at the table. This latter sight gave them great joy, but it was a still greater joy that they saw the same body in the Sacrament through the interior eyes of faith. Not one of them asked him, "Master, how is this possible?" for they well knew that he who had created heaven and earth and all things from nothing could certainly also transform one substance into another whenever he wished to do so. After all, it was he who in a single instant had turned all the waters of Egypt into blood, had changed Lot's wife into a stone figure, and had made a great stream of water flow from a dry rock, not to mention many other great wonders which are described in the Old Testament and also in the New. For him all things are possible; to him all things are subject.

Note further that all the bread which Christ had before him at the consecration and which all the priests of the entire world have before them in every place and upon every altar is but one single nature of bread. Gathered together in all these consecrations it is but one single matter, which becomes one simple substance—the body of our Lord—through the priest's correct intention and the words of consecration. Everything which previously was bread becomes the body of our Lord. Even though the hosts are dispersed to the ends of the earth, the Sacrament is one and the living

---

3. The text of this paragraph is based on the Roman Canon of the Mass as it existed in Ruusbroec's day. Since the Second Vatican Council, the wording of this Eucharistic Prayer has been somewhat revised.

body of our Lord is one, undivided in the entire Sacrament. You should believe the same as regards the consecration of the wine into the blood of our Lord: His blood is wholly in each chalice and is not more fully in all the chalices of the world than it is in a single chalice, for it cannot be divided, increased, or decreased.

Although the consecration of the body of our Lord and the consecration of his blood are separate and distinct as regards their matter and the form of their words and also as regards their shape and their signification, they nevertheless constitute a single truth and are one Sacrament and one Christ. The living body of our Lord is not in the host without his blood, and his blood cannot be in the chalice without his body in which it lives. Christ is thus whole and undivided in each part of the Sacrament.

Only unleavened wheat bread and wine mixed with a little water may be used for our Sacrament. This signifies that Christ was innocent, gentle, and humble among all persons; that he was that noble grain of wheat which died and fell into the earth and brought forth much fruit for us (cf. Jn 12:24–25), namely, the life of us all in the Christian faith; and that he is the true vine which his Father has planted in our vineyard (cf. Jn 15:1).

The third point: the manner of Christ's self-giving

From his wounds balm and wine flow upon us, and their fragrance and taste make the lovers of God drunk. Whoever wishes to be drunk with love should observe, note, and wonder at two marks of love which Christ has shown us in the blessed Sacrament. They are so great and so profound that no one can fully grasp or understand them.

Christ as our nourishment

The first of these teaches us that Christ gave his flesh to be our soul's food and his blood to be our soul's drink. Such a marvel of love had never been heard of in previous times. Now it is the nature of love always to give and to take, to love and to be loved; these two aspects are found in everyone who loves. Christ's love is both avid and generous. Although he gives us all that he has and all that he is, he also takes from us all that we have and all that we are and demands of us more than we can accomplish. His hunger is incomparably great: He consumes us right to the depths of our being, for he is a voracious glutton suffering from bulimia and consuming the very marrow from our bones. Still, we grant him all this willingly, and the more willingly we grant it, the more does he savor us. No matter how much of us he consumes, he cannot be satisfied, for he is suffering from bulimia and so has an unquenchable appetite. Even though we are poor, that does not matter to him, for he does not wish to leave us.

First of all, he prepares his food by burning all our sins and transgressions. Then, when we have been purified and roasted in the fire of love, he opens his mouth as wide as a vulture ready to devour everything, for by consuming our sinful life he wishes to transform it into his own life, which is full of the grace and glory which he keeps always ready for us if only we are willing to deny ourselves and renounce our sinful ways. If we could comprehend Christ's passionate desire for our salvation, we would not be able to refrain from casting ourselves down his throat. Although these words of mine sound strange, those who love know what I mean.

Jesus' love of us is so noble that at the very moment it consumes us it also wishes to nourish us. Although he absorbs us completely into himself, he gives us himself in return, together with a spiritual hunger and thirst which make us want to savor him eternally. To satisfy our spiritual hunger and heartfelt affection, he gives us his body as our food, and when we eat and consume it with fervent devotion, his glorious, warm blood flows from his body into our human nature and into all our veins. In this way we become enflamed with love and heartfelt affection for him, and our body and soul become thoroughly flooded with longing and spiritual savor. He thus gives us his life full of wisdom, truth, and instruction, so that we might follow him in all the virtues. He then lives in us and we in him. He also gives us his soul with its fullness of grace, so that we might always stand firm with him in love, in virtue, and in the praise of his Father. Above all this he reveals and promises us his divinity for our everlasting enjoyment. What wonder is it, then, if those who experience and savor this should break forth in cries of jubilation?

When the queen of the Orient saw the riches, the majesty, and the glory of King Solomon, her spirit succumbed in deep amazement, so that she fell in a faint (cf. 1 Kgs 10:4–5). Now note how small Solomon's riches and glory were compared to the riches and glory which Christ himself is and which he has prepared for us in the blessed Sacrament. Even if we are able to receive into ourselves all that belongs to his humanity and still remain in control of ourselves, nevertheless, when we contemplate his divinity which we have before us in the Sacrament, we fall into such wonderment that we must rise above ourselves in spirit to a state of superessential love or else must faint away in a transport of amazement at the Lord's table.

With devotion and heartfelt affection we eat our Lord's humanity and take it into our own nature, for affection draws to itself all that it loves. With like affection our Lord draws our nature to himself and consumes it, filling us with his grace. We then grow large and transcend ourselves, entering a state of divine affection which is above reason. When we there eat and take our nourishment and with our spirit strive after our Lord's divinity in pure love, we then encounter his Spirit—that is, his love—which is infinitely great and which burns up and consumes our spirit and all its works, drawing them into unity with itself, where we experience a blessed rest. It is in this way that we will always eat and be eaten and will always ascend and descend in love. This is our eternal life, which is what Christ meant when he said to his disciples: "I have greatly desired to eat this Passover meal with you before I suffer" (Lk 22:15).

For us, the Passover meal means Christ himself, whom we eat in the Sacrament, just as the Apostles who were gathered with Christ at the Last Supper all together received the blessed Sacrament just like any other food which nourishes the body. In the Sacrament each one therefore received our Lord's body as his eternal nourishment because of his faith, love, and desire, for faith and love are the soul's mouth, with which the Apostles received and consumed the Lord's body with all its members. They received it, however, not in its physical size as they saw it there seated at the table, for he had hidden its physical size in the substance of his body as well as in the Sacrament. His body was at that time still mortal, and if they had bitten it with their teeth it would have hurt him. Rather, above and beyond his human nature he gave them the lovable life of his flesh and blood, of his soul and divinity. It is that which was their spiritual food, as it was also his and is all of ours. Nevertheless, in himself he remained all that he had been, undivided and unchanged in nature.

He gave his disciples the entire substance which he had received from the Virgin Mary, his mother, namely, his human nature. In doing this he gave himself wholly and indivisibly in two ways, giving his body under the form of bread and his blood under the form of wine. In each of these he is whole and undivided, for his body is the living support of his blood and his blood is the living support of his body, while his soul is the life of them both. Together these three constitute one undivided life which is Christ himself, and it is this which he gave to his disciples and left to all of us in the Sacrament.

In the same way that all the hosts which all priests have before them at the time of consecration are all the single, undivided substance of bread, so too are they after the consecration the single substance of our Lord's body, which no one can divide. I say the same as regards the wine, which is changed by consecration into our Lord's blood. For this reason each drop from the chalice and each particle of the consecrated host—no matter how small, as long as it retains the appearance of bread—is Christ whole and entire, just as he is in heaven. Although the particles and hosts are dispersed in every country in many a way, the Sacrament itself is one and Christ is one and undivided in the entire Sacrament all over the world. In the same way that a person's soul lives in all his members and is complete in each member without being divided or bound to any place, so too does the glorified body of our Lord live in the entire Sacrament all over the world without being divided or bound to any place, in order that he might be present to all his members in common, that is, to all who desire to receive him in Christian faith. To each such person he is complete in a special way, in accordance with each one's need and desire. This is called communion, that is, common participation, for in the Sacrament we all receive our Lord's body in common, each in particular receiving all that the others receive in common. Even though the priests at Mass receive the blessed Sacrament under two species, they still do not receive more than the laity, for although the consecration of the cup and the consecration of the hosts are separate, Christ is wholly and indivisibly present in each.

It could happen that some foolish, unbelieving person might think and reason in the following way: Since the Sacrament which Christ consecrated was eaten completely by the Apostles who were with him at that time, what is it that priests do nowadays? Christ himself answered this question when he said to his Apostles immediately after the consecration: "As often as you do these things, do them in memory of me" (Lk 22:19; 1 Cor 11:24)—in other words, do them in memory of my love, my passion, and my death, and of my being truly divine and human and having all power in heaven and on earth. The Apostles received these words from the mouth of our Lord just as he meant them, namely, as his prophecy and commandment and as his divine authority given to them and their successors to perform this office until the Last Day. Therefore immediately after his ascension, when they had received the Holy Spirit who taught them all truth, they began to celebrate Mass in the person of our Lord Jesus Christ. It was his Spirit who spoke through them at the consecration: "This is my body; this is my blood." They also ordained bishops and priests on his behalf and in his name and gave them the power which they had received from God to serve as priests throughout the world.

It was in this way that the holy Church was founded on Christ. Christ lives in the Church and has been one with it from the beginning. It will remain constant in its service until the Last Day. In the consecration of the blessed Sacrament, all priests are willing instruments of our Lord Jesus Christ, who says through the mouth of one and all: "This is my body; this is my blood." Each priest truly consecrates the body of our Lord, and all of them together truly consecrate no more than one and the same body. I hereby conclude my remarks about the first mark of love which Christ has shown and taught us in the blessed Sacrament.

Christ as our consecrated sacrificial offering

The second mark of love, following the first, is evident in Christ's words at the consecration: "This is the cup of my blood, which will be poured out for you and for many for the forgiveness of sins." He spoke these words when he consecrated his blood as drink for his Apostles and for us all, blood which he shortly afterward would shed in dying out of love on account of the sins of us all. Greater love was never seen than when God's Son handed over his life to death and through that death redeemed us by making satisfaction to his Father so that we might live with him for all eternity. In his lowly death he offered himself and us to his Father's mercy, while the Father received us together with him into his Son's eternal inheritance. This is why Christ divided the consecration, so that we might be mindful of the cup of his suffering which he drank out of love and through which he delivered us from eternal death and purchased for us from his Father a life of grace and glory. This is what the consecration of his holy blood teaches us, whereas the consecration of our Lord's body reveals to us the greatness of his love, for he wishes to feed and nourish us spiritually with himself so that he might live in us and we in him, just as I said earlier. He died out of love that we might live, and he lives in us so that we might remain living eternally in him.

These two marks of love are so great that no one can fully comprehend them. Whenever we attend Mass or approach the Sacrament, we should reflect on these things and think of Christ's love, so that we might forget ourselves and, for his glory, renounce all love of anything else. And whenever pain and suffering come our way, we should think of his suffering and follow him in obedience and self-abandonment, even unto death. It is thus that we will come to savor his love, with which he has chosen and loved us from all eternity, without beginning.

Four signs of God's love for us

I find there are four signs of God's eternal love which are so sublime and so great that all of Holy Scripture, from its very beginning, is rooted in them. The first of these is that out of love God created us to his image and likeness. The second is that the Son of God, who is the eternal wisdom, assumed a human nature out of love and impressed upon it his own Person. The third is that this same Son of God, Jesus Christ, died out of love, redeemed us with his precious blood, and washed away all our sins in baptism. He also united us with himself above our own nature in the Spirit of his love. The fourth sign of his love is that he gave us his flesh and blood, together with all that he had received from our human nature and all that he is—both God and a human being—to be our food and drink, so that he might live eternally in us and we in him, who is both divine and human. Now note these four points very carefully as I explain them in greater detail.

Our creation to God's image and likeness. God, from all eternity, so loved the world that he gave us his only Son in these four ways. As regards the first of them, Holy Scripture teaches us that God, the heavenly Father, created all human beings to his image and to his likeness. His image is his Son, his own eternal wisdom. All things live in him, as St. John says: "All that was made was life in him" (Jn 1:3–4). That life is nothing other than God's image, in which God has known everything from all eternity and which is also the cause of all creatures. This image, which is the Son of God, is therefore eternal, prior to all creation.

It is to this eternal image that we have all been made, for in the most noble part of our soul—namely, in the ground of our higher powers—we have been created as a living and eternal mirror of God, on which God has impressed his eternal image and on which no other image can ever be impressed. This mirror remains constantly before the face of God and therefore participates in the eternity of the image which it has received. In this image God knew us in himself before we were created, and now that we have been created in time he knows us in this image as destined for himself. This image exists essentially and personally in all persons. Each person possesses it wholly and indivisibly, and all persons together do not possess more of it than a single person does. We are therefore all one, united in our eternal image, which is the image of God and the source of us all—of all our life and all our becoming. Our created being and life are directly dependent on this image as on their eternal cause. Nevertheless our created being does not become God, nor does God's image become a creature, for we are created to the image, that is, created so as to receive the image of God, and that image is the uncreated and eternal Son of God.

As regards God's essential being, this image is that very being and is therefore essential, and as regards the divine nature it is that nature itself.

This nature is fruitful, comprising both fatherhood and the Father. In this fruitful nature the Father is in the Son and the Son is in the Father, but in the Father the Son is filial and unbegotten, being the immanent fruit of the divine nature. Here the nature acts both paternally (by always begetting) and filially (by ceaselessly being begotten). But in the begetting itself, the Son is a distinct Person, eternally proceeding from the Father, while the Holy Spirit, the third Person, flows forth in burning ardor as the love of both Father and Son into all creatures who are prepared to receive the Spirit.

Now the topmost part of our soul is always thus prepared, for it is bare and devoid of images and is always gazing at and tending toward its source. It is therefore an eternal and living mirror of God which ceaselessly receives the eternal birth of the Son, who is the image of the Holy Trinity. In this image God knows himself and all that he is according to both his essential being and the Persons, for in the essential being of God and in each of the Persons the image is all that the Person is in the divine nature.

We all possess this image as an eternal life—apart from ourselves, prior to our creation—while in our created being this image is the super-essential being of our essential being and is eternal life. From this the substance of our soul has three attributes, which are but one in nature. The soul's first attribute is an essential bareness devoid of images. Through it we are like the Father and are also united with him and with his divine nature. The second attribute may be called the soul's higher reason. This is a mirrorlike resplendence through which we receive the Son of God, the eternal wisdom. Through this resplendence we are like the Son, and through receiving him we become one with him. The third attribute is what I call the spark of the soul, which is the soul's natural tendency toward its source. Through it we receive the Holy Spirit, who is God's love. Through this tendency we are like the Holy Spirit, and through receiving him we become one spirit and one love with God.

These three attributes constitute the undivided substance of the soul, its living ground and the proper ground of the higher powers. The likeness and the union are in all of us by nature, but in the case of sinners they are hidden in their proper ground because of the coarseness of sin. Therefore, if we wish to find and experience the kingdom of God which is hidden within us, we must lead an interiorly virtuous life and be exteriorly well ordered in genuine charity, following Christ in every way so that grace, love, and virtue might raise us up to the highest part of our being, where God lives and reigns. Without grace we cannot contemplate or experience the blessedness which is God himself—neither by any natural light nor by any artifice or skill of our own. It is for this reason that God created the higher powers of our soul, namely, in order that we might receive his likeness, that is, his grace and his gifts. We are thereby renewed and elevated above our own nature and are made like him in love and virtue.

Through the supernatural likeness to God which we have through grace and virtue, our memory is raised up to a state of imageless bareness, our understanding to a state of simple truth, and our will to a state of divine freedom. We are thus like God through grace and virtue and are united with him above and beyond the likeness in a state of blessedness. This is the first sign of the love which God showed for human nature: his creating us to his image and likeness.

God's sending of his Son to us. But when Adam, the first human being, was disobedient and broke our Lord's commandment, he became unlike God because of his sin. He, and we with him, forfeited Paradise and access into the kingdom of God. This led to the second sign of love which God has shown for us all, namely, the fact that he sent his only Son to share our nature and so become a fellow human being and the brother of us all. Christ humbled himself but exalted us, made himself poor but us rich, and brought disgrace upon himself but honor to us. But even though he humbled himself, he did not thereby lose his nobility, for he remained all that he had been when he took upon himself what he had not been: He remained God in becoming a human being, so that human beings might become God. He clothed himself with the humanity of us all, just as a king might clothe himself with the garments of his household and of his servants, in order that all of us might wear the one garment of human nature together with him. But in a special way he clothed in a royal garment— namely, in his divine personhood—the soul and body which he received from the immaculate Virgin Mary. This garment belongs by nature to no one but him alone, for he is both divine and human in one Person.

If we are to be clothed with him, this can come about only through his grace. If we love him so much that we are able to deny ourselves and transcend our created personality, we will be united with his Person, which is eternal truth. You well know that by nature we have all been born as children of wrath (cf. Eph 2:3), as murderers and oppressors in the kingdom of God. This is due to the disobedience of the first human being, who lost the grace which he had received for the benefit of all who were to be born of him as members of the human race. To expiate this sin the Father sent us his Son, who took on our nature and through the Holy Spirit was born into our humanity.

Our redemption through Christ's death. The Son's coming was not enough

215

for the forgiveness of sins, for the Father wanted to make satisfaction for sin in accordance with justice. He therefore delivered his Son to death because of sin, and the Son was obedient to him even unto death, while the Holy Spirit brought this work to completion through love. This is the third sign of God's love: that the Son of God saved us by his death, purchasing and redeeming us before his Father's face with his precious blood so that we might have life through his death. He washed us in the spring of water which flowed from his side (Jn 19:34), saved us with his blood, and united us with his Spirit in love. We therefore remain always in him, for in him we are a single spiritual life. All this is signified by the water which is mixed with the wine in the chalice when his blood is consecrated, for the water which is united with the wine at the consecration represents Christ's people united with him and living in his blood. No one can have or experience such a life except believing Christians who are united with Christ in his love.

Christ's gift of himself in the Eucharist. There follows the fourth sign of love, one which Christ left his chosen friends who live in him. It consists in the fact that he feeds and sustains them with the noble food and drink of his flesh and blood, which by right belong to him alone. He himself says: "Whoever eats my flesh and drinks my blood lives in me and I in him" (Jn 6:56), and again: "He will not die but will live forever" (cf. Jn 6:58). Living forever means living spiritually, just as do the angels and saints. They eat and drink Christ without employing teeth or mouth, for Christ is that living bread of heaven which the Father sent into the world so that through love we might eat and consume it in our spirit, just as the angels and saints do in heaven and just as Christ himself, through his love, consumes us all in himself.

Those who consume and are consumed in this way have an eternal and blessed life in Christ and are able to eat and drink as often as they think lovingly of their Beloved. All the same, they desire the Sacrament itself more avidly than other persons and are more apt and ready to receive it, for they love the ways and practices of the holy Church which Christ ordained and established for his own glory and for the benefit of his people. These persons are accordingly always growing and increasing in grace and in all the virtues, both interiorly and exteriorly, for all that they possess interiorly in their spirit they also receive exteriorly in the blessed Sacrament. They are therefore blessed in receiving, still more blessed in possessing, and most blessed of all in both possessing and receiving. Those, however, who receive the blessed Sacrament unworthily, in a state of mortal sin, are passing judgment on themselves. So too, those who receive neither in spirit nor in the Sacrament are dead in the sight of God, for they are living merely according to nature, apart from grace. As regards the way in which we should receive Christ and in which we should eat and be eaten, I have already spoken about that.

The fourth point: the hidden nature of Christ's presence

Now there are some coarse, foolish persons who think they are wiser than Christ, who is the very wisdom of God. Such persons reflect on and ask about the reason why Christ is present in the blessed Sacrament in a hidden and concealed way, not in a visible way as he was then and as he is now in heaven. Holy Scripture gives the answer thus: "Everything which God has done is very good, and everything which comes from God is well-ordered" (cf. Gn 1:31). Again, the Prophet Isaiah says that "a light has arisen for the people who were walking in the kingdom of darkness and death" (cf. Is 9:1). That light is Christ, and St. John says that this light "shines in the darkness, and the darkness is not able to comprehend it" (Jn 1:5), for St. Paul writes that we now see as in a mirror and in likenesses, but that in eternal life we will see the glory of our Lord Jesus Christ face to face and will know him as clearly as he now knows us (cf. 1 Cor 13:12). But here on earth we are able to know him in the light of our faith, just as the Apostles did both before his death and also after his resurrection. They saw a human being but believed that he was God and that his divinity was hidden beneath his humanity. In the same way we see the blessed Sacrament with our bodily eyes but believe that the body of our Lord is hidden for us within the Sacrament. If we were to see our Lord in his glorious resplendence as he is in heaven, we would not be able to bear it, for our eyes are mortal and would lose their power of sight, just as all our senses would fail before the resplendence of our Lord's body.

From this you can judge how inconceivably great must be the spiritual resplendence of his soul and his divinity, and you can accordingly understand that all the gifts in which our Lord Jesus Christ placed our spiritual life are concealed and enveloped in sacraments and exterior, perceptible signs. Thus holy baptism, which constitutes our entry into eternal life, is actualized through water and the appropriate words. Many other gifts which Christ gives us in the holy Church are all concealed in particular ways, such as through chrism, oil, words, acts, signs, and sacraments, all according to right order and the needs of each person. In a special way the Lord of all gifts, Jesus Christ, through the power of his words, concealed and hid his flesh and blood from us in the blessed Sacrament, so that here on earth we would have to live amidst all his gifts with a firm faith rather than with a clear and glorious sight of them, for it is through a complete and integral faith that we will merit this eternal sight.

Those persons are therefore foolish who want to bring eternal life and God's glory into the temporal order, or the things of time into eternity, for all this is impossible. If we were to see our Lord as he is in heaven, it would be impossible as well as inhuman for us to eat his body or drink his blood. But at present it is the Sacrament which we eat with our teeth, while it is in the Sacrament and through our faith and love that we eat his flesh and drink his blood in our soul. In this way we are united with him and he with us.

Christ, the wisdom of God, conceived of this loving union in his spirit and brought it to realization in his works of truth, just as it had been pre-figured through types and likenesses from the beginning of the world. You should therefore note the loving union which Christ wishes to have with us all. All the hosts which lie before priests throughout the world are to-gether the single substance of bread prior to their consecration. At the con-secration, through the power of God, the substance of bread is changed into the substance of our Lord's body. This is the same substance and the same body which is in heaven, and in the Sacrament all of us in common receive it substantially. In this substance we receive all that is essentially one with it, such as length, breadth, and magnitude, together with all that belongs to the body as it is one with the substance—we receive all of this in the Sacrament. It is therefore by means of the Sacrament that the body of our Lord is in all countries, all places, and all churches, and that we are able to lift it up and lay it down, to hold and carry it in pyxes and ciboria, and to take, give, and receive it in many different ways.

As regards the way he now sits in heaven—with hands, feet, and all his members, and being contemplated in the fullness of his glory by the angels and saints—he does not move from there but remains ever present to those heavenly beings; we are therefore not able to receive him in this form, neither now nor ever. But after the Last Day, when we come to heaven with our own glorified body, we will all be near him and with him. There we will behold his glorious countenance with our bodily eyes and hear his loving, sweet voice with our bodily ears. At this our heart and all our senses will be filled with his glory and we will be immersed in him through love and joy, and he in us. All this is the least of the glories of heaven, because it comes from without and is perceptible by the senses. Nevertheless, as long as we are here on earth we cannot behold the coun-tenance of our Lord with such clarity, for our senses would not be able to bear it. We must therefore now walk in Christian faith and receive the Sacrament devoutly, reverently, and lovingly, so that after this life we might experience and savor eternal bliss.

The fifth point: the different groups who receive the blessed Sacrament

The first group

We have now to consider the different kinds of persons who receive the blessed Sacrament, both those in the clerical state and those who are laypersons. The group with which I will begin is comprised of those who are weakhearted by nature. When such persons are touched by God's grace and respond docilely and obediently to its promptings, their affectivity and desires become so hot and so strongly moved by an affective love of our Lord's humanity that they easily scorn and renounce everything in the world so as to be able to give themselves to their Beloved in accordance with their longing and for the satisfaction of their desires. Since they cannot come any nearer our Lord than in the Sacrament, they fall into a state of restlessness because of the fervent affection and insatiable desire which they have for the blessed Sacrament. At times it even seems to them that they will go mad and die if they cannot receive the Sacrament.

There are not many such persons. They are usually women or girls, seldom men, for they are of a weak temperament and are not raised up and enlightened in their spirit. For this reason their exercises are on the level of the senses and desires and are completely filled with representations of our Lord's humanity. They are unable to feel or understand how anyone could receive our Lord in spirit, apart from the Sacrament. This is the reason why they languish interiorly in their desire and longing for our Lord. No one can advise them, calm them, or bring them help or peace before they have received the Sacrament. But afterward they are all at peace and give themselves to their Beloved in rest, spiritual savor, and a superabundant sweetness of soul and body. This lasts until a new grace and exercise take possession of their nature and of all the powers of their soul. Then they fall back into a state of longing, desire, and restlessness as though they had never before received the Sacrament. They seem to be out of their mind, so much does their heart open wide in yearning to receive the blessed Sacrament once more.

Such persons are like the royal official who asked our Lord to come down to Capernaum and heal his son, who was close to death. Our Lord replied: "Unless you see signs and wonders, you do not believe" (Jn 4:48), at which the official said: "Lord, come down before my son dies." He did not believe that our Lord could heal his son without coming to him at his house, laying his hands on his head, and performing other signs with which to heal him. These persons behave in the same way in their affection for the blessed Sacrament, which is a genuine sign of the Lord's body there present. They accordingly languish in a restless desire and longing for the Sacrament and call out to the priest and to our Lord: "Lord, come down here in the blessed Sacrament into my house before I die of love."

Such persons are bold and daring and are untouched by grave sin. They have been set free by God for as long as they remain in this state. They may therefore receive the Sacrament on Sundays and on such other days as they receive permission. But if this permission is not granted, that is God's will, and they should then reflect and meditate on what our Lord said to the royal official: "Go, your son lives" (Jn 4:50). The soul which believes, loves, and desires to receive the blessed Sacrament is full of grace; it lives in God and God in it. They should console themselves with this reflection as best they can.

Now these persons are generally of a weak temperament and are subject to natural inclinations. Therefore, when they pray or when they wish to meditate on our Lord's humanity with desire and affection, they are sometimes touched and moved, against their will and intention, by their lower appetites, for their exercises are still in the realm of the senses and live in flesh and blood. The more they think of themselves and of the inordinate inclinations of their body at such times, the more do these inclinations increase and the more strongly is their nature drawn to disorder and transgression. If they are to win the victory and keep their nature pure in the service of the Lord, they must forget themselves and turn their face entirely toward him whom they love. Then they will be filled with his image in soul and body, in heart and senses, and will thus become pure and overcome every obstacle. Such is the first group of persons who receive the blessed Sacrament worthily.

The second group

There follows the second group, which is more advanced than the first. It is composed of persons whose spirit is astute and understanding but whose nature is inclined toward impurity. When such persons receive God's grace and abide in it, they often have to struggle, for the flesh is opposed to the spirit. It is for this reason that they choose a way of life in which they can turn inward and practice spiritual exercises in the Lord's sight. They thereby escape all temptations, all outbursts of emotion, and the incitements of flesh and blood. If they place more faith, hope, and trust in God than in their exercises and works, they will be raised up above their rational understanding to the divine light. Moreover, if they remain raised up in this divine light and set their mind and desires more on what is above reason and comprehension than on what they can discover and understand through the power of reason, then their faith reaches its perfection and their love is grounded on its true foundation. They are set free and come to the knowledge of God, of truth, and of the root of all virtues.

All the same, their nature retains its life in flesh and blood, with all the appetites, torpor, sloth, and inordinate inclinations which they experienced formerly. When such persons observe and experience this within themselves, they abandon and scorn everything in themselves which is opposed to God and to their spirit and which hinders their pursuit of perfection. They let go of all sensuousness and flee inward in spirit in the sight of God with faith, devotion, and humble prayer, just as St. Paul did when he was tempted in the flesh (cf. 2 Cor 12:7–9). The spirit of God then answers their humble prayer, assuring them that God's grace is strong enough to withstand every temptation, "for strength is made perfect in weakness" (2 Cor 12:9). This is true in the case of all who struggle and who turn prayerfully in spirit to God's presence.

We may rightly compare such persons to the centurion in the Gospel, who was spiritually a believer even though by nature he was an uncircumcised pagan. He had under him a hundred soldiers who served him obediently at all times. He also had a servant who lay sick at his house, grievously afflicted by paralysis. The centurion therefore asked our Lord to heal him, to which our Lord replied: "I will come and heal him." Then the centurion said, "Lord, I am not worthy that you should come under my roof; but say only a word and my servant will be healed" (Mt 8:8). Our Lord praised his faith, and in that very hour his servant was healed. In the same way, as long as these persons experience in their nature impure appetites and inclinations to sin, just so long is their desire and affection for our Lord's humanity blocked and hindered and just so long is their servant (that is, their corporeal nature) opposed to God and to their spirit and grievously afflicted by the enemy, for they are not willing to follow their spirit with desire and affection in our Lord's service.

Such persons have no fervent desire for the blessed Sacrament as long as they struggle in this way, but they say with a humble heart: "Lord, I am impure and am not worthy that your holy body should come in the Sacrament under the roof of my impure body. Lord, I am also unworthy of all the honor, goodness, and consolation which good persons receive from you. I must therefore always weep and lament and walk with firm faith in your sight. Even though I am poor and abandoned, I will not leave you but will call upon you and pray to you without ceasing until the time when your grace and my faith have healed my servant. Then I will praise and serve you with soul and body, with the entirety of my being, and with all my powers."

This is the way the second group of spiritual persons lives. They are more pleasing to God than the first group, for even though they are sick and tempted in their nature and live without God's consolation and sweetness, their spirit is nevertheless full of faith, devotion, and divine love. They often have to struggle against the devil, the world, and their own flesh and therefore require a strong spiritual fare with which they can win the victory. This fare is the Lord's body in the Sacrament, which they will receive as often as accords with their rule, their office, or the good custom of other spiritual persons with whom they live.

The third group

The third group of good persons is composed of those who are still holier and much more advanced in spirit and nature. These are recollected persons who, with God's grace, walk in his presence with a spirit which is free and exalted and which draws inward their heart and senses, their soul and body, and all their corporeal powers. Such persons have mastered their spirit and nature and have thereby found true peace. Even though they might at times experience some incitement in their nature, they quickly win the victory. No inordinate movement can long continue within them, for they truly know our Lord in both his divinity and his humanity. They exercise this knowledge with a spirit which is free of images both when they turn inward with a pure love which is raised up to the nature of the Godhead and when they turn outward with a heartfelt affection which is conformed to the image of our Lord's humanity. The more they know and love, the more do they savor and experience, and the more they savor and experience, the more do they desire, long for, seek, ground, and find what they love with their heart, soul, and spirit.

These persons are very much like Zacchaeus, a man of whom we read in St. Luke's Gospel (19:1–9). He wished to see our Lord Jesus as he was, but he could not do so because of the crowd of people, for he was short and small of stature. He therefore ran ahead of all the people and climbed a tree at a place where Jesus would pass. When Jesus drew near, he saw the man and said: "Zacchaeus, come down quickly, for I must stay at your house this very day." Zacchaeus received our Lord into his house with great joy, saying: "Lord, I give half of my possessions to the poor, and if I have wronged anyone, I repay him fourfold." To this, our Lord replied: "Today salvation has come to this house, for this man has spiritually become a son of Abraham," for it was through his faith that he climbed up the tree and saw and knew Jesus, whom he desired. He then descended obediently and humbly received Jesus, whom he knew and loved, into his house. With an outflowing generosity he distributed his possessions and paid back any wrongs fourfold. In this way he became righteous. Such was his life and his name, and thus did he become holy and blessed. Jesus remains living within him, both here on earth and in eternity.

Now note how the persons I have previously mentioned resemble this man. They desire to see Jesus as he is. All power of reason and all natural light are too short and small for this, so they run ahead of all crowds and all the multiplicity of creatures. Through faith and love they climb up to the highest part of their mind, where their spirit lives in its freedom, devoid of images and obstacles. It is there that Jesus is seen, known, and loved in his divinity, for there he is always present to the free and exalted spirit which has risen above itself in love of him. Jesus there flows forth with a fullness of grace and favors, but he says to all: "Come down quickly, for the exalted freedom of the spirit cannot be maintained except through lowly obedience of mind. You must know and love me as both God and a human being, higher than all and lower than all. You will savor me when I raise you up above all things and above yourself to myself, and when you lower yourself beneath all things and beneath yourself to me and for my sake. Then I will have to come to your house and remain living with you and in you, and you with me and in me."

When these persons know, taste, and feel this, they come down quickly in great disdain of themselves, and with a humble heart and true displeasure over their life and all their works they say: "Lord, I am not worthy—but am truly unworthy—that I should receive your glorious body in the blessed Sacrament into the sinful house of my body and soul. But be gracious to me, Lord, and have mercy on my poor life and all my transgressions." As long as these persons look at themselves and at their transgressions and failings, they are displeased with themselves and give themselves to the practice of a loving fear, a humble self-disdain, and a genuine hope in the sight of God. To the degree that they come down through displeasure with and disdain of themselves in true humility, to that degree do they please God and ascend before his face with true reverence.

Their life and exercises therefore consist in turning inward to God and outward to themselves. The turn inward is characterized by their spirit's being raised freely in loving reverence to God and in God, while the turn outward to themselves means displeasure with and renunciation of themselves. All the good works which they do or are able to do, whether exteriorly or interiorly, are completely unnoticed by them and are of no importance to them, seeming to be as nothing in the sight of God. They stand in the middle of these two turnings, sometimes looking inward, sometimes outward, and are always in control of themselves and therefore able to turn either way whenever they want. Their outward vision is governed by the power of reason, rooted in charity and in the practice of good customs and holy works, ordered to every virtue, and always exercised in the sight of our Lord. They accordingly remain chaste and pure of conscience and are always growing and increasing in grace and every virtue before God and all other persons. Their inward vision is at times governed by reason and characterized by particular forms and images, while at other times it is above reason and devoid of particular forms and images. When governed by reason, it is also full of desire and wisdom, since such persons are standing in the sight of God's love and goodness, where we learn all wisdom.

These persons are truly humble and free. They therefore represent to themselves the humanity of our Lord Jesus Christ and speak to him in the following way: "Lord, you have said, 'Without me you can do nothing' (Jn 15:5). You have also said, 'Unless you eat my flesh and drink my blood, you have no life in you' (Jn 6:53). You have said in addition, 'Whoever eats my flesh and drinks my blood lives in me and I in him' (Jn 6:56). Lord, I am presently a poor sinner and unworthy of the heavenly food which you yourself are. Nevertheless, Lord, you have given and left yourself for the sinner who is displeasing to himself, who contritely confesses and laments his sins, and who has a genuine trust in you. Such a person is pleasing to you, for you have taught us that you came to call not the just but the sinner (cf. Mt 9:13), so that he might repent and do penance for his sins. I am therefore bold and outspoken, forgetful of myself and of all my transgressions because of your grace, for you yourself have said, 'Come to me, all you who labor and are burdened, and I will refresh you' (Mt 11:28). You have also said that you are our living bread which has come down from heaven and that anyone who eats it will live forever (cf. Jn 6:51). You are also the living spring which flows out of your Father's heart by means of the Holy Spirit. As a consequence, Lord, the more I eat, the more hungry I become, and the more I drink, the more thirsty I become, for I cannot take you fully into myself and consume you. But I ask you, Lord, of your great nobility, that you take me fully into yourself and consume me, so that I might become one life with you and in you and that I, in your life, might be able to rise above myself and above all particular forms and exercises to a state devoid of forms—that is, to a state of formless love where you are your own beatitude and that of all the saints. It is there that I will find the fruit of all the sacraments, of all particular forms, and of all holiness."

However, we must seek this fruit in particular forms, in the sacraments, and in a holy life; only then will we find it in a state devoid of form and measure, in eternal and fathomless love. We will eternally remain within ourselves and be blessed and well ordered in particular forms of glory, each of us in a special way according to the degree of our virtue and love, and we will blissfully enjoy God above and beyond ourselves and live in him apart from particular forms and above ordered divisions, in that fathomless love which he is himself. Those who understand this and live accordingly may receive the blessed Sacrament every day that it is given to them, for they are well ordered and full of grace and virtue in all their exercises, whether these are directed inward or outward.

These comprise the third group of persons, the most advanced of all who nobly approach the Sacrament. Their life and exercises consist of four qualities, of which the first is a conscience free from all grave sin. The second quality is their supernatural knowledge and wisdom in looking both inward and outward, that is, in contemplating and acting. The third quality is their genuine humility of heart, of will, and of spirit, practiced in their bearing, their words, and their deeds. The fourth quality is that they have died to all self-centeredness, that is, to all self-will, for the sake of God's free will, and that they have also died to all images which occupy the understanding for the sake of that imageless truth which is God himself. This bare simplicity of mind is the dwelling place of the Godhead.

Now note that these four qualities were characteristic of our Lady's life and exercises when she conceived our Lord. She was chaste, pure, and virginal, full of God's grace. She was also knowledgeable and wise in the way she questioned and answered the angel, who taught her the complete truth. She was humble to the core of her being, a quality which drew the Son of God from heaven to our earthly valley. And she said: "I am the handmaid of the Lord and it is his will which I must desire. Let it be done to me according to your word." When the Holy Spirit heard these words, they were so pleasing to God's own love that the Spirit sent God's Son into Mary's womb, the Son who freed us from every evil.

Now note what follows and learn from it. Although Mary was chosen above all creatures to be the mother of God and the queen of heaven and earth, she nevertheless chose to be the handmaid of God and of all the world. Therefore, when she had conceived our Lord, she went with great haste into the hill country to serve St. Elizabeth, the mother of St. John the Baptist, as her humble handmaid until the time when St. John was born. In the same way her Son, our dear Lord Jesus Christ, who is both divine and human, after he had consecrated the blessed Sacrament, given it to his disciples, and received it himself, wrapped a linen towel around himself, knelt before his disciples, washed their feet, and dried them with the towel, saying: "I am giving you an example, that as I have done to you, so you also should do in service to one another" (cf. Jn 13:15).

Accordingly, as regards persons in religious orders, however advanced they may be in contemplation and in their way of life and however frequently they receive our Lord in the Sacrament—even if daily—if an office is entrusted to them or they are chosen to be superior so that they have to serve the community in things which are beneficial to it and without sin, they should do this gladly and lovingly. Even if during their periods of recollection and prayer they feel hindered and distracted because of the things which have been entrusted to their care, and even if they are full of cares over the external affairs of the community, they should not for these reasons be negligent of these matters or resign their office to free themselves of the burden. Rather, they should be obedient unto death toward God and their own superior and community in every matter which is good and honorable and beneficial to the community, as long as in turning inward to God they preserve their love, fear, and reverence, and as long as in turning outward they disdain and renounce themselves. In genuine humility they should consider everything they can do or suffer as being of little or no account. When dealing with members of their community or any other persons they should be gentle, cheerful, and generous, ready to lend appropriate help to everyone in his need with true equanimity.

Those who observe these rules, whether they be religious superiors or their subjects, may receive the Sacrament as often as they want, just as they did previously, for they are now even more conformed to the life of our Lord Jesus Christ, to the Scriptures, and to the greatest saints than they were before, and they possess the true foundation of genuine contemplation, action, and virtue. I say the same concerning all who live outside religious orders if they maintain a state of being turned inward to God in unity with him and if they turn outward to their fellow Christians in works of charity in every necessary way. All such persons are nobler, more advanced, and nearer and more like our Lord than those who merely turn inward in contemplation without turning outward in works of charity, provided that the former have mastered themselves and that their neighbor stands in need of them. Those who wish only to turn inward in contemplation and so leave their neighbor in need do not live a recollected and contemplative life but are deceived to the core of their being. Above all things, beware of such persons.

The fourth group

There follows the fourth group of spiritual persons who may receive the Sacrament. These are persons of good will who sincerely set their minds on God's glory and their own salvation. They strive to follow the rule of their religious order and all the good usages which they have learned orally or in writing from those who preceded them and who established these regulations through their words and deeds. I am referring to such things as behavior in choir, chapterhouse, refectory, dormitory, and infirmary; times and places for silence and for speaking; and all that concerns fasting and other matters of discipline for both those who are sick and those who are healthy—these things to be observed always with true discretion in accordance with the rule of the order and the capabilities of human nature. The common rule of all good monks and nuns is that they renounce all self-will through humble obedience, that they always be doing something good when they are healthy and always be meek and patient when they are sick, and that they constantly struggle to overcome flesh and blood and all worldly things. If, however, they are negligent in what they do or leave undone or if they fall into spiritual disorder by doing too much or too little, so that their conscience accuses them of sin, they should humbly and contritely lament and confess this to a priest, do the penance which he assigns, and place their trust in God. Then, relying on God's grace, they may freely approach the Sacrament as often as is common according to good custom or the practice of their order. As regards other spiritual persons, who are not in a religious order but who follow good rules of conduct in obedience to God, the holy Church, and their superiors in such matters as fasting, liturgical celebrations, and all the regulations which are observed by good Christians, these persons may also approach the Sacrament in accordance with the advice of their confessor and the customs of the place where they live.

The fifth group

There follows the fifth group of those who approach the Sacrament. These are conceited persons who take pleasure in thinking that they are holier and more righteous, wiser and more understanding than anyone else in what they do and what they leave undone. They are not enlightened by God and accordingly think that they and their works are great. They act in ways that make a fine show, for they want to appear holy and have others consider them holy. They seek to have the advantage over others in going to confession or receiving Communion. When anyone gets ahead of them in any way, they become displeased and peevish, for they consider it an injustice that anyone should take precedence over themselves. They are melancholy and easily offended; they like to be praised and honored but are averse to being humbled or brought low. They gladly accept commendation, a reputation for holiness, and whatever is flattering to their nature. In no respect do they wish to be advised, admonished, or instructed, but they themselves wish to advise, instruct, and admonish anyone who draws near them. Even though they are well behaved in church—reading, praying, kneeling, and bearing themselves nicely—as soon as they return home they become intractable, gruff, tart, contemptuous, and rude to their servants and to all with whom they live. They make bold to approach the Sacrament often, for they consider their behavior justified and proper, or else a minor failing or the fault of those with whom they live.

As long as such a person is pleased with himself, he will remain proud in spirit and be unable to recognize clearly the transgressions which arise from this pride, for he thinks himself deserving of everything and always right in all that he does. Even though such behavior might not be mortally sinful—on account of these persons' lack of understanding and their many confessions—their way of life is nevertheless very dangerous. In confession they must often be treated severely by being reprimanded and chastised for their pride and by being told the truth in the following way: "With fear, relying on the mercy of our Lord, a priest may give you the blessed Sacrament on major feastdays so that you may not fall into despair or become impatient. But if you were to become meek and humble, you could always be fed on Christ, living in him and growing and increasing in every virtue."

The sixth group

The sixth group of persons who may receive the blessed Sacrament is in general made up of all those who love our Lord and their own salvation so much that they wish never again willingly and knowingly to commit a deliberate mortal sin. Out of their fear and love of God and of themselves, they wish to keep his commandments and those of the holy Church in things to be done or left undone and in everything which is right and necessary. Once a year, namely, at Eastertime, they wish sincerely to confess their sins to a priest—both great and small sins, just as they committed them and insofar as they recall them and are guilty of them. Afterward they wish to receive the blessed Sacrament according to the law and custom of good Christians. They are resolved always to be obedient with a willing heart and to do penance for their sins in accordance with the will of their confessor and the nature and manner of their transgressions. Those who live in this way are following the common way to heaven, which all Christians have to follow if they wish to be saved, even though it be accompanied by severe acts of penance or a long time in purgatory.

The seventh group

There follows the seventh group, made up of all those whom God has scorned and rejected. These should not be given the blessed Sacrament, neither during their lifetime nor at the time of their death, unless they repent. The first category within this group consists of pagans, Jews, and all unbelievers. A second category includes bad Christians who scorn and blaspheme Christ and do not revere his holy sacraments or who do not believe that Christ is present in his flesh and blood in the blessed Sacrament of the Altar. Such persons are all damned. However, suggestions and temptations against faith apart from the consent of our will can well coexist with the state of grace. A person should therefore struggle to win the victory through faith, for in this way a person merits a reward rather than damnation. But it is holier, easier, and better simply to walk in faith above reason, without suffering or struggle.

There are other diabolical persons who say that they themselves are Christ or God, that their hand created heaven and earth, that heaven and earth and all things depend on their hand, and that they have been raised above all the sacraments of the holy Church, so that they neither need nor desire them. They disdain and attach no importance to the rules and customs of the holy Church and to all that the saints have written, whereas they consider the lack of regulations and the beastly practices of their evil sects, which they themselves have invented, to be holy and great. They have expelled the fear and the love of God from themselves and wish to have no knowledge of good and evil. They have discovered within themselves a formless state above reason and therefore think in their folly that on the Last Day all rational creatures—both the good and the wicked, both angels and devils—will become a single formless being. That being, they claim, will be God, blessed in nature and having no knowledge or will.

Pay close attention, for this is probably the most foolish and perverse opinion that has ever been heard since the creation of the world, and yet through this and similar opinions many persons, who appear to be spiritual but who are more wicked than the devil, have gone astray. Their unbelief is refuted by pagans and Jews; by nature, the law, and reason; by all the writings of the good and bad alike; by the angels and devils; and by God's words and works. The faith common to us all teaches us that God is three in one and one in three and that it is his nature to know himself, to love himself, and to enjoy himself in himself. These three activities are change-less and eternal, without beginning or end. In himself God is order and form and a mirror of all creatures, and in accordance with this exemplar he created all things with order, form, measure, and weight. He is thus in all things and all things are in him.

The life which we have in God is one with him and is blessed by na-ture. But we, with the angels, have another life, which God created out of nothing and which will last forever. This life cannot be blessed by nature, but it can become blessed through God's grace. If we obtain grace—faith, hope, knowledge, and love—then we practice virtues pleasing to God and so are raised up above ourselves and united with God. But no creature can become God. In the same way, the angels in heaven were not created blessed by nature, but they received God's grace. Those who turned to him in knowledge and love became blessed and were firmly established and united with God in a state of eternal enjoyment. Nevertheless they still did not become God and can never do so, but they all remained before the Lord's face, each in a particular way in accordance with the distinctions of state and order which they had received from God in nature, grace, and glory as well as through their own merits. They will remain like this for all eternity, and we with them all, knowing and loving God, thanking and praising him, and above all enjoying him, each in his own state and order with the angels in accordance with the degree of his worthiness and the merits he acquired through his virtues here on earth. It is for this reason that our Lord says that our angels always behold the face of the Father in heaven (Mt 18:10).

Just as the good angels turned to God and are blessed, the bad angels turned away from God to themselves in their pride, for they took pleasure in the nobility and beauty which God had given to their nature and scorned grace and any turning to God. They suffered immediate damnation and fell from heaven into the accursed darkness, where they must remain forever. But more wicked than any devil are these hypocritical unbelievers who scorn God and his grace, the holy Church and all its sacraments, and Holy Scripture and all virtuous practices. They say that they live in a formless way above all forms, that they are as empty as if they did not exist at all, and that they have neither knowledge nor love, neither will nor desire, nor any exercise of virtue, being empty of everything. Because they want to sin and to perpetrate their impure wickedness without fear or qualms of conscience, they go on to say that at the Judgment on the Last Day both angels and devils, both good persons and wicked persons will all become a single, simple divine substance, in which they will all be but one essential beatitude without any knowledge or love of God. Consequently, according to them God will neither will, know, nor love any creature.

This is the greatest error and the most perverse and foolish heresy that has ever been heard. No one should give the blessed Sacrament to such persons, neither during their lifetime nor at the time of their death, nor should they be given a Christian burial. Rather, they should rightly be burned at the stake, for in God's eyes they are damned and belong in the pit of hell, far beneath all the devils.

You should also know that the Sacrament should be withheld from all who live in a state of mortal sin and follow the ways of the world in the manner of beasts, without fear, love, or reverence toward God and without obeying God, the holy Church, and the law of Christ. The same holds true in the case of those who are proud or who oppress their neighbor. Consider also the following kinds of persons: those who are avaricious, miserly, and unmerciful; those who are wrathful, envious, cruel, and malfeasant; those who revile, curse, swear, and quarrel; those who commit usury and buy up everything without restraint; those who are sly, cunning, deceitful, and misleading; those who are false and untrustworthy in everything they do; those who are lazy, slothful, and unprepared for any virtue, but are avid and eager to turn quickly to sin; and those who are as intemperate and gluttonous as swine, drunken from morning till evening—no wonder they act so foolishly, for with their eating and drinking their belly has become their god (cf. Phil 3:19), while they, wishing only to fill all their vats with food and drink without measure, have become the mockery of the devil. There is seldom anything to be done for such persons, for all this gives rise to an unchaste life in which they give their body its satisfaction through their words, bearing, and actions. Such persons are just like the devil's vats, for they are slaves of sin and so have the devil as their master. Now note the evil circle in which they find themselves: They have fallen out of the state of God's grace and therefore no one should let them receive the Sacrament. Their whole life is nothing but a living death unless they repent and seek the Lord's pardon, for God's grace is always available for those who wish to make amends for their misdeeds.

Accordingly, when a sinner repents, confessing his faults before a priest and being willing to do penance, then he has received God. The priest will then rejoice together with the angels and saints and will give that person the blessed Sacrament, regardless of what time of year it is. But as for those who remain without self-knowledge and do not repent of their wickedness, they should not be given the blessed Sacrament whether they are dying or are still in good health, nor should they receive a Christian burial. As long as a person persists in his evil will and lives without sorrow for his sins, neither the pope nor all the priests on earth can absolve him, and if he dies in such a state he is damned.

The eighth group

There are some persons who are of a good nature and temperament—cheerful, generous, compassionate, and warmhearted. They are easily moved and swayed toward the good or the bad, depending on the company in which they find themselves, and so they sometimes fall into various grave sins. But when they see or hear something good from good persons, they are easily stirred to fear and anxiety over their sins and contritely turn back to God and do penance. Others come to self-knowledge through sickness and the fear of death, while still others do so at propitious times, such as Lent, through the sermons and penitential practices which are regularly carried out in the holy Church at such times. These persons are then touched with sorrow from within; they recognize their transgression and, following the lead of God's grace, accuse themselves of their sins in confession and seek to make reparation to God, to the holy Church, and to all persons as best they can. In this way they come to be of one will with God and may approach the Sacrament in reliance on God's mercy. Even if they fall often into sin, they are always more easily moved to repentance and readier to arise than persons who are refractory and intractable by nature. If they stand firm, they also advance farther in grace and virtue than those who are callous and less good-natured.

Furthermore, all those who, in conformity with good custom, sincerely confess their sins during Lent with true contrition, who receive their penance from their confessor, and who also resolve to live according to God's will in what they do and leave undone—all in genuine charity toward God and their neighbor—may receive our Lord with his grace at Easter, in accordance with the advice of their confessor and in true humility of soul and body.

Now you should understand that there are many persons who live in the world in a state of life which is compatible with God and with the holy Church and who are of such good will that they stand firm with the help of God and refrain from grave sins. Some are married, others are not; some hold offices of authority, others are servants; some are buyers, others are sellers in all sorts of business; some are laborers, others are engaged in some honest trade. They never knowingly and willingly deceive or cheat anyone, nor take or hold back what belongs to another. Rather, being just and upright in all things, they wish and intend to follow God's commandments. They have no hate, envy, or aversion toward anyone but are merciful and compassionate to anyone who is in need. They like to attend Mass and hear sermons, and have a fear, reverence, and love of God and of all good persons. They humbly accuse themselves of their transgressions in confession before a priest and are obedient in doing penance and other good works. Even though such persons are occupied with many cares in external matters in order to gain a livelihood for themselves and their families or in order to be able to share their goods with the poor, they may nevertheless freely receive the blessed Sacrament in reliance on God's mercy on every feastday that they wish. Although they often commit venial sins, they are, to the best of their ability, persons of good will, living uprightly in all things.

Note carefully what is involved in being a person of good will, someone who is of one will with God in all that he does, leaves undone, or suffers. Goodness of will is engendered and born of the Holy Spirit. This makes the will a living and willing instrument with which God accomplishes his ends. Goodness of will in a person is God's infused love, with which a person practices the things of God and all the virtues. Goodness of will is God's grace and our own supernatural life, with which we struggle against every sin and win the victory. United with God's grace, a good will sets us free, raising us up above ourselves and uniting us with God in a contemplative way of life. In turning inward to God, a good will is a spirit crowned with eternal love, while in turning outward it is the master of its exterior good works. It is itself the kingdom in which God reigns with his grace. In it lives charity, which is our loving affection for God. When raised above itself, it is blessed and united with God. Through it we die to sin and acquire a virtuous way of life, and in it we possess peace and harmony with all things. If we live in this way, we may receive our Lord in the Sacrament as often as we wish, or may do so spiritually through love.

PART THREE: THE LIVING LIFE

A. THE CORRECT UNDERSTANDING OF THIS LIFE

There are some persons who, over and above all virtuous exercises, find and experience within themselves a living life, which joins together the created and the uncreated, both God and creatures.[4] You should know that we possess an eternal life in the image of God's wisdom. This life always remains in the Father, flows out with the Son, and turns back toward the same nature with the Holy Spirit. We thus live eternally in our image of the Holy Trinity and of the paternal Unity. From this we also have a created life, which flows out of the same wisdom of God; in it God knows his power, wisdom, and goodness, and this is the image through which he lives in us. From this image of God our life acquires three properties, through which we become like the image of God which we have received; these are the properties of being, seeing, and tending toward the source of our creatureliness. There we live out of God and toward God, God in us and we in him. This is a living life, which is in all of us essentially, in our bare nature, for it is above hope and faith, above grace and all virtuous exercises. This is why its being, its life, and its works are all one. This life is hidden in God and in the substance of our soul. Because it is in all of us by nature, some persons are able to perceive it apart from grace, faith, and the practice of virtue. These are persons who have idly turned inward, above and beyond perceptible images, to the bare simplicity of their being. There they think they are holy and blessed, and some even think they are God. They consider nothing to be either good or evil, since they are able to transcend images and to possess their own being in bare emptiness. These are those false, unbelieving persons whom I described earlier as

---

4. The term "living life" (*levende leven*) may derive from St. Bernard's distinction between a *vita vitalis* and a *vita mortalis* at the beginning of his seventeenth sermon on Psalm 91 (*Qui habitat*).

forming the seventh group, those to whom no one should give the blessed Sacrament, for they are all in error and under the curse of God and of the holy Church.

Now raise your eyes above reason and all virtuous exercises and with a loving spirit and fixed attention look at that living life which is the source and cause of all life and all holiness. It will be seen as a glorious abyss of God's riches and as a living spring in which we feel ourselves to be united with God and flowing out in all our powers through grace and a multiplicity of gifts, each in his own way in accordance with his needs and merits. In this living spring we are all united with God, but in the streams of his grace we are divided and receive everything in different ways, so that everyone receives what is proper to him. Even so, we always remain united with one another in charity, in our human nature, and above all in that living life in which we are all united with God.

This union which we have with God is above reason and the senses. In it we are united with God in one spirit and one life, No one can perceive, find, or possess this life unless through love and God's grace he has died to himself in the living life, been baptized in the spring, and been born again of God's Spirit in divine freedom. He will then always remain dwelling in God, united with him in the living life and, through the richness and fullness of his love, will always be renewed and flow out with God's grace in every virtue. This is an eternal and heavenly way of life, born of the Holy Spirit and always renewed in love between God and ourselves. God's activity in the emptiness of our soul is eternal. We all have an eternal life with the Son in the Father; the same life flows forth and is begotten with the Son from the Father; and the Father, with the Son, has eternally known and loved this life in the Holy Spirit. We thus possess a living life, which has been in God from all eternity, before anything was created.

It is out of this life that God created us, though not from this life nor from God's substance, but rather from nothing. Our created life depends on our eternal life in God as on its eternal cause, which is by nature proper to it. For this reason our created life is one life, without intermediary, with the life which we have in God, while this eternal life which we have in God is one with God without intermediary, for God is the living exemplar of all that he has made and is also the cause and principle of all creatures. He knows himself and all things in one and the same act of seeing, and all the things which he knows in their distinctness in the mirror of his wisdom— in images, orders, forms, and reasons—are truth and life. This life is God himself, for there is within him nothing but his own nature. Nevertheless all things are in God apart from themselves, as in their own cause. That is why St. John says: "All that was made was life in him" (Jn 1:3–4), and that life is God himself. All of us, above and beyond our created being, have an eternal life in God as in the living cause which made and created us from nothing. But we are not God, nor did we make ourselves. We also did not flow forth from God by nature; rather, since God knew and willed us eternally in himself, he created us not by nature or out of necessity, but out of the freedom of his will.

God also knows all things and is able to do everything he wishes, both in heaven and on earth. He is in us as light and truth and reveals himself in the topmost part of our created being, raising our memory to a state of purity, our spirit to a state of divine freedom, and our understanding to a state of imageless bareness. He enlightens us with his eternal wisdom and teaches us to see and contemplate his fathomless riches. There there is life without labor, at the fountainhead of all grace; there there is the taste and experience of eternal blessedness, fully satisfied, with no tinge of anything unpleasant. Let us then transcend all that is passing with time; then we will be able to rejoice in love, for eternal life has been prepared for us.

B. THE SOUL AS A LIVING MIRROR

At the beginning of the world, when God resolved to create the first human being, he said in the Trinity of Persons: "Let us make man to our image and to our likeness" (Gn 1:26). God is a spirit, so his word is his knowledge and his action is his will. He is able to do all that he wills, and all his acts are full of grace and good order. He has created each person's soul as a living mirror, on which he has impressed the image of his nature. In this way he lives imaged forth in us and we in him, for our created life is one, without intermediary, with this image and life which we have eternally in God. That life which we have in God is one in God, without intermediary, for it lives in the Father with the unbegotten Son and is begotten with the Son from the Father, flowing forth from them both with the Holy Spirit. We thus live eternally in God and he in us, for our created being lives in our eternal image, which we have in the Son of God. This eternal image is one with God's wisdom and lives in our created being.

For this reason the eternal birth is always being renewed, and the flowing forth of the Holy Spirit into the emptiness of our soul is always occurring without interruption, for God has known, loved, called, and chosen us from all eternity. If we resolve to know, love, and choose him in return, then we are holy, blessed, and chosen from all eternity. Our heavenly Father will then reveal his divine resplendence in the topmost part of our soul, for we are his kingdom, in which he lives and reigns. Just as the sun in the heavens pervades and enlightens all the world with its rays and makes it fruitful, so too does God's resplendence as it reigns in the topmost part of our mind, for upon all our powers it sheds its bright, brilliant rays, namely, its divine gifts: knowledge, wisdom, clear understanding, and a rational, discerning insight into all the virtues. It is in this way that the kingdom of God in our soul is adorned.

For its part, that infinite love which is God himself reigns in the purity of our spirit like the glow of burning coals. It sends forth brilliant, burning sparks which, in the fire of love, touch and enflame the heart and senses, the will and desires, and all the powers of the soul to a stormy transport of restless, formless love. These are the weapons with which we must do battle against the awesome, immense love of God, which strives to burn up and devour all loving spirits in their very being. Nevertheless God's love arms us with its own gifts, enlightening our reason and commanding, advising, and teaching us to defend ourselves in the struggle and to maintain our own rights in love against it as long as we can. For this purpose it gives us fortitude, knowledge, and wisdom, and it draws all our sensible powers together into an experience of interior fervor. It makes our heart love, desire, and savor, gives our soul the power to fix its gaze in contemplation, bestows upon us the gift of devotion, and makes us ascend on its fiery flames. It also gives knowledge and the taste of eternal wisdom to our understanding, touches our amorous power, and makes our spirit burn and melt away in veneration before its face.

Here our reason and every activity characterized by the making of distinctions must give way, for our powers now become simply one in love, grow silent, and incline toward the Father's face, since this revelation of the Father raises the soul above reason to a state of imageless bareness. There the soul is simple, spotless, and pure, empty of everything. In this pure emptiness the Father reveals his divine resplendence, which neither reason nor the senses, neither rational observation nor distinctions can attain. Rather, all these things must remain below, for this infinite resplendence so blinds the eyes of reason that they have to give way before this incomprehensible light. However, that simple eye which dwells above reason in the ground of our understanding is always open, contemplating with unhindered vision and gazing at the light with the light itself—eye to eye, mirror to mirror, image to image.

With these three—eye, mirror, and image—we are like God and

united with him, for this vision in our simple eye is a living mirror which God created to his image and on which he impressed his image. His image is his divine resplendence, with which he fills the mirror of our soul to overflowing, so that no other light or image can enter there. But this resplendence is not an intermediary between God and ourselves, for it is both the very thing which we see and also the light with which we see, though it is distinct from our eye which does the seeing. Even though God's image is in the mirror of our soul and is united with it without intermediary, still the image is not the mirror, for God does not become a creature. The union of the image in the mirror is, however, so great and so noble that the soul is called the image of God. Furthermore, the very image of God which we have received and which we bear in our soul is the Son of God—the eternal mirror and the wisdom of God—in whom we all live and are eternally imaged forth. Nevertheless we are not God's wisdom, for in that case we would have created ourselves, which is impossible and contrary to faith, for all that we are and have comes from God and not from ourselves.

Even though the nobility of our soul is great, it is hidden from sinners and even from many good persons. All that we can know in natural light is imperfect, lacking in savor and feeling, for we cannot contemplate God or find his kingdom within our soul without his help and grace and without our own efforts practiced genuinely in his love and in the name of our Lord Jesus Christ, who is a willing mirror of himself.

C. THE IMMEDIATE CONDITIONS FOR THIS LIFE

God reveals himself to those he wishes, namely, to those who renounce themselves, who follow his grace in what they do and leave undone and in their practice of all the virtues, and who through faith, hope, and love are raised above all their words to their soul's bare act of seeing. This is that simple eye which is always open in the ground of our understanding, above reason. It is there that the eternal wisdom reveals itself and fills our bare act of seeing, that is, the simple eye of our soul, whose being, life, and activity are to contemplate, to fly, to run, and always to transcend our created being without looking around or turning back. Blessed are the eyes which see and to which God reveals his kingdom and his glory, that is, himself, for our heavenly Father lives in the kingdom of our soul as in himself. He there bestows his incomprehensible resplendence upon us, above our power of understanding, in the proper ground of our understanding.

The Father and the Son have their fathomless love flow into us, above our will and activity. In the ground of our will's goodness, our will is a fiery spark, the very life of the soul. It is there that the Father begets his Son and that their mutual love flows forth in a fathomless way. But we cannot comprehend this activity of God nor can our power of comprehension enter it, for all our powers, together with their activities, have to give way and passively undergo the transformation wrought by God. When we undergo God's action and the influx of the Spirit of our Lord, we are sons of God (cf. Rom 8:14)—by grace and not by nature. We then become simple and unified, for all our powers fall short as regards their own activity, melting and flowing away to nothingness before the face of God's eternal love. That is why this is called a life of annihilation in love.

Now you should understand that this life is lived in the self-transcendence of our spirit, for here a person transcends all his powers and their activities and enters his state of emptiness, his simple nature, and his spirit's purity. Our state of emptiness refers to a bare absence of images; our simple nature refers to the contemplation of eternal truth; and the purity of our spirit refers to our being united with God's Spirit. There we experience our union with God and our unity in God, feeling that we are breathed forth with God and breathed out of our own being into God.

The living union with God which we experience is active and is always being renewed between ourselves and God. Insofar as we embrace and touch each other, we feel a duality which does not allow us to remain in ourselves. Although we are above reason, we are not without reason and therefore feel that we are both touching and being touched, loving and being loved, and always being renewed and returning to ourselves. We feel ourselves coming and going like lightning in the heavens, for such striving and straining in love is like swimming against the current: we cannot break through or pass beyond our creaturely state. For this reason God's touch and our secret, interior striving constitute the last intermediary between ourselves and God, in which we become united with him in a mutual encounter in love. The living spring of the Holy Spirit is where we become united with God, and it has a welling vein of water, namely, God's touch, which is so strong and powerful that we cannot break through it to the abyss of God's fathomless love. We therefore always remain standing above reason in our very selfhood—imageless, gazing, and striving in incomprehensible richness. These are the three properties of the soul's nature, life, and activity; through them the soul is like God in its highest nobility. When it corresponds to God's eternal Trinity, the nature of the soul is imageless and empty—the dwelling place of the Father, his temple and kingdom. He begets his Son, that is, his resplendence, in the eye which is open in its gazing, and he has his Spirit, that is, his love, flow forth in the fervent striving of our spirit as the latter continues its eternal striving.

In our own works we always remain like God in the purity of our spirit, for we feel that we are seeing and striving after someone who is different from ourselves. It is through this that we are like God. In God's works, on the other hand, we undergo the action of his Spirit and the transformation wrought by his resplendence and love. There we are above likeness, being sons of God by grace. Whenever we feel that we are working and striving in him and that we are passively undergoing his action, we recognize all of this through his light, just as we savor and experience his love through his Spirit.

In our union with God we are one spirit and one life with him, but we always remain creatures, for even though we are transformed through his light and breathed out of ourselves into him through his love, we know and feel ourselves to be distinct from him. We must therefore always fix our gaze upon him and strive after him, an activity which will last forever, for we cannot lose our creaturely state or so purely transcend ourselves as not to remain eternally distinct from God. Although the Son of God assumed our nature and became a human being, he did not make us God. Indeed, many persons live in a state of sin and are not saved but damned.

But the Son of God has a soul created from nothing, and in addition a body taken from the pure blood of the Virgin Mary. He took up this soul and body and united them with himself in such a way that he is both the Son of God and the Son of Mary, both God and a human being in one Person. In the same way that a soul and body constitute a single human being, so too is God's Son and Jesus, the Son of Mary, a single, living Christ, the Lord and God of heaven and earth, for his soul is informed by the wisdom of God. Nevertheless his soul is not God nor is it God's nature, for God's nature cannot become a creature. But the two natures, remaining distinct, are united in the one divine Person, which is Jesus Christ, our dear Lord. He alone is with God in a way transcending all creatures—a powerful, living prince both in heaven and on earth, unlike anyone else. His humanity was filled with all God's gifts and with the fullness of sanctity. Everything which other holy persons have possessed since the beginning of the world or will ever be able to possess is divided among them, in accordance with God's will; our Lord's humanity alone received an undivided fullness of all gifts, with which he has filled all creatures and can fill them still further. He alone is the source and cause of all the good things which we have obtained or are able to obtain from God.

It is the grace of our Lord Jesus Christ which must enlighten us in all the truth of which we stand in need. In the beginning, when his soul was created and was united with the wisdom of God, his power of reason was so clear and his understanding so enlightened that his soul knew distinctly every creature which had ever existed or ever would exist. His humanity received from his heavenly Father on high both power and might over all things in heaven and on earth, so that he was able to give and to take, to put to death and to raise to life, to perform as many signs and wonders as he wished, to forgive sins, and to grant grace and eternal life, for everything which God had created was subject to Christ's humanity, to do with as he wished. Moreover, the Holy Spirit rested in his soul and in his human nature with all his gifts, making him rich, generous, and overflowing toward all who needed and longed for him. He was humble, patient, gentle, merciful, full of grace and faithfulness, obedient, submissive of will, and innocent of any fault. He delivered himself up to the scorn and revilement of all, bending his knees in prayer to his God and Father. He handed himself over to death so that we might be saved and live with him forever. He is the rule and mirror according to which we ought to live. His humanity is a lamp of God's resplendence which has shed its light upon heaven and earth and will continue to do so forever. His blessed name, Jesus, was foreseen, designated, and chosen from all eternity and was announced by the angel to his mother, the Virgin Mary, so that he might be both God's Son and her Son, both God and a human being in one Person. It is in this way that he was given to us, lived for us, served and taught us, redeemed and delivered us with his death, and washed away our sins in his holy blood. He afterward ascended above all the heavens and all the angelic choirs and now sits enthroned at the right hand of his Father, equal to him in glory and power. All knees bend before him, for he is the Lord of Lords and King of Kings, and of his kingdom there is no beginning or end.

Nevertheless some unbelieving and foolish persons say that they are Christ or God, but in fact they possess neither wisdom nor God's grace, neither power nor virtue. They accordingly belong in the fires of hell, for there is only one God and only one Christ, who alone is both divine and human. On the Last Day, when he will judge the good and the wicked, these persons will discover that they are damned instead of being God. That they are also not Christ is something which I will now prove to you with all clarity. The humanity of our Lord Jesus Christ does not subsist in itself, for it is not its own person—as is the case among all other human beings—but instead the Son of God is its hypostasis and form. It is therefore of one form with God and by means of this union is wise and has power over everything which is beneath God. <u>The humanity of our Lord is thus taken up into God and is noble, wise, holy, and blessed above and beyond all creatures.</u> He alone is the heir in God's kingdom, both by nature and by grace, for he is the firstborn of his Father and mother, the sovereign Prince of all his brothers. If he wishes, and if we are worthy of it through his grace, he will make us coheirs with himself and sharers of his Father's kingdom. He has promised us—on the condition that we serve him—that we will be where he is, that is, with soul and body in the palace of God's glory. We will be with him there forever, each of us glorified in the state proper to himself, clad in our works and adorned and perfected in love and virtues. Jesus will reveal to us his glorious countenance, more resplendent than the sun, and we will hear his lovely voice, which is sweeter than any melody. We will sit down at his table and he will serve us (cf. Lk 12:37) as a noble prince serves his beloved family and chosen friends. He will bestow upon us the honor and glory which he has received from his heavenly Father, while we will desire that honor and glory more for him than for ourselves. This is what he meant when he said: "Father, I will that all whom you have given me may be with me where I am, so that they may see the glory which you have given me" (Jn 17:24). We will indeed see this and will be clothed with it more than with all of our own works and merits. We will thus rejoice and glory both in ourselves and in him. This joy will be in our heart, senses, soul, and body, full and overflowing forever without end. Yet this is but the least bliss which we will have with our dear Lord Jesus Christ in his eternal kingdom.

D. FOUR POINTS CONSTITUTIVE OF THE LIVING LIFE

Now raise your mind and your bare vision above all the heavens and above all that has been created, for I wish to show you the living life which is hidden in us and in which our highest bliss resides. I have spoken about it already but did not clarify it sufficiently. Even though I did not proceed through this material in an orderly way, I was aware of that and did it on purpose. What I then left unsaid I will now fill in.

Now see and understand, all you who have been raised up into God's light; I am addressing no one else, for others would not be able to understand. The living life which God has established in us consists of four points: the first point is the nature of this life, the second is its practice, the third is its essential being, and the fourth is its superessential being.

THE FIRST POINT: THE NATURE OF THIS LIFE

The nature of eternal life has been born of God for us. It is union with God and lives out of God in us and out of us once more in him. Of his own free will the heavenly Father chose us and won us back in his Son. We are therefore sons of God by grace, not by nature, for God's grace is our supernature and eternal life, which no one can see or find without grace. If we wish to see and find eternal life in ourselves, we must through love and faith raise ourselves up above reason to our simple eye. There we will find God's resplendence born in us. This resplendence is the image of God, which has transformed our simple eye so that no other image can enter there. Nevertheless, through an infused light we can know all that is less than God, provided that he wishes to reveal it to us.

Each one's vision receives the entire image of God, whole and undivided. It is given entirely to each, yet remains in itself an undivided whole. We know the image through itself when we receive it, but when we are transported and transformed in its resplendence we forget ourselves and become one with it. We thus live in it and it in us, though we always remain distinct in substance and nature.

This resplendence of God which we see in ourselves has no beginning or end, no time or place, no way or path, no form, figure, or color. It has wholly embraced, grasped, and pervaded us and has opened the eye of our simple vision so widely that this eye must remain open forever, for we cannot close it. This is the first point, which concerns the nature of this eternal life which is born of God.

THE SECOND POINT: THE PRACTICE OF THIS LIFE

There follows the second point, which will treat the practice of this living life between ourselves and God. Now understand, and raise your inner eye to the highest part of your being, where you are united with God. To be united with God is a living and eternal state in which God lives in us and we in him. This union is living and fruitful and cannot be empty or idle, for it is always being renewed in love and in new visits through that mutual indwelling which cannot be disrupted. Here there is drawing and following, giving and taking, touching and being touched. Our heavenly Father dwells within us, visiting us with himself and raising us up above reason and rational observation. He empties us of all images and draws us into our source. There we find nothing other than a wild desert of imageless bareness, which always responds to the call of eternity.

There the Father gives us his Son, who comes to our imageless vision with the groundless resplendence which he is himself, inviting and teaching us to gaze at and contemplate this resplendence in and through itself. We there find God's resplendence in ourselves and ourselves in it, united with it. Although it has laid hold of us, we cannot lay hold of it, for our power of comprehension is creaturely whereas this resplendence is God. We therefore allow our vision to run with it and after it along a way which is endlessly long and wide, endlessly high and deep, devoid of form and measure. Although we are united with it in a simple way, we cannot overtake or grasp what is incomprehensible to us. We here see the Father in the Son and the Son in the Father, for they are one in nature. They live within us and bestow upon us the Holy Spirit, the love of them both, who is one nature and one God with them both and who lives within us together with them both, for God is indivisible. The Holy Spirit gives himself to us, visiting us and touching the burning spark of our soul. This is the beginning and source of an eternal love between ourselves and God.

The practice of love is free and is not ashamed of itself. Its nature is both craving and generous, for it constantly wishes both to demand and to offer, to give and to take. On the one hand, God's love is full of craving, for it demands of the soul all that it is and all that it can do. For its part, the soul is rich and generous, ready to give to love's craving all that it demands and desires, but it cannot do this fully, for its created nature must remain forever: The soul can neither escape it nor leave it behind. For this reason, however much love swallows, devours, and consumes, demanding of the soul what is beyond its power, and however vehemently the soul desires to melt away to nothing in love, the soul must nevertheless remain forever and not pass away.

On the other hand, God's love is also fathomlessly generous. It reveals and offers to the soul all that it is, and it wishes to give all of this freely to the soul. For its part, the loving soul is now especially gluttonous and full of craving, opening itself in the desire to possess everything which is revealed to it. But since it is a creature, it cannot devour or grasp the immensity of God. It must therefore be filled with longing and yearning in a state of hunger and thirst which will never end. The more it yearns and strives, the more keenly does it feel itself falling short of God's riches. This is what is meant by unsatisfied striving.

It is in this way that love both gives and takes and that love is practiced in our living life. Those who live such love are able to see and experience that all this is true.

THE THIRD POINT: THE ESSENTIAL BEING OF THIS LIFE

There follows the third point, which concerns the living essential being in which we are one with God above and beyond all exercises of love in a state of eternal enjoyment—that is, above works and virtues in a state of blessed emptiness, and above union with God in unity, where no one can work except God alone. God's work is his very self and his nature, and in his works we are empty and transformed, becoming one with him in his love. But we do not become one with him in his nature, for then we would come to nought in ourselves and be God, which is impossible. There, however, we are above reason and also without reason in a state of clear knowing, in which we feel no difference between ourselves and God, for we have been breathed forth in his love above and beyond ourselves and all orders of being. There we have no demands or desires and we neither give nor take. There there is only a blessed and empty being, the crown and essential reward of all holiness and all virtue.

This is what our dear Lord Jesus Christ desired when he said: "Father, I desire that all whom you have given me may be one as we are one" (cf. Jn 17:11, 24). He did not mean one in every respect, for he is one with his Father in nature, since he is God, and also one with us in our nature, since he is a human being. He lives in us and we in him through his grace and our good works, and so he is united with us and we with him. In his grace, and with him, we love and revere our heavenly Father. In this love and veneration we are united with our heavenly Father but are not one with him, for the Father loves us and we love him in return, and in this loving and being loved we always feel a difference and a duality; this is the nature of eternal love. But when we are embraced and enveloped by the Father and the Son in the unity of the Holy Spirit above all exercises of love, then we are all one, just as Christ, both God and a human being, is one with the Father in their fathomless mutual love. In this same love we are all brought to perfection in a single state of eternal enjoyment, that is, in a blessed and empty being which is incomprehensible to all creatures.

THE FOURTH POINT:
THE SUPERESSENTIAL BEING OF THIS LIFE

Furthermore, in our state of emptiness, in which we are one with God in his love, there begins a superessential contemplative experience which is the highest which anyone could express in words. This is a dying life and a living death, in which we go out of our own being into our superessential beatitude. It occurs when, through grace and God's help, we have so mastered ourselves that we can become free of images every time we wish, right up to that empty state of being where we are one with God. This takes place in the fathomless abyss of his love, where we find full satisfaction, for we have God within us and are blessed in our very being through the interior working of God. There we are one with him in love, though not in being or nature. Rather, we are blessed—and blessedness itself—in God's essential being, where he enjoys both himself and all of us in his sublime nature. This is the core of love, which is hidden from us in darkness and in a state of unknowing which has no ground.

This unknowing is an inaccessible light which is God's essential being; it is superessential to us, being essential to him alone, for he is his own blessedness and enjoys himself in his own nature. In his blissful enjoyment we die, for by being immersed in him we become lost as regards our enjoyment, though not as regards our being. Our love and his love are always alike and one in this state of enjoyment, in which his Spirit absorbs our love, swallowing it up into himself in a single state of blessedness and enjoyment with himself.

Now whenever I write that we are one with God, this is to be understood as a oneness in love and not in being or nature, for God's being is uncreated and ours is created, so that God and creatures are immeasurably different. They may therefore unite, but cannot become one. And if our being were annihilated, we would neither know nor love nor be blessed. Our created being is to be regarded as a wild and barren desert, in which God lives and reigns over us. In this desert we must wander about without mode or manner, for we cannot transcend our own being and arrive at our superessential being except through love. If, then, we live in love, we are blessed in our very being; and if we die to ourselves in love and in the enjoyment of God, then we are blessedness itself in God's being. We always live in our own being through love and always die in God's being through blissful enjoyment. That is why this is called a dying life and a living death, for we live with God and die in God. Blessed are the dead who live and die in this way, for they are heirs of God and of his kingdom (cf. Rv 14:13).

THE LITTLE BOOK OF CLARIFICATION

PROLOGUE

The prophet Samuel wept over King Saul, although he well knew that God had repudiated and rejected him as king of Israel—both him and his descendants (1 Sm 15:10–23). This was because of his pride and his disobedience toward God and toward the Prophet himself, who had been sent by God. We also read in the Gospel that our Lord's disciples begged him to dismiss the pagan Canaanite woman by granting everything that she was requesting, since she kept crying after them (Mt 15:21–28). So I can now say that we would do well to weep over certain deceived persons who think that they are kings in Israel, for they fancy that they have been raised above all other good persons to a high and contemplative way of life, whereas in fact they are proud and are willingly and knowingly disobedient toward God and his Law, toward the holy Church and all the virtues. Just as King Saul tore the mantle of the Prophet Samuel into pieces (1 Sm 15:27–28), so do they try to tear apart the unity of the Christian faith and all true teaching and virtuous living. Those who persist in this are cut off and separated from the kingdom of eternal contemplation, just as Saul was cut off from the kingdom of Israel. But that humble little Canaanite woman believed and hoped in God, even though she was a foreigner and a pagan. She acknowledged and confessed her lowliness in the presence of Christ and his Apostles. She therefore received grace and health and all that she desired, for God exalts the humble and fills them with every virtue, but he resists the proud, who remain empty of all that is good.

Some of my friends desire and have asked me to express and clarify—in a few words and as precisely and clearly as I can—the truth which I understand and feel concerning all the most profound teaching which I have written, so that no one might be led astray by my words and everyone might be helped.[1] I am pleased to do this. With God's help I will instruct and enlighten the humble, those who love virtue and truth, and with the same words I will interiorly unsettle and darken those who are false and

---

1. As noted in the Introduction to this volume, these friends of Ruusbroec were Brother Gerard and other Carthusians of the charterhouse at Herne. Their concerns centered above all on certain passages from Ruusbroec's first treatise, *The Kingdom of Lovers.*

proud. To these latter my words will be contrary and displeasing, and that is something the proud cannot endure without being provoked to anger.

Note that I have said that a contemplative lover of God is united with God through an intermediary and also without intermediary and, thirdly, without difference or distinction. I find this to be so in the realm of nature and also in the realms of grace and of glory. I have further said that no creature can become or be so holy that it loses its creatureliness and becomes God—not even the soul of our Lord Jesus Christ, which will eternally remain something created and different from God. Nevertheless, if we are to attain salvation we must all be raised above ourselves to God and become one spirit with God in love. Therefore note well my words and my meaning and understand me correctly as I describe the way of our ascent to our eternal beatitude.

PART ONE: UNION THROUGH AN INTERMEDIARY

A. THE NATURE OF THIS UNION

In the first place, I say that all good persons are united with God through an intermediary. This intermediary is God's grace, together with the sacraments of the holy Church, the divine virtues of faith, hope, and love, and a virtuous life in accordance with God's commandments. To these there is joined a dying to sin, to the world, and to all the inordinate desires of our nature. In this way we remain united to the holy Church, that is, to all good persons, and are obedient to God and of one will with him, just as a good religious community is united with its superior. Apart from this union no one can be pleasing to God or be saved.

Whoever maintains this union through this intermediary till the end of his life is the person of whom Christ speaks to his heavenly Father in St. John's Gospel: "Father, I will that where I am, there my servant may be, so that he may see the glory which you have given me" (cf. Jn 17:24). In another place he says that his servants will sit down at the banquet—that is, in the richness and fullness of the virtues which they have exercised—and that he will pass before them, ministering to them with the glory which he has merited (cf. Lk 12:37). He will generously give this glory and reveal it to all his beloved, in a greater or lesser degree to each in particular according to his merit and his ability to understand the sublimity of Christ's glory and honor, which he alone merited through his life and death. In this way all the saints will be with Christ for all eternity, each in his order and in the degree of glory which, with God's help, he merited through his works. And Christ, according to his humanity, will be above all the saints and angels, like a prince of all the glory and honor which belong to his humanity alone above all creatures.

You can thus understand that we are united with God through an intermediary, both here in grace and later in glory. There is much difference and diversity in this intermediary as regards both the way persons live and the reward they receive, just as I have told you. St. Paul understood this well when he said that he wished to be freed from the body and to be with Christ (Phil 1:23). But he did not say that he himself would be Christ or God, as some unbelieving and perverse persons now claim, saying that they have no God but are so dead to themselves and so united with God that they have become God.

B. THE AUTOTHEISTIC-QUIETISTIC DEVIATION FROM THE TRUTH

These persons have turned inward to the bareness of their being by means of an undifferentiated simplicity and a natural inclination, with the result that they think eternal life will be nothing other than a purely existing, blessed state of being which has no distinctions of order, holiness, or merit. Some of these persons are so insane that they say that the Persons in the Godhead will disappear, that nothing will remain there for all eternity except the essential substance of the Godhead, and that all blessed spirits will be so simply absorbed with God in a state of essential blessedness that nothing will remain apart from this—neither will nor action nor the distinct knowledge of anything created.

These persons have gone astray into the empty and blind simplicity of their own being and are trying to become blessed in their bare nature, for they are united in so simple and empty a way to the bare essence of their soul and to God dwelling within them that they have no ardor or devotion to God, whether exteriorly or interiorly. At the highest point of their introversion they feel nothing but the simplicity of their own being, dependent upon God's being. They take this undifferentiated simplicity which they possess to be God himself, because they find natural rest in it. They accordingly think that they themselves are God in the ground of their simple oneness, for they lack true faith, hope, and love. Because of this bare emptiness which they experience and possess, they claim to be without knowledge and love and to be exempt from the virtues. They therefore strive to live apart from conscience, however much evil they do. They ignore all the sacraments, all the virtues, and all the practices of the holy Church, for they think they have no need of these, believing that they have passed beyond them all—according to them, only those who are imperfect need such things. Some of them are so hardened and deeply rooted in their simplicity that they are empty and heedless of all the works which God ever wrought and of all the Scriptures, just as if no word of them had ever been written, for they fancy that they have found and possessed that for the sake of which all of Scripture was composed, namely, this blind, essential rest which they experience. But in fact they have lost God as well as all the ways which lead to him, for these persons have no more interior fervor, devotion, or holy exercises than a dead animal. Nevertheless, some of them receive the sacraments and occasionally quote Scripture so as better to disguise and conceal themselves. They like to take up some dark passages of Scripture and falsely twist their meaning to accord with their own opinions, so that they might please other, simple persons and lure them into that false state of emptiness which they experience.

Such people think that they are wiser and more astute than anyone else, whereas in fact they are the dullest and coarsest persons alive, for what pagans, Jews, and bad Christians—whether learned or unlearned—have come to discover and understand through the power of their natural reason is something which these wretched persons are neither willing nor able to attain. You may make the sign of the cross to protect yourself against the devil, but guard yourself with great care against these perverse persons and pay close attention to their words and deeds. They wish to instruct, and to be instructed by no one; to reprove, and to be reproved by no one; to give orders, and to be obedient to no one; to oppress others, and to be oppressed by no one; to say what they wish, and to be contradicted by no one. They follow their own will and are subservient to no one, and this they take to be spiritual freedom. They practice freedom of the flesh by giving the body what it desires, and this they take to be nobility of nature. They have united themselves to the blind and dark emptiness of their own being, believing that there they are one with God and that this is their eternal beatitude. In turning inward they have attained this state through their own will and natural inclination, but as a result they think that they are above the Law and the commandments of God and of the holy Church, for they experience neither God nor any otherness above this essential rest which they possess. The divine light has not revealed itself in their darkness because they have not sought it through active love and supernatural freedom. For this reason they have fallen away from the truth and all virtues into a perverse state devoid of any likeness to God. They claim that the highest holiness consists in a person's following his own nature in every respect, without restraint, so that he might live in a state of emptiness according to the inclination of his spirit and turn outward to satisfy the flesh in accordance with every movement of corporeal desire, so as all the more quickly to be freed of such an image and be able to return without hindrance to the bare emptiness of his spirit.

This is the hellish fruit which grows out of their unbelief and nourishes that unbelief right up to the death which is eternal, for when the time has come and their nature is weighed down with bitter woe and the fear of death, then they are interiorly filled with images, restlessness, and anxiety. They lose their state of empty, restful introversion, fall into such despair that no one can console them, and die like rabid dogs. Their emptiness brings them no reward, and those who have performed evil deeds and die in them go to the eternal fire, as our faith teaches.

I have set the good and the evil side by side before you, so that you may better understand the good and be guarded against the evil. You should shun and flee from these persons as the mortal enemies of your soul, however holy they seem to be in their conduct, their words, their dress, or their appearance, for they are the devil's emissaries and the most nefarious people alive for simple, unexperienced persons of goodwill. I will now lay all this aside and return to the subject with which I began.

PART TWO: UNION WITHOUT INTERMEDIARY

A. THE PREPARATION
NECESSARY FOR THIS UNION

You know that I have told you previously that all the saints and all good persons are united with God through an intermediary. I will now further show how they are all united with God without intermediary. In this life there are few who are able and sufficiently enlightened to experience and understand this. Therefore, if anyone is to discover and experience within himself the three unions of which I am speaking, he must live wholly and entirely for God, in such a way that he responds docilely to God's grace and movements in the practice of every virtue and interior exercise. He must be raised up through love and die in God to himself and all his works, so that he yields himself up with all his powers and undergoes the transformation wrought by the incomprehensible truth which is God himself. Living he must go forth in virtues and dying he must enter into God; a perfect life consists in these two movements, which are joined together within a person as closely as matter and form or soul and body. Through their practice a person's understanding becomes clear and his feelings overflow in all their richness, for he has dedicated himself to God with his powers uplifted, with a pure intention, with heartfelt desire, with unsatisfied craving, and with the living ardor of his spirit and nature. Because he conducts himself in this way in God's presence, love vanquishes him in every respect—in whatever way it moves him, he constantly grows in love and all the virtues, for love always moves a person for his benefit and in accordance with his ability.

The most beneficial movement which such a person can experience and of which he is capable is a sense of heavenly well-being and of hellish pain, together with his response to these two with works which are proper to each. Heavenly well-being raises a person above all things through a free

257

Tribulation

ability to praise and love God in every way that his heart and soul desire. There follows a sense of hellish pain, which makes a person sink into a state of misery in which he is deprived of all the savor and consolation which he ever experienced. When a person is in this state of misery, the sense of well-being sometimes manifests itself, bringing with it a hope which no one can shake, but then he falls back into such despair that no one can console him.

What I am calling heavenly well-being occurs whenever a person feels God within him with the full richness of his grace. At such times he is wise and clear in understanding; rich and outflowing in heavenly teaching; warm and generous in charity; drunk and overflowing with joy and feeling; strong, valiant, and undaunted in everything which he knows to be pleasing to God; and so on in countless other ways which only those who experience such things can know. But whenever the scale of love goes down and God conceals himself together with all his grace, then a person falls back into such despair, torment, and dark misery that it seems he will never again come out of it. He feels he is nothing but a poor sinner who knows little or nothing of God. Any consolation which creatures might afford him is distasteful, and the consolation and taste of God are not given him. At this, his power of reason says within him: "Where is your God now? What remains of anything you ever experienced of God?" Then are his tears his food day and night, just as the Prophet says (Ps 42:4).

If a person is to recover from this torment, he must reflect on and experience the truth that he does not belong to himself but to God. He must therefore renounce his own will for the free will of God and allow God to have his way with him in both time and eternity. If he is able to do this in the freedom of his spirit and without feeling oppressed at heart, then he recovers at once and brings heaven into hell and hell into heaven, for however much the scale of love goes up or down, he is always evenly balanced. Whatever love wishes to give or take away is a source of peace to a person who denies himself and loves God. Whoever lives in suffering without rebelling has a spirit which remains free and undisturbed. Such a person is capable of experiencing unity with God without intermediary, for in the richness of his virtues he already possesses the unity which is through an intermediary. Because he is of one mind and one will with God, he feels God within him in the fullness of his grace, as the life-giving health of his entire being and of all his works.

You might ask why it is that not all good persons reach the point of being able to feel this. Pay attention and I will tell you the reason: They do not respond to God's movement with a renunciation of themselves and therefore do not stand in God's presence with living fervor. They are also not careful in the way they interiorly observe themselves and accordingly remain always turned more to outward multiplicity than to interior simplicity. They perform their works more out of good custom than out of interior experience and pay more attention to particular methods and the greatness and multiplicity of good works than to having their intention and love directed to God. They therefore remain caught up in the exterior, multiple concerns of the heart and are not aware of how God lives within them in the fullness of his grace.

B. A MORE PRECISE DESCRIPTION OF THE UNION WITHOUT INTERMEDIARY

I will now tell you how an interiorly fervent person who enjoys health despite all his afflictions will feel himself to be one with God without intermediary. Whenever a person who lives in this way raises himself up with the entirety of his being and with all his powers and devotes himself to God with a living and active love, then he feels that his love—in its very ground where it begins and ends—is blissful and devoid of any ground. If he then wishes to penetrate further into this blissful love with his active love, all the powers of his soul will give way and will have to suffer and endure that penetrating truth and goodness which is God himself. In the same way that the air is pervaded with the radiance and warmth of the sun or a piece of iron is penetrated by fire, so that with the fire it does the work of fire, burning and giving light just as fire does (and I say the same about the air, for if the air had the power of understanding it would say, "I give light and warmth to all the world"), and yet each retains its own nature— for the fire does not become iron, nor the iron fire, but the union is without intermediary, for the iron is within the fire and the fire within the iron, even as the air is in the light of the sun and the light of the sun is in the air—so too is God constantly in the being of the soul.[2] Whenever the higher powers turn inward through active love, they are united with God without intermediary in a simple knowledge of all truth and in an essential experience and savoring of all goodness. This simple knowledge and experience of God is possessed in essential love and is practiced and maintained

---

2. Ruusbroec's images of the air pervaded by the sun's light and warmth and of a piece of iron penetrated by fire may derive from St. Bernard, who uses the very same images in *De diligendo Deo*, ch. 10.

through active love; for the powers it is therefore accidental, occurring whenever they die to themselves by turning inward in love, but for the essential being of the spirit it is essential, always remaining within it. We must accordingly always turn inward and be renewed in love if we are to experience love with love. St. John teaches us this when he says, "Whoever abides in love abides in God and God in him" (1 Jn 4:16).

Even though the union between the loving spirit and God is without intermediary, there is nevertheless a great difference, for the creature does not become God nor does God become the creature, just as I said concerning the iron and the air. If material things which God created can unite without intermediary, much more can God unite himself with his beloved when he wishes, provided they turn and prepare themselves for this by his grace. For this reason, when an interiorly fervent person whom God has adorned with virtues and has also raised to a contemplative life turns within himself in the most profound way, there is no intermediary between himself and God except his enlightened reason and his active love. Through these two intermediaries he cleaves to God, and this is what it is to become one with God, as St. Bernard says.[3] But he is also raised above reason and above active love to a state of bare seeing in essential love, apart from works, and then he is one spirit and one love with God, as I said earlier. In this essential love and by means of the unity with God which such a person has in an essential way, he infinitely transcends his understanding. This is what is meant by the common life of contemplatives, for at this exalted level a person is capable of knowing all creatures in heaven and on earth together with the distinctions in their lives and in their rewards, provided that God wishes to reveal this to him in a single vision. But before God's infinity a person must give way and must pursue it in an essential and unending way, for no creature can comprehend or attain that, not even the soul of our Lord Jesus Christ, which has received the highest union granted to any creature.

This eternal love which lives in the spirit and with which the spirit is united without intermediary bestows its light and grace upon all the powers of the soul. This is the source of all virtue, for God's grace touches the higher powers and this gives rise to charity and knowledge of the truth, a

---

3. See St. Bernard, *Sermones super Cantica canticorum* 71.6: "Even though I am dust and ashes, through reliance on the words of Scripture I am not at all afraid to say that I am one spirit with God, provided only that I become convinced by certain experience that I am cleaving to God in the manner of those who abide in love and who therefore abide in God and God in them. . . . I think it was concerning such adherence that it was said: 'Whoever cleaves to God is one spirit with him' (1 Cor. 6:17)."

love of all righteousness, the exercise of God's counsels in a discerning way, an imageless condition of freedom, the effortless overcoming of all things, and a transport into unity through love. As long as a person perseveres in such exercises, he remains capable of contemplating and of experiencing union without intermediary. He also experiences God's touch within himself, which brings about a renewal of grace and of all his virtues.

You should know that God's grace flows right into the lower powers and touches a person's heart. This gives rise to heartfelt affection and a felt desire for God. This affection and desire pervade heart and senses, flesh and blood, and all of a person's bodily nature, creating such strain and impatience in his members that he often does not know how to act. He feels like a drunken person who is not in control of himself. This produces many strange kinds of behavior, which such weakhearted persons cannot easily control: With restless longing they often raise their heads to heaven with eyes wide open; at one moment they are full of joy, at another they are weeping; at one moment they are singing, at another shouting; first they feel weal, then woe, and often both at once; they jump and run about, clap their hands together, kneel and bow down, and flurry about in many similar ways. As long as a person remains in this state and stands with his heart open and raised up toward the riches of God, who lives in his spirit, he will experience new touches of God and a new restlessness of love. It is in this way that all these things become renewed. Through this corporeal feeling a person will therefore at times pass to a spiritual feeling which is in accordance with reason; through this spiritual feeling he will pass to a divine feeling which is above reason; and through this divine feeling he will be immersed in a feeling of changeless beatitude.

PART THREE: UNION WITHOUT DIFFERENCE

A. THE GROUND OF THIS UNION WITHIN THE GODHEAD

That last-named feeling is our superessential beatitude, which consists in the enjoyment of God and of all his beloved. This beatitude is the dark stillness which always stands empty. To God it is essential, but to all creatures it is superessential. Here the Persons give way and lose themselves in the maelstrom of essential love, that is, in the blissful Unity, and nevertheless remain active as Persons in the work of the Trinity. You can therefore see that the divine nature is forever active as regards the Persons but stands eternally empty and modeless as regards the simplicity of its essential being. Accordingly, everything which God has chosen and embraced with eternally personal love he has also possessed essentially and blissfully in the Unity with essential love. The divine Persons embrace one another in an eternal sense of contentment through fathomless active love in the Unity, and this activity is constantly renewed in the living life of the Trinity. Here there occurs a perpetually new birth in new knowledge, together with a new sense of contentment and a new breathing forth of the Spirit in a new embrace accompanied by a new flood of eternal love.

All the elect—both angels and humans, from the last to the first—are embraced in this sense of contentment. On this contentment depend heaven and earth and the being, life, activity, and preservation of all creatures, with the single exception of any turning away from God in sin, for this arises from the blind perversity of creatures themselves. From God's contentment flow grace and glory and all gifts in heaven and on earth, bestowed upon each person in a particular way according to his need and his ability to receive them, for God's grace stands ready for everyone and awaits each sinner's conversion. Whenever such a sinner, touched by grace, decides to have pity on himself and trustfully to call upon God, he always finds pardon. So whoever through grace is brought back with a loving sense of contentment to God's eternal contentment is enveloped and embraced in the fathomless love which is God himself; such a person is constantly renewed in love and virtue.

In this reciprocal activity in which we are pleasing to God and God is pleasing to us, love and eternal life are practiced. God has loved us and found us well pleasing to himself from all eternity, and this is something we should rightly reflect upon, for then our love and sense of contentment will be renewed. By means of the relations of the Persons in the Godhead, there is an ever-new sense of contentment accompanied by a new outflow of love in a new embrace in the Unity. This is beyond time, that is, without any before or after, in an eternal now. In this embrace in the Unity all things are brought to their perfection; in the outflow of love all things are accomplished; and in the living, fruitful nature all things have their possibility of occurring. In this living, fruitful nature the Son is in the Father and the Father is in the Son, while the Holy Spirit is in them both, for this is a living, fruitful Unity which is the source and beginning of all life and all becoming. Here all creatures are therefore one being and one life with God—apart from themselves, in their eternal origin. But as the Persons proceed outward in distinct ways, then the Son is from the Father and the Holy Spirit is from them both; it is here that God has created and ordered all creatures in their own essential being. He has also re-created human beings to the greatest extent possible through his grace and his death and has adorned with love and virtues those who belong to him, bringing them back with him to their source. There the Father, the Son, and all the beloved are enveloped and embraced in the bond of love, that is, in the Unity of the Holy Spirit. This is the same Unity which is fruitful in the procession of the Persons and which in their return is an eternal bond of love which will never be broken.

B. OUR THREEFOLD PARTICIPATION IN GOD'S BEATITUDE

All who know themselves to be enveloped in this bond will remain eternally blessed. Such persons are rich in virtue, clear in contemplation, and simple in their enjoyable rest, for as they turn inward God's love reveals itself as flowing out with all that is good, as attracting inward into unity, and as being superessential and devoid of mode in eternal rest. They are therefore united with God through an intermediary and without intermediary and also without difference.

Union through an Intermediary

In their inward vision, God's love is seen as a good common to all as it flows forth in heaven and on earth. They feel the holy Trinity inclined toward them and being within them in the fullness of grace. They are therefore adorned with every virtue, with holy exercises, and with good works, both from without and from within, and are thus united with God through the intermediary of his grace and of their own holy way of life. Because they have given themselves over to God in what they do, in what they leave undone, and in what they suffer, they have a constant peace and interior joy and a consolation and savor which cannot be experienced by the world, by any hypocritical creature, or by anyone who seeks himself and directs his mind more to himself than to God's glory.

Union without Intermediary

Secondly, in their inward vision these same interior and enlightened persons have God's love before them whenever they wish, drawing or calling them to union, for they see and feel that the Father and the Son, through the Holy Spirit, have embraced themselves and all the elect and are being brought back with eternal love to the Unity of their nature. This Unity is constantly drawing and calling to itself all that has been born of it, whether in a natural way or through grace. Enlightened persons are therefore raised up with a free mind above reason to a vision which is bare and devoid of images. Here lives the eternal call of God's Unity. With a bare and imageless understanding these persons pass beyond all activity, all exercises, and all things, and enter the topmost part of their spirit. There their bare understanding is pervaded with eternal resplendence, just as the air is pervaded with the light of the sun. So too is their bare and uplifted will transformed and pervaded with fathomless love, just as a piece of iron is penetrated by fire, while their bare and uplifted memory feels itself caught up and set firm in a fathomless state devoid of images. In this way the created image is united above reason in a threefold way with its eternal image, which is the source of its being and life. This source is held fast and possessed essentially and in unity through a simple act of contemplating in imageless emptiness. A person is thus raised above reason, threefold in unity and one in trinity.

Nevertheless, the creature does not become God, for this union occurs through grace and through a love which has been turned back to God. For this reason the creature experiences in his inward vision a difference and distinction between himself and God. Even though the union is without intermediary, the manifold works which God performs in heaven and on earth are hidden from the spirit. Although God gives himself as he is with clear distinction, he does so in the essential being of the soul, where the soul's powers are unified above reason and undergo a transformation wrought by God in an undifferentiated way. There everything is full and overflowing, for the spirit feels itself to be but one truth, one richness, and one unity with God, but there is nevertheless an essential inclination to go onward, and that is an essential distinction between the soul's being and God's being. This is the highest distinction which a person can experience.

Union without Difference

After this follows the unity without difference, for God's love is to be considered not only as flowing forth with all that is good and as drawing back to unity, but also as being above and beyond all distinction in a state of essential enjoyment in accordance with the bare essential being of the Godhead. For this reason, enlightened persons find within themselves an essential act of gazing inward which is above reason and apart from reason; they also find an inclination toward blissful enjoyment which transcends all particular forms and beings and which immerses them in a modeless abyss of fathomless beatitude, in which the Trinity of the divine Persons possess their nature in the essential Unity. There the state of beatitude is so simple and so modeless that in it every essential act of gazing, every inclination, and every distinction of creatures pass away, for all exalted spirits melt away and come to nought by reason of the blissful enjoyment they experience in God's essential being, which is the superessential being of all beings. There they fall away from themselves and become lost in a state of unknowing which has no ground. There all light is turned into darkness and the three Persons give way before the essential Unity, where without distinction they enjoy essential bliss.

This bliss is essential to God alone; to all spirits it is superessential, for no created being can be one with God's being and have its own being perish. If that happened, the creature would become God, and this is impossible, for God's essential being can neither decrease nor increase and can have nothing taken away from it or added to it. Nevertheless, all loving spirits are one enjoyment and one beatitude with God, without difference, for that blessed state of being which is the enjoyment of God and of all his beloved is so simple and undifferentiated that there is within it neither Father nor Son nor Holy Spirit as regards the distinction of Persons, nor is there any creature either. Rather, all enlightened spirits are there raised above themselves into a modeless state of blissful enjoyment which overflows whatever fullness any creature has ever received or ever could receive. There all exalted spirits are, in their superessential being, one enjoyment and one beatitude with God, without difference. This beatitude is so simple and undifferentiated that no distinction could ever enter within it. This is what Christ desired when he prayed to his heavenly Father that all his beloved might be made perfectly one, even as he is one with the Father in blissful enjoyment through the Holy Spirit (cf. Jn 17:21–23). He thus prayed and desired that he might be one in us and we one in him and in his heavenly Father in blissful enjoyment through the Holy Spirit. I consider this the most loving prayer which Christ ever prayed for our salvation.[4]

THESE THREE UNIONS AS THE
FULFILLMENT OF CHRIST'S PRAYER

You should also note that his prayer was threefold, as St. John has described it for us in this same Gospel. He first prayed that we should be with him, so that we might see the glory which his Father had given him (Jn 17:24). It is for this reason that I said in the beginning that all good persons are united with God through the intermediary of God's grace and their own virtuous life. God's love is always flowing into us with new gifts. All who take heed of this are filled with new virtues, with holy exercises, and with all good things, just as I have told you previously. This union

---

4. This paragraph shows very clearly that Ruusbroec's "union without difference" is to be understood as a datum of mystical consciousness—a nondualistic experience of "enjoyment" and "beatitude"—and not as an assertion of ontological identity with God. For a contemporary, philosophical analysis of this immediate awareness of union with the transcendent source of the self, see Louis Dupré, "The Mystical Experience of the Self and Its Philosophical Significance," in *Understanding Mysticism*, ed. Richard Woods (Garden City, N.Y.: Doubleday, Image Books, 1980), pp. 449–66.

through the fullness of grace and glory, in both body and soul, begins here and lasts for all eternity.

Secondly, Christ prayed that he might be in us and we in him. We find this in many places in the Gospel. This is the union without intermediary, for God's love not only flows outward but also draws inward toward unity. All who experience and perceive this become interior and enlightened persons and have their higher powers raised above all their exercises into their bare essential being. There these powers are simplified in their essential being, above reason, and thereby become full and overflowing. In this simplicity the spirit finds itself united with God without intermediary. This union, together with the exercises which are proper to it, will last for all eternity, just as I have said previously.

Thirdly, Christ prayed the highest prayer, namely, that all his beloved might be made perfectly one, even as he is one with the Father (Jn 17:23)—not in the way that he is one single divine substance with the Father, for that is impossible for us, but in the sense of being one in the same unity in which he, without distinction, is one enjoyment and one beatitude with the Father in essential love.

Christ's prayer is fulfilled in those who are united with God in this threefold way. They will ebb and flow with God and constantly stand empty in possession and enjoyment; they will work and endure and fearlessly rest in their superessential being; they will go out and enter in and find their nourishment both without and within; they are drunk with love and sleep in God in a dark resplendence.

CONCLUSION

I could say much more about this, but those who possess it do not need my words, and as for those to whom this has been shown and who cleave to love with love, love will certainly teach them the truth. But as for those who turn outward and find their consolation in things separate from God, they will not even miss what is lacking to them; even though I said much more, they would understand nothing of it, for those who give themselves completely to exterior works or to interior idleness without any activity cannot understand this.

Even though it is true that reason and all corporeal feeling must yield and give way to faith, to the spirit's gazing, and to those things which are above reason, nevertheless reason and the life of the senses remain in a state of potency even when not active and cannot perish any more than human nature can perish. And even though it is also true that the spirit's act of gazing and its inclination toward God must give way to enjoyment in a condition of simplicity, nevertheless this gazing and inclination remain in their habitual state of potency, for this constitutes the inmost life of the spirit. In the enlightened person who is ascending to God, the life of the senses adheres to the spirit. For this reason his sensory powers are turned to God with heartfelt affection and his nature is filled with all good things. He feels that the life of his spirit is joined to God without intermediary. His higher powers are thereby raised to God with eternal love, pervaded with divine truth, and set firm in a freedom devoid of images. With this he is filled with God and overflowing without measure. In this overflow occurs that essential flowing away or immersion of oneself in the super-essential Unity where the union without distinction is found, as I have often said. All our ways end in this superessential being. If we are willing to walk with God along the lofty ways of love, we will rest with him eternally and without end. In this way we will eternally approach God and enter into him and rest in him.

At this time I cannot set forth my meaning any more clearly for you. I submit myself to the judgment of the saints and of the holy Church as regards everything I understand or feel or have written, for I wish to live and die as Christ's servant in the Christian faith and desire to be, with the help of God's grace, a living member of the holy Church. For this reason, just as I have told you previously, you should beware of those deceived persons who—by means of their empty, imageless state and through a bare, simple act of gazing—have found in a natural way God's dwelling within them and have wished to become one with God without his grace and without the practice of virtue, in disobedience toward God and the holy Church. With all their perversity of life, which I have previously described, they wish to be sons of God by nature. Now if the prince of the angels was cast out of heaven because he had exalted himself and wished to be like God, and if the first human being was driven out of Paradise because he wished to be like God, how will the most wicked of sinners—namely, the unbelieving Christian who himself wishes to be God without any likeness to God through grace and virtue—ascend from earth to heaven? No one ascends to heaven through his own power except the Son of Man, Jesus Christ (cf. Jn 3:13). We must therefore be united with him through grace and virtues and Christian faith, and then we will rise up with him to where he has gone before us. On the Last Day we will all rise, each with his own body. Those who performed good works will then enter eternal life, while those who performed evil deeds will enter the eternal fire. These are two opposite ends which can never converge, for they constantly flee from one another.

Pray fervently for the one who has composed and written this that God may have mercy on him, so that his poor beginning and his and our miserable middle course may be brought to perfection in a blessed end. May Jesus Christ, the living Son of God, grant this to us all. Amen.

SELECT BIBLIOGRAPHY

Works of Ruusbroec

1. Editions

Werken. Edited by Jan Baptist David. 6 vols. Ghent, 1858–1868.
  The first printing of all Ruusbroec's treatises in the original Middle Dutch.
Werken. Edited by the Ruusbroecgenootschap. 4 vols. Mechelen: Het Kompas, 1932–1934; 2d ed., rev., Tielt: Uitgeverij Lannoo, 1944–1948.
  Based on two manuscripts, one originating from Groenendaal in the late fourteenth century, the other from Brussels in the late fifteenth century.
Opera Omnia. Edited by the Ruusbroecgenootschap. 2 vols. to date. Tielt: Uitgeverij Lannoo; Leiden: E. J. Brill, 1981–.
  A critical edition, projected to comprise ten volumes. The original text is accompanied by new English translations as well as the sixteenth-century Latin translation of Surius.

2. Translations

Opera Omnia. Edited and translated by Laurentius Surius. Cologne, 1552; Farnborough: Gregg Press, 1967.
  A Latin translation that for centuries provided the text for translations of Ruusbroec into other European languages.
The Adornment of the Spiritual Marriage; The Sparkling Stone; The Book of Supreme Truth. Translated by C. A. Wynschenk. London: J. M. Dent and Sons, 1916.
  Includes an Introduction and notes by Evelyn Underhill.
Oeuvres de Ruysbroeck l'Admirable. Translated by the Benedictine monks of Wisques/Oosterhout. 6 vols. Brussels and Paris: Vromant, 1912–1938.
Ruysbroeck: Oeuvres choisies. Translated by J.-A. Bizet. Paris: Aubier, 1946.
  Contains excellent French translations of *The Kingdom of Lovers* and *The Spiritual Espousals.*

JOHN RUUSBROEC

The Spiritual Espousals. Translated by Eric Colledge. London: Faber and Faber, 1952. Westminster, Md.: Christian Classics, 1983.

Ruusbroec hertaald (Ruusbroec translated) is the name of a series of translations of Ruusbroec into modern Dutch by Lodewijk Moereels and published in ten volumes. Each volume has its own title and includes the original Middle Dutch on facing pages. Tielt and Amsterdam: Uitgeverij Lannoo, 1976–1982.

WORKS BY OTHER AUTHORS

As an aid to the reader, the works in this section of the Bibliography have been grouped in four categories, according to the major focus of each work. It is recognized, of course, that in many cases a work will include material pertaining to more than one of these categories.

1. The Spirituality of the Low Countries

Axters, Stephanus. *Geschiedenis van de vroomheid in de Nederlanden.* 4 vols. Antwerp: De Sikkel, 1950–1960.
   Begins with the Roman period and goes up to the early eighteenth century. The section devoted to Ruusbroec is in vol. 2, pp. 213–91.
———.*The Spirituality of the Old Low Countries.* Translated by Donald Attwater. London: Blackfriars, 1954. Originally published as *La spiritualité des Pays-Bas: L'évolution d'une doctrine mystique.* Bibliotheca Mechliniensis, ser. 2, fasc. 1. Paris: J. Vrin; Louvain: E. Nauwelaerts, 1948.
   Summarizes in a more popular form the author's multivolume history of Netherlandic spirituality listed in the preceding entry.
Deblaere, Albert. "The Netherlands [School of Mysticism]."In *Sacramentum Mundi: An Encyclopedia of Theology,* edited by Karl Rahner, 4:143–46. New York: Herder and Herder; London: Burns and Oates, 1969.
Mommaers, Paul. "Bulletin d'histoire de la spiritualité: L'école néerlandaise." *Revue d'histoire de la spiritualité* 49 (1973): 465–92.

2. The Cultural, Religious, and Theological Background of Ruusbroec's Works

Ampe, Albert. "Bernardus en Ruusbroec." *Ons Geestelijk Erf* 27 (1953): 143–79.
   Shows the considerable extent to which Ruusbroec was influenced by the writings of St. Bernard.
Axters, Stephanus. "Hadewijch als voorloopster van de zalige Jan van Ruusbroec." In *Dr. L. Reypens Album,* edited by Albert Ampe, pp. 57–74. Antwerp: Ruusbroecgenootschap, 1964.

Argues that the thirteenth-century beguine Hadewijch of Antwerp was one of the most important influences on Ruusbroec's own writings.

Cognet, Louis. *Introduction aux mystiques rhéno-flamands.* Paris: Desclée, 1968.
Perhaps the best general introduction to Eckhart, Tauler, Suso, and Ruusbroec, with useful material on lesser figures as well.

Hadewijch. *Hadewijch: The Complete Works.* Translated by Mother Columba Hart. The Classics of Western Spirituality. New York: Paulist Press, 1980.
The writings of one of Ruusbroec's most important predecessors.

Leff, Gordon. *Heresy in the Later Middle Ages: The Relation of Heterodoxy to Dissent c. 1250–c. 1450.* 2 vols. Manchester: Manchester University Press; New York: Barnes and Noble, 1967.
The heresy of the Free Spirit is the subject of chapter 4 (vol. 1, pp. 308–407).

———.*The Dissolution of the Medieval Outlook: An Essay on Intellectual and Spiritual Change in the Fourteenth Century.* New York: New York University Press, 1976.
The fourth and final chapter, "The Spiritual World," is particularly helpful as background for the study of the fourteenth-century mystics.

Le Goff, Jacques, ed. *Hérésies et sociétés dans l'Europe pré-industrielle: 11e–18e siècles.* Paris and The Hague: Mouton, 1968.
The proceedings of a colloquium held 27–30 May 1962 at Royaumont. The work contains a lengthy and well-organized bibliography prepared by Herbert Grundmann.

Lerner, Robert E. *The Heresy of the Free Spirit in the Later Middle Ages.* Berkeley and Los Angeles: University of California Press, 1972.
Includes a chapter on the response of Ruusbroec and other mystics to this heresy.

Orcibal, Jean. "Le 'Miroir des simples âmes' et la 'secte' du Libre Esprit." *Revue de l'histoire des religions,* tome 176 (July–Sept. 1969): 35–60.
A careful analysis of the actual teaching of *The Mirror of Simple Souls.*

Reynaert, J. "Ruusbroec en Hadewijch." *Ons Geestelijk Erf* 55 (1981): 193–233.
A thorough treatment of the question of Hadewijch's influence on Ruusbroec. Reynaert sees this influence particularly in the concepts of spiritual liberty and the common life.

Southern, R. W. *Western Society and the Church in the Middle Ages.* New York: Penguin, 1970.

Van Mierlo, Jozef. "Over het ontstaan der Germaansche mystiek." *Ons Geestelijk Erf* 1 (1927): 11–37.
The lead article in the very first issue of this journal. Van Mierlo argues for the distinctness of Low Countries spirituality as over against spiritual currents east of the Rhine.

Verdeyen, Paul. "De invloed van Willem van Saint-Thierry op Hadewijch en Ruusbroec." *Ons Geestelijk Erf* 51 (1977): 3–19.
Originally a lecture, this article summarizes the "enormous influence" of William on such beguines as Hadewijch and, through her, on Ruusbroec.

3. Works Relating to Ruusbroec's Life and Writings

Alaerts, Joseph. "La terminologie 'essentielle' dans *Die gheestelike brulocht.*" *Ons Geestelijk Erf* 49 (1975): 248–330.

———."La terminologie 'essentielle' dans *Die gheestelike brulocht* et *Dat rijcke der ghelieven.*" *Ons Geestelijk Erf* 49 (1975): 337–65.

These two articles by Alaerts present a thorough linguistic study of the term "essential" and related terminology, central to Ruusbroec's mysticism.

Ampe, Albert. *Kernproblemen uit de leer van Ruusbroec.* Studiën en textuitgaven van ons geestelijk erf, vols. 11–13. Tielt: Uitgeverij Lannoo, 1950–1957.

A massive study of Ruusbroec's Trinitarian doctrine, his theology of creation and grace, and his teaching on the soul's ascent to God.

———."La théologie mystique de l'ascension de l'âme selon le bienheureux Jean de Ruusbroec." Parts 1, 2. *Revue d'ascétique et de mystique* 36 (1960): 188–201, 303–22.

A summary of the final volume of the author's *Kernproblemen*, listed in the preceding entry.

———. "Jean Ruusbroec (bienheureux)." *Dictionnaire de spiritualité* 8:659–97.

Auger, Alfredus. *De Doctrina et Meritis Joannis van Ruysbroeck.* Louvain: J. van Linthout, 1892.

A harbinger of the revival of Ruusbroec studies in the twentieth century.

Bonny, Johan. "Jan van Ruusbroec." *La vie spirituelle,* no. 136 (Nov.–Dec. 1982): 666–94.

Includes a brief account of Ruusbroec's life, works, and influence, followed by commentary on selected texts from the mystic's writings.

d'Asbeck, Melline, ed. and trans. *Documents relatifs à Ruysbroeck.* Paris: Ernest Leroux, 1931.

French translations of Brother Gerard's Prologue and other early documents relating to Ruusbroec's life and writings.

Deblaere, Albert. "Essentiel (superessentiel, suressentiel)." *Dictionnaire de spiritualité* 4, pt. 2:1346–66.

Explains the significance of this terminology in Ruusbroec's mysticism.

———."Giovanni (Jan van) Ruusbroec." *Dizionario degli istituti di perfezione* 4:1291–96.

de Vreese, Willem, ed. *Bijdragen tot de kennis van het leven en de werken van Jan van Ruusbroec.* Ghent, 1896.

Materials in this book first appeared in numbers of the journal *Het Belfort* in 1895 and 1896. Included is the Prologue of Brother Gerard.

Dupré, Louis. *The Common Life: The Origins of Trinitarian Mysticism and Its Development by Jan Ruusbroec.* New York: Crossroad, 1984.

The edited text of five lectures given at Gethsemani Abbey in 1982.

Fraling, Bernhard. *Mystik and Geschichte: Das "ghemeyne leven" in der Lehre des Jan van Ruusbroec.* Regensburg: Friedrich Pustet, 1974.

SELECT BIBLIOGRAPHY

Geraert van Saintes and Hendrik Utenbogaerde. *De twee oudste bronnen van het leven van Jan van Ruusbroec door zijn getuigenissen bevestigd.* Translated by the Benedictine nuns of Bonheiden. Mystieke teksten met commentaar, no. 4. Bonheiden, Belgium: Abdij Bonheiden, 1981.
Modern Dutch translations of the Prologue of Brother Gerard and of Pomerius's life of Ruusbroec. (Utenbogaerde is the Middle Dutch equivalent of the Latin name Pomerius.)

Henry, Paul. "La mystique trinitaire du bienheureux Jean Ruusbroec." Parts 1, 2. *Recherches de science religieuse* 39–40 (1951–1952): 335–68; 41 (1953): 51–75.

Jan van Ruusbroec, 1293–1381: Tentoonstellingscatalogus. Brussels: Koninklijke Bibliothek Albert I, 1981.
Catalog of an exhibition of manuscripts, books, paintings, and other Ruusbroec memorabilia to commemorate the six hundredth anniversary of the mystic's death. The book contains a valuable bibliography of modern studies of Ruusbroec.

Mommaers, Paul. *The Land Within: The Process of Possessing and Being Possessed by God according to the Mystic Jan van Ruysbroeck.* Translated from the Dutch by David N. Smith. Chicago: Franciscan Herald Press, 1975.
Treats Ruusbroec's writings "primarily as a personal testimony to his own experience."

———, and Norbert De Paepe, eds. *Jan van Ruusbroec: The Sources, Content, and Sequels of His Mysticism.* Mediaevalia Lovaniensia, ser. 1, stud. 12. Louvain: Leuven University Press, 1984.
Contains eleven papers read at a colloquium held at Louvain in 1981 to commemorate the six hundredth anniversary of Ruusbroec's death.

Pomerius, Henricus. *De origine monasterii Viridisvallis et de gestis patrum et fratrum in primordiali fervore ibidem degentium.* In *Analecta Bollandiana* 4 (1885): 263–322.
One of the earliest sources of information about Ruusbroec, but much more in the genre of hagiography than of strict biography. Pomerius wrote this work about 1420.

Reypens, Leonce. "Ruusbroec-studiën: I, Het mystieke 'gherinen.' " *Ons Geestelijk Erf* 12 (1938): 158–86.

Ruusbroecgenootschap, ed. *Jan van Ruusbroec: Leven, Werken.* Mechelen: Het Kompas, 1931.
Essays published on the occasion of the five hundred and fiftieth anniversary of the mystic's death. Leonce Reypens's essay on Ruusbroec's mystical doctrine is particularly important.

Teasdale, Wayne. "Ruysbroeck's Mystical Theology." Parts 1, 2. *American Benedictine Review* 35 (1984):82–96, 176–93.
Relies on inaccurate sources for its biographical information but provides a useful synopsis of Ruusbroec's mystical theology.

Underhill, Evelyn. *Mysticism: A Study in the Nature and Development of Man's Spiritual Consciousness.* London: Methuen, 1911.

A classic work that has gone through many editions and reprintings. It contains numerous references to Ruusbroec, especially in the tenth and final chapter, "The Unitive Life."

————. *Ruysbroeck*. London: G. Bell, 1915.

A study of Ruusbroec's life and writings by one who considered him "my own favorite of all the mystics."

Van de Walle, A. "Is Ruusbroec pantheïst?" Parts 1, 2. *Ons Geestelijk Erf* 12 (1938): 359–91; 13 (1939): 66–105.

Shows why charges of pantheism against Ruusbroec are unfounded.

Van Mierlo, Jozef. "Ruusbroec's bestrijding van de ketterij." *Ons Geestelijk Erf* 6 (1932): 304–46.

Traces the evolution in Ruusbroec's opposition to heresy in the course of his writings.

Verdeyen, Paul. *Ruusbroec en zijn mystiek*. Louvain: Davidsfonds, 1981.

An introduction to Ruusbroec's life and writings, with a selection of texts from the mystic's works in modern Dutch translation.

4. Ruusbroec's Influence on or Similarities to Later Writers

Ampe, Albert. *Ruusbroec: Traditie en werkelijkheid*. Antwerp: Ruusbroecgenootschap, 1975.

A detailed study of the understandings—and misunderstandings—that writers have had of Ruusbroec over the centuries.

Combes, André. *Essai sur la critique de Ruysbroeck par Gerson*. 3 vols. Paris, J. Vrin, 1945–1959.

Volume one includes the texts of Gerson's critique of Ruusbroec and of John of Schoonhoven's response to Gerson.

Emery, Kent, Jr. "The Carthusians, Intermediaries for the Teaching of John Ruysbroeck during the Period of Early Reform and the Counter-Reformation." *Analecta Cartusiana* 43 (1979):100–29.

Hatzfeld, Helmut. "The Influence of Ramon Lull and Jan van Ruysbroeck on the Language of the Spanish Mystics." *Traditio* 4 (1946): 337–97.

Argues in part for the direct literary influence of Ruusbroec on St. John of the Cross.

Mommaers, Paul. "Benoît de Canfeld et ses sources flamandes." Parts 1, 2. *Revue d'histoire de la spiritualité* 48 (1972): 401–34; 49 (1973): 37–66.

Orcibal, Jean. *Saint Jean de la Croix et les mystiques rhéno-flamands*. Paris: Desclée de Brouwer, 1966.

A wide-ranging account of literary and doctrinal resemblances, with carefully qualified conclusions. See especially the next-to-last chapter, "Les grands thèmes communs."

Reypens, Leonce. "Ruusbroec en Juan de la Cruz: Hun overeenstemming omtrent het toppunt der beschouwing." *Ons Geestelijk Erf* 5 (1931): 143–85.

    Illustrates the similarities between these two mystics on the nature of mystical contemplation.

Ricard, Robert. " 'La fonte' de saint Jean de la Croix et un chapitre de Laredo: I." *Bulletin hispanique* 58 (1956): 265–74.
    A critical response to Hatzfeld's article, listed above.

INDEX TO INTRODUCTION

INDEX

INDEX TO TEXTS

INDEX

Devotion to God, 79, 175
Discretion, 66
Disobedience, 56
Dog days, 88–89
Dropsy, 93–94

Eckhart, Meister, 117n14
Elizabeth, St., 226
Emptiness, false, 136, 139–42
Emptiness, true, 132–33
Enemy, 41, 192, 194
Enlightenment, 74–75, 178
Envy, 60
Ephesians, Letter to the, 215
Eternal birth, 237
Eternal fire, 256
Eternal life, 45, 187–88, 214, 244
Eucharist: 201–19, 225–34
Exemplarism, doctrine of, 142n17
Exercises, interior, 112, 116, 165, 192

Faith, 162, 230
Fear of hell, 164
Fear of the Lord, gift of, 122–23, 164
Fervor, 79, 105, 119
Fevers, 94–96
Fickleness, 95–96
Flesh, 64
Fog, 83
Fortitude, 65, 94, 124
Freedom, spiritual, 75, 157

Gabriel, Angel, 41, 202
Gemini, sign of, 81–82
Generosity, 51, 60–61
Genesis, Book of, 217, 237
Gerard, Brother, 251n1
Gluttony, 63, 138
God: is able to do all that he wishes, 237; our ascent to, 170; we belong to, 198; we are born again in, 199; ceaselessly calls all persons, 163; and Christ, 48; conceals himself, 258; contemplation of, 146–47; craving and desire for, 80, 133–34, 176–77, 204, 261; devotion to, 79; dying in, 169–70, 189; to enjoy, 113–14, 158–59, 182–83, 262–65; es-

sential being of, 213–14, 246–47, 266; estrangement from, 96; our eternal being in, 148, 214; exalts the humble, 251; to experience, 174–77, 190, 259–60; faithfulness of, 99, 102; faithful servants of, 163–65, 169; Father, 100–01, 119, 129–30, 151–52; generosity of, 51; gifts from, 163; is a common good to all, 43–44; grace of, 43–45, 71, 74, 99, 112, 120–27, 132, 163, 165, 177, 179, 191, 195, 200, 214, 230, 253, 261, 262; heirs of, 248; hidden sons of, 168–69; hired servants of, 163–65, 169; Holy Spirit, 101, 114, 119, 151–52; and human spirit, 110, 115; our immersion in, 173; inclines himself to every creature, 110; Kingdom of, 111; to know, 113, 202, 203; knows all things, 237; life in, 172, 190; becoming like, 122; our likeness to, 121–23, 213–14, 215, 238; love for, 135, 233; love of, 43, 47, 115, 133, 200, 212–19, 238, 245, 263–65; lover of, 252; mercy of, 51, 67; nature of, 62, 67; obedience, 6, 98; as a oneness, 67; praise of, 80, 175; prayer to, 104–05; resplendent glory of, 114–15, 143, 147, 150, 167, 171, 172, 173–75, 179, 244, 267; resting in, 68–69, 268; reveals himself, 239; secret friends of, 165–67, 169; shadow of, 178–79; Son (Word) of, 101, 119, 147, 149, 151–52, 171, 179; and the soul, 238, 261; is a spirit, 237; thanksgiving to, 79–80, 175; touches us, 177, 240; transcends every creature, 110; union with, 117, 157–61, 167, 173–74, 128, 236, 240–41, 244–47, 253–68; unity of, 120, 158–59, 181–82, 189; will of, 125, 199; *See also*: Christ Jesus; Grace; Holy Spirit; Union

Godhead: essential substance of, 254; Father as origin of, 129; nature of, 100; stillness of, 177; Unity of, 71, 100–01, 262

Good works, 192

Grace: of God, 43–45, 71, 74, 99, 112, 120–21, 127, 132, 163, 165, 177, 179, 191, 195, 200, 214, 230, 253, 261, 262; of

283

INDEX

INDEX

Zacchaeus = climbing Tree 69/70

L's S = special dessert hot

raised to God 181